Binge

Binge

Campus Life in an Age of Disconnection and Excess

What Your College Student Won't Tell You

Barrett Seaman

WILEY

John Wiley & Sons, Inc.

Published by John Wiley & Sons, Inc., Hoboken, New Jersey
Published simultaneously in Canada

Previously published in hardcover by John Wiley & Sons, Inc., as *Binge: What Your College Student Won't Tell You*.

For general information about our other products and services, please contact our Customer Care Department within the United States at (800) 762-2974, outside the United States at (317) 572-3993 or fax (317) 572-4002.

Wiley also publishes its books in a variety of electronic formats. Some content that appears in print may not be available in electronic books. For more information about Wiley products, visit our web site at www.wiley.com.

Library of Congress Cataloging-in-Publication Data:

Seaman, Barrett.
    Binge: campus life in an age of disconnection and excess / Barrett Seaman.
      p. cm.
    Includes index.
    ISBN-13 978-0-471-49119-4 (cloth)
    ISBN-10 0-471-49119-5 (cloth)
    ISBN-13 978-0-470-04918-1 (paper)
    ISBN-10 0-470-04918-9 (paper)
    1. College students—Social conditions—United States—Case studies.
  2. College students—United States—Attitudes. I. Title.
    LB3605.S382   2005
    378.1'98'0973—dc22

                                              2005001252

Printed in the United States of America

10 9 8 7 6 5 4 3 2 1

For Sidney Wertimer,
a model of what college teaching was
and can be again

Contents

Acknowledgments

The fingerprints of many knowledgeable and thoughtful people are all over this book. Because the benchmark for all my observations about college life was my own experience, first as a student and more recently as a trustee of Hamilton College, I owe a debt to all of my colleagues on the Hamilton board as well as to the administrators and faculty members who helped steer my thinking. I am particularly grateful to Eugene M. Tobin, Hamilton's eighteenth president, who encouraged me to tackle this complex topic and to be forthright in my opinions about it. Professor Sidney Wertimer, to whom I have dedicated this book, and his wife, Eleanor, were constant sounding boards throughout the many evenings I haunted their living room on College Hill Road over the years. And Nancy Thompson, the college's dean of students, patiently fielded my many questions and requests.

Todd Shuster of Zachary Shuster Harmsworth was instrumental in reshaping my proposal for *Binge* from a linear look at contemporary student behavior into a richer examination of campus culture. Tom Miller, my editor, furthered that growth by urging me to seek out and report the more varied student voices that are heard throughout these pages. Elizabeth Sampson, Georgetown class of 2002, chased down facts and anecdotes beyond the twelve campuses I covered.

My three college-educated daughters, Kate, Maggie, and Lily, listened patiently to my theories, enriched my understanding of their generation's experiences, and tried at least to prevent me from embarrassing myself. No one was more supportive than their mother and my wife, Laura, who patiently endured my long absences while I was off visiting campuses—and an even longer absence while I sat writing in my office under the same roof. Laura read and synopsized for me numerous books about modern parenting. She also read my manuscript with the discerning eye of the careful reader that she is.

I thank the many college administrators who not only allowed me to hang out on their campuses but also detailed for me the exigencies of modern college life from their perspective. Above all, I owe thanks to the hundreds of college students who took the time to educate a visitor to their world. So many were articulate and extraordinarily forthcoming. Some were particularly gracious in reaching out to their peers on my behalf: Claire Bourne, Middlebury class of 2004; Catherine Dale, Dartmouth class of 2004; Jessie Duncan, Stanford class of 2005; Mina Pell, Harvard class of 2004; Cory Schouten, Indiana class of 2004; and Anthony Vitarelli, Duke class of 2005 each took the time and effort to find others on their campuses who could personalize the issues I explore in this book.

Introduction

Those of us who were privileged to attend a four-year residential college tend to wear the experience like an identity badge. For better or worse, our college years helped to shape us. But our memories of them remain frozen in frames that might have been taken from an old movie about campus life. We likely missed all the changes that occurred on campus after we left and went about our adult lives, leaving us with anachronistic assumptions of what it must be like to be a student today.

My hiatus lasted nearly twenty years. In the mid-1980s, I was invited to reinvolve myself with Hamilton College in Clinton, New York, from which I had graduated in 1967. I was in Washington, D.C., by then, covering the White House for *Time* magazine. My reengagement rapidly escalated, and within a few years I was elected to the college's board of trustees. I started returning to Hamilton's picture-postcard campus. Each time I drove up College Hill Road and saw the chapel spire rising above the weathered dolomite walls of the buildings surrounding the main quadrangle, I was filled with nostalgia and a sense of deep personal identity with the place. I saw it just as it had been when I was a student.

College board meetings tend to be well-orchestrated affairs. Once a quarter, along with other trustees, many of whom were also graduates of a Hamilton that was all male prior to 1978, I returned for two days of meetings where we listened as administrators reported on the state of the college, asked probing questions, and eventually approved expenditures. The few students who joined us for meetings were invariably the campus leaders—able, articulate, and generally supportive of the administration. A couple of times a year, we were afforded opportunities to meet with larger groups of students, usually seniors, at receptions and dinners, where they spoke eloquently about what they'd learned and what they aspired to do next.

Occasionally, a student would make a caustic aside about the latest rule governing parties or the prep school atmosphere that students claimed was choking all the fun out of college life. Having spent four years at a prep school myself, I thought such comparisons seemed harsh: the Hamilton I knew was a libertarian dream compared to life at Phillips Academy–Andover. And Andover was considered one of the least restrictive of the New England prep schools.

Gradually, I began to understand how different a place Hamilton had become from the essentially uncomplicated and loosely governed community of eight hundred young men and their teachers and coaches I had known in the mid-1960s. We board members who had been on College Hill when single women were only occasional visitors found it hard to fathom how students of both sexes could comfortably share the same dorms, even the same bathrooms. Not only are women there now but also many more African Americans, Hispanics, and out and organized gays. The athletes are a lot bigger and their coaches have full-time assistants. There are also many people employed by the college who do not teach but seem more involved with the students than are the professors. They work in a division known as Residential Life, or, in the campus vernacular, Res Life.

There are people known as area coordinators who oversee more than fifty residential advisors—students paid to proctor other students in campus residence halls. In my day, there were just six seniors who kept watch over the entire freshman class in the one dorm assigned to us; thereafter, we were on our own. Now there is a full-time student activities director who assists campus clubs. I don't recall anyone performing that function in the sixties, except professors who had a personal interest in the French club or the biology club or the Charlatans, the campus drama society. Whereas a single night watchman guarded the college then, Hamilton now has a security force of about ten officers who seem to spend as much time protecting students from themselves as they do from outsiders. Those of my contemporaries who had psychological problems usually went home to work things out; now the college has a full-time psychological counselor. When my classmates sought advice about what to do after graduation, they usually relied on a favorite professor; now students are wired into a wholly separate career center. Whereas communications technology used to consist of a pay phone at the end of the corridor, modern students are doing everything by computer, cell phone, and PDA (personal digital assistant).

When I joined the board, a few men who had been faculty members while I was an undergraduate were still teaching. But the vast majority were new to me. Now there are almost as many women as men, and quite a few used to be on the faculty of Kirkland, the coordinate all-women's college that had lasted nine years and graduated six classes before being absorbed by Hamilton in 1978. Sitting in on meetings in which tenure decisions were presented for our approval, I was often struck by the attention given to the faculty's scholarly writing as the criterion for promotion to lifelong employment as well as by the often arcane nature of their academic expertise—all in a small liberal arts college long known for its emphasis on teaching.

After my stint in Washington, I moved to *Time*'s headquarters in New York, where I was appointed the magazine's special projects editor. Part of that job was to develop and edit a college guidebook. *The Best College for You* series offered prospective applicants and their families tips on what to look for in a college as well as a directory of 500 four-year colleges and universities compiled by *The Princeton Review*, *Time*'s partner in the venture. Working on this series allowed me to meet with many college presidents and deans as they periodically made the rounds of guidebook editors in the vague hope of receiving favorable attention. I used those meetings to test whether the trends I saw at Hamilton were evident elsewhere, and through them I began to realize how much colleges were truly changing.

In 2001, following the merger of America Online with Time Warner, the parent company of *Time*, I took advantage of an opportunity for early retirement. At the age of fifty-five, after thirty rewarding years of working for one company, I wanted to try something else, and one of the projects I had in mind was to pursue my growing fascination with contemporary college life. I hoped to utilize the reporting skills I had developed at *Time* in order to get a closer view of what it was like being a student in a residential college. I naturally decided to start at Hamilton.

Founded in 1812 and named for Alexander Hamilton, a founding father of the country and principal benefactor of the college's predecessor, Hamilton-Oneida Academy, Hamilton was for its first 160 years an intimate ivory tower for men reputed in New York circles to be capable in a quiet, self-confident way, good on their feet, thanks to an unusual four-year public speaking requirement, and generally proficient writers. With the absorption of Kirkland in 1978, the college stumbled into coeducation and went through a period of adjustment that lasted longer than similar periods at other coeducational colleges. The nineties were marked by a critical self-examination during the presidency of Eugene Tobin, which led to significant curricular and student life reforms, notably an end in 1995 to the residential fraternity system that dominated Hamilton's social scene when I was a student.

What remains special about Hamilton is the intimacy that comes with a small, rural, liberal arts college: a sense that everyone, including faculty members and their families, is familiar. With the arrival of women and some modest growth beyond that, the student body of 1,750 is now more than twice as large as it was in the 1960s. But the student/faculty ratio (less than 10:1) is still such that almost every class is conversational. *The Princeton Review* describes Hamilton's professors as highly demanding but "very helpful and available" both as teachers and advisors.

As a trustee, I had no problem winning permission to live with students for a couple of weeks. I joined seventeen of them as a resident of Rogers House, a converted estate nearly half a mile from the main campus. Rogers was not a typical college dorm. The rooms were like upstairs bedrooms at home; mine had a private bath. The students who chose Rogers were juniors and seniors, most of whom seemed to be studious. I had wonderful conversations with them over meals cooked by our own chef five nights a week and served in an elegant paneled dining room. During the day, I met with Res Life staff members and hung out in the Beinecke Student Village, Café Opus, and other places where Hamilton students go to see and be seen.

While I didn't attend regular classes, I participated in several seminars. I listened as student government representatives wrestled with campus issues at their regular meetings. I hung out with the staff of the weekly paper, the *Spectator*, while they closed a couple of issues. I worked out at the fitness center, which was in use throughout the day and night, mostly by women. I spent several evenings at the Little Pub, an on-campus haven for seniors, where I could count on good conversation over a few beers. Late on a Saturday night, I rode around with a uniformed campus safety officer as he monitored the weekend party scene. I watched as student EMTs carried a freshman girl, barely conscious after consuming vast quantities of vodka, to an awaiting ambulance— an all-too-familiar college event these days.

My two-week stay made me realize how very different student life was compared to what I had experienced. The young people I met went about their days at a frenetic pace, looking for adult guidance wherever they could find it, which more often than not was from student life professionals trained to handle personal and social issues. They exhibited an intensity that seemed far removed from the blithe atmosphere I recalled from my college days. At night, they entered a world of their own, operating under their own rules, almost as if the adults had taken their rules home with them. Being with them at night felt like orbiting around the moon and getting a glimpse of its dark side.

How representative, I wondered, was student life as I had seen it at Hamilton? What would a similar visit to another campus reveal? As iconic as they are, classic residential colleges and universities catering to eighteen- to twenty-four-year-olds are not where most college graduates earn their degrees these days. As of the last census, four out of ten undergraduates were twenty-four years old or older. More were getting all or part of their education through online programs like the University of Phoenix. Four-year residential programs represent only 15 percent of the more than four thousand colleges and universities in the United States. But even within that category there is a wide range of campuses—from small liberal arts colleges like Hamilton to urban campuses like New York University, from Emory in Atlanta to the great sprawling state universities like Texas and Penn State. How different could student life be in each of these or in schools down South or out West?

I decided to try to match my Hamilton experience against a sample of other college campuses. Within the constraints of time and resources, I picked twelve from the ranks of both private and public institutions with a range in size and geographical location. I decided to stay within the coeducational mainstream, ruling out single-sex schools, religiously or racially affiliated schools, and specialized (e.g., art, engineering, military) schools. I ruled out community and commuter colleges whose students, many of them part-time, go home at night to jobs and families rather than to residence halls and extracurricular activities.

If there was a bias in my selection, it was toward the most selective institutions. While I recognize that academic demands on students vary widely from one campus to another, I concluded that the institutions to which most college-bound students aspire are also the highly ranked places whose practices other colleges emulate.

It was easy to pick Harvard, which the *Fiske Guide to Colleges* accurately describes as "the benchmark against which all other colleges are compared." Its student body represents a level of accomplishment and potential that is the envy of everybody else in the business, so everybody else tends to follow in Harvard's footsteps if they can afford to, whether by offering early admissions, diversifying the curriculum, or recruiting minority intellectuals to their faculties. On an admissions tour I joined inside Harvard's famous Yard, the father of a prospective applicant asked the guide why he had chosen Harvard. The young man paused, apparently baffled by the question. "I guess I didn't have a good reason *not* to come to Harvard," he finally managed, adding with that youthful shift in intonation that makes an assertion sound like a question, "Harvard is Harvard."

Though Harvard's campus is urban, 97 percent of undergraduates live in college housing dispersed among twelve residential houses to which they are randomly assigned after freshman year. While the student body now numbers over six thousand, the house system has the effect of shrinking the size of the place and making it homier.

Despite the accomplishments of its students and the comfort of its residences, Harvard has its problems, including several well-publicized suicides in recent years and widely circulated reports about sexual assaults and the administration's controversial method of adjudicating date rape cases—a persistent issue at many colleges.

While also a member of the Ivy League, Dartmouth College is a very different place from Harvard. Nestled along the east bank of the Connecticut River separating New Hampshire from Vermont, Dartmouth is as rustic as Harvard is urbane. Dartmouth students often compare themselves to Harvard students. They attend an institution that is almost as old, almost as selective, almost as prestigious—but not quite. The schools attract different kinds of students. Harvard tends to be more intellectual, artier; Dartmouth is heartier, more outgoing. Drive into Hanover on an early evening almost any time other than winter and you will see physically fit young men and women running a few miles before dinner. Sports are a big part of life here, and the Dartmouth Outing Club is a major extracurricular force.

Thanks to a local ordinance that requires food to be served in any commercial establishment that serves alcohol, there are no student bars in Hanover. Student social life centers around Dartmouth's fraternity houses, most of which line Webster Avenue to the northwest of the signature Green. There were fifteen fraternities and six sororities in operation when I visited, although that number varies according to which ones are on probation or suspension for social violations. Since Dartmouth began admitting women in 1972, its robust fraternity system has fallen under siege as it runs up against demands for social equality both from women and from a growing number of minority students. I knew that Dartmouth had embarked on an ambitious effort to reform its fraternity culture and I was curious to see how it was working.

Unlike many of the New England private colleges, Middlebury in central Vermont has been coed since its inception in 1800. But until the 1970s, men and women might as well have gone to different schools. Women were housed separately and protected by parietal hours; the college even calculated their class standings separately. The men, with their fraternity houses, were the social hosts. Anxious to have students safely on campus instead of driving the hour or so it took to get to nearby New York State where the drinking age was eighteen, the administration turned a blind eye to the technically illegal consumption of alcohol that went on in those houses.

I chose Middlebury in part because I wanted to see how another northeastern liberal arts college compared to Hamilton, and also because Middlebury was in the process of creating a new housing system that divided the student body of twenty-three hundred into five residential and dining units loosely modeled on the residential colleges at Yale, Harvard, and elsewhere. The administration has invested tens of millions of dollars in new facilities specifically designed to put students and their professors into daily contact outside the classroom—an aspect of Res Life that had gone missing in recent years.

The University of Virginia in Charlottesville—U-VA, as everyone calls it—is at or near the top of the list of so-called public Ivies—state schools that offer a first-rate education. Students who are not Virginia residents vie for a limited number of out-of-state spots. U-VA is all about tradition. The campus is not just any campus but the Grounds. Its signature is the Lawn, around which is built the Academical Village that Thomas Jefferson designed. Students refer to Mr. Jefferson, Mr. Madison, and Mr. Monroe as if the three founding fathers were still walking around the place in their revolutionary period britches.

Indeed, U-VA students keep up a lot of the old ways. Some still join secret societies, like IMP or Z, with occult rituals. They speak with reverence about their "community of trust," in which lying, cheating, and stealing are not tolerated. A student-run honor court enforces that standard with a Single Sanction, which is permanent banishment from the Grounds for anyone caught and convicted of those fundamental offenses.

The Princeton Review noted in its 2004 edition of *The 351 Best Colleges* that U-VA has a well-deserved reputation as a haven for preppies. Beyond the pillared porches of its thirty-four fraternities and twenty-two sororities, there is a highly visible element of that vestige of old Virginia's moneyed aristocracies. All male and all white less than fifty years ago, U-VA is now about half women and a quarter students of color. Yet Virginia shares a feature of so many campuses these days: a palpable sense that there are two different student bodies. One is established, middle class, and white; the other is a loose coalition of women, gays, and minorities. I was curious to see how the elements of this emerging dichotomy, evident on so many campuses, interacted.

There is something mildly schizophrenic as well about Duke University, a private campus in Durham, North Carolina. I was familiar with Duke, having spent a month there in 1993 as a Terry Sanford fellow, a program for journalists invited to Duke to do research, take classes, and spend time with professors. Five years later I was back, leading a team of journalists in producing a *Time* special report titled "The Week in the Life of a Hospital," about the Duke University Medical Center.

Duke is a curious patchwork of cultures. Though there are still remnants of a good old boy network of comfortable white southern families, Duke's student body of six thousand is now almost as racially diverse as the Ivies. Athletes live in a world of their own. It is commonly observed at Duke that the school has two religious shrines: the gothic chapel that soars above the West Campus and Cameron Indoor Stadium, where the chronically powerful Blue Devils play basketball. As its academic reputation climbed throughout the second half of the twentieth century, Duke became as tough to get into as some Ivies and began to attract a significant number of folks from outside the South, including a lot of New England boarding school types looking for an alternative to the cold, competitive northeastern schools. Between classes on the main quad, you notice a lot of Andover, Hotchkiss, Taft, and other private boarding school sweatshirts.

Hidden beneath the multicultural mélange of preppies, jocks, and Bubbas is another divide—between men and women. A recent study revealed a shocking disconnect between the achievements and capabilities of Duke women and their self-perceptions as second-class citizens beholden to their male counterparts for their social lives.

Indiana University–Bloomington has long enjoyed a reputation as a first-rate public university. Its school of music boasts one of the country's finest opera faculties, Kevin Kline is an alumnus of the dramatic arts program, and the Kelley School of Business competes with some of the well-known MBA programs on the coasts. It is also home to the Kinsey Institute for the Study of Human Sexual Behavior.

Dominated by massive buildings made from locally mined Bedford limestone, the campus is breathtaking, especially in spring around the running of the Little 500 bicycle race featured in the film *Breaking Away.* The Indiana Memorial Union, the nation's second largest student union building, has its own hotel, bowling alleys, a travel agency, a hair salon, a four hundred–seat movie theater, and six different eateries ranging from a Burger King to a white-tablecloth formal dining room. The building devotes five floors of office space to student activities.

Sprawled out over 903 acres between two lakes, the University of Wisconsin–Madison offers every type of student housing imaginable to its twenty-eight thousand undergraduates plus another thirteen thousand grad students: high-rise freshman dorms, learning communities, language houses, an old-fashioned women-only residence hall with visiting hours, fraternities, sororities, and the full range of off-campus apartments.

Wisconsin students are renowned for their activity: there are more than six hundred student organizations, and it is the only campus in the country with two daily student newspapers. It was also a cradle of the student revolution. Campus guides still take visitors past the old Army Math Center, where a bomb planted by antiwar activists in 1969 killed a graduate student. The scars of the blast are still visible on the outside walls of the building. Madison was one of those places in the sixties where students discovered the extent of their power over adults and in doing so led to the reshaping of American higher education. I wondered how today's students wore the mantle, if they wore it at all.

The other cradle of sixties student activism was Berkeley, the flagship of the University of California system. It is hard to imagine a school more different from cozy Hamilton College than this sprawling hillside campus overlooking San Francisco Bay. Berkeley is as political as any campus in America, but it is nowhere near the cauldron it was four decades ago when three thousand Cal students surrounded the squad car holding free speech movement leader Mario Savio to prevent him from being jailed.

The passion may still be there, but it struck me as diffused among a hundred disparate causes and groups. Four out of ten Berkeley students are of Asian descent; when combined with

Hispanics and blacks, this statistic puts Caucasian students in the minority. But diversity here is about much more than skin color. "There are hippies and stoners and gutter punks and preppy Abercrombie & Fitch–donning, cell phone–carrying socialites," a student said in *The Princeton Review*. "There are frat boys and oddball co-opers, the politically zealous and the religious fanatics, the athletes and the trannies." I saw them all as I strolled north-ward through Sproul Plaza past the sign-up tables for pro-Israeli and pro-Palestinian groups, Naderites, Berkeley College Repub-licans, the National Organization for Women (NOW), the Nav-igator (a Christian evangelical group), the Asian Business Associ-ation, and followers of Lyndon LaRouche. Just outside the old campus gate, a men's a capella group serenaded wide-eyed coeds with the Beach Boys' "Help Me, Rhonda."

This quintessential research university—where vitamins B, K, and A were first identified; from which teams of archaeologists dis-covered dinosaur bones in Hell Creek, Montana; whose Campbell Hall observatory aided in the discovery of black holes and dark galaxies—is no place for students who need hand-holding. "If I have to name one drawback for Cal, it's that we can't afford to have professors sitting next to you at dinner or baking cookies with you," said a student guide on an admissions tour I joined. I was curious to see if students at big universities like Wisconsin and Berkeley could develop relationships with their teachers as we could at Hamilton.

Stanford is an academic country club to Berkeley's factory. It is a place no one ever seems to want to leave except maybe to move a few miles down Silicon Valley to start up another fortune-making dot-com. Stanford has it all—renowned professors, state-of-the-art libraries, and just about everything its highly diversified student body might want. Though wags have called it the world's largest Spanish restaurant, Stanford's red tile–roofed, Mission-style architecture reflects the open, inclusive character of the school. To keep students abreast of all that is going on every day on "the Farm," as Stanford students incongruously refer to their

campus, the administration was installing a comprehensive electronic calendar called ISIS, designed to alert all to concerts, lectures, cooking contests, and athletic events. When I asked Gene
Awakuni, the vice provost for student life, about life inside the
Stanford "bubble," as students sometimes characterized their college environment, he laughed and acknowledged, "It's a Disney-
land type of experience."

Looking to balance my list with another small liberal arts college outside the Northeast, I considered many schools, including
Ohio's Oberlin, Denison, and in particular Kenyon, which had
been the subject of an insightful book about college life in the
early nineties. Carleton and Macalester in Minnesota, Grinnell in
Iowa, Davidson in North Carolina, and Reed in Oregon all mer-
ited attention. But only Pomona in southern California served a
regular late-night meal of comfort foods called Snack. Snack is
more than a funky meal; it is a symbol of the extent to which colleges today are willing to cater to the lifestyles of their students.
My decision was made.

There were substantive reasons to look at Pomona as well.
Tiny (1,550 students), highly selective (it accepts only about one
in five applicants), and cerebral, Pomona is a western alternative to
small, intellectual eastern schools like Swarthmore and Amherst.
Pomona is part of the Claremont Colleges, all of which fit like
tiles into a mosaic laid out in a valley some thirty miles west of
Los Angeles. The five schools gain economies of scale by sharing administrative services and a student health center. Because
these colleges are small enough to need help competing athleti-
cally, they team up in football and other big men's sports: Pomona
with Pitzer, Claremont with Harvey Mudd. (The fifth college is
Scripps, an all-women's institution.) Otherwise, they are surprisingly independent; each has its own faculty, administration, and
endowment, which in Pomona's case is over $1 billion.

My final selection was beyond the U.S. border: McGill in
Montreal, probably the best known of the Canadian universities.
There are more Yanks at McGill—about two thousand in any

given year—than there are students altogether at Hamilton College. This English-speaking school in a French-speaking city is a
hybrid of American and European educational styles, with less
emphasis on extracurricular activities, sports, and other aspects of
collegiate life.

It is also situated in a province where the drinking age is still
only eighteen. The first surprise Americans get at McGill comes
during Frosh Week, when members of the various faculties invite
new students to join them under a tent on the lawn off Rue Sher-
brooke for a few beers. The beginning of the fall semester is a bit
of running revelry that some neophyte drinkers from south of the
border find hard to handle at first. But by November, when the
work piles up, they usually settle down.

McGill assumes its students are adults and treats them as
such—even first-years. Most upperclassmen and women live in
apartments in a section near the university known affectionately
as "the ghetto." They pay their own rent, buy their own food, and
deal with life's little inconveniences on their own. I suspected that
even American students, when offered the chance, were capable
of living up to such expectations.

While I am confident that these twelve institutions reasonably
represent the top tier of mainstream colleges and universities, it is
fair to ask whether their students behave differently from students at less competitive and less equipped schools—the literally
thousands of second-, third-, and fourth-tier colleges where most
undergraduates matriculate. Given the level of achievement needed
to get into these schools in the first place, you would expect that
students would feel more pressure to succeed and might be more
constrained in their behavior.

Certainly the students talked a lot about stress. But there is
also a tacit assumption on the part of American college students
that they have an irrevocable license to let off steam. From
national surveys measuring student attitudes and behaviors, I

found that the sexual behavior, attention to studies, proclivity toward cheating, levels of depression, alcohol and drug use I found at these twelve schools, while sometimes different in degree from the general college population, were not different in kind. On some campuses, drinking is a big issue; at others, it's hard drugs or racial tensions. But what struck me in my preliminary research was that every institution was wrestling with the same issues and none had a formula for success.

Throughout my reporting for this book, I tried to mirror the methodology I used at Hamilton. I approached each school through official channels, requesting and in most cases receiving permission to live in student housing. While I was primarily interested in students' opinions, I also looked to administrators and teachers for a perspective that was vital to the central question of this book: To what degree does the contemporary undergraduate experience differ from what it was in the past?

Reaching these two groups often made for long days. The faculty and staff were typically available during normal working hours, sometimes early in the morning, whereas students were best approached well after dark. I tried to arrange to ride along with campus security officers to see the kinds of issues they faced in the hours past midnight, when students were often on their worst behavior—not that I was looking only for the bad news. I also saw students at their best, running student government meetings, closing an edition of the campus newspaper, wrestling with complex ideas, and articulating their thoughts over a cup of coffee or a beer. College students today are often a compilation of seeming contradictions, unfinished works in progress but full of promise.

I hope that *Binge* reaches deeply into the many different audiences that have a stake in higher education. Parents can learn a lot that will help them prepare for the years just ahead when their child will be off someplace that in all likelihood will become part of his or her future identity. For those baby boomers whose vision of college life remains fixed in the sixties or seventies, I hope to disabuse you of many of those images. It's a different world today, and you need to know which way those differences cut for your child and why your alma mater acts as it does. I also believe that despite some of the more disturbing attributes of modern campus life, you will do your sons and daughters as well as the colleges they attend a big favor by standing back. It's their time to grow up. Let them.

Current college students and recent graduates should not be surprised by what they read in these pages; after all, it is a portrait of them. But they can benefit from a perspective that I suspect is different from what they have heard from parents, professors, deans, and their own peers. While this book will not help prospective students choose one college over another since it is not a guide or a ranking system, it should help them look for certain benchmarks of campus life at the various colleges they consider.

There is another audience I hope to reach as a journalist and as a longtime college trustee: the administrators, professors, deans, and others who oversee our colleges, including the politicians who pass laws affecting student life. The serious policy implications in this book concern how oversight of student affairs should be managed, what the reward system should be for faculty members, and whether laws intended to help make higher education better actually accomplish that goal.

Colleges and the life of students on their campuses are changing, though they are always aimed at producing enlightened, articulate, and responsible citizens. I hope that in some way this book might help achieve that end.

I

Daily Res Life

O n a crisp November Monday evening just past six-thirty, I arrived at the large, rambling cedar-shingled building on the outskirts of the University of California's Berkeley campus. I was there to seek the approval of the governing council of a student co-op, hoping they would allow me to spend a week living among them. I made my way inside. Midway down a broad lobby strewn with mattresses, beer kegs, and empty liquor bottles, I found a lounge where the meeting was already under way. As I felt that old twist of anxiety you get on the first day of anything new or intimidating, I forgot for a brief moment that I was a fifty-something adult.

Apparently as an enticement to improve attendance, the council president had structured the meeting around a word game. From an exposed overhead pipe that created the impression we were below decks on an aging cargo ship dangled two scrolls of printer paper. Each contained a list of scatological and obscene words or phrases (e.g., "salty dog snot," "sand in my vagina") written in thick black marker. As I listened from the back of the lounge, I gathered that the object of the game was to use as many of these words or phrases as possible in the course of articulating whatever point of house business a student wanted to make. So here were a couple of dozen Cal-Berkeley students, women as well as men, lacing their otherwise earnest questions or points of order about housework assignments or budgetary matters with language more appropriate for the lower decks of an aging cargo ship. In recognition of a particularly well-turned phrase or richly inflected sentence, the president would toss a can of beer across the room to the eloquent student.

At most campuses I visited to do research for this book, I requested student housing through the administration and was assigned a vacant room. At Berkeley, however, I had no luck with the administration and decided to seek student housing through the University Students Co-operative Association (USCA), a self-governing alliance of nineteen cooperatives, separate from the university, that provide room and board for some 1,300 Cal students. Scattered around the edge of the campus, Berkeley's co-ops range from cozy houses with fewer than two dozen occupants to apartment complexes with over 400. The largest single co-op with a common kitchen accommodates 151 men and women. A few of the co-ops are for women only. One is for vegetarians. Another caters to gays and lesbians.

I had to contact each house, find out if a room was available, then present myself to the residents, who in the tradition of co-op self-governance would vote on whether they would have me among them. This was the moment to sell myself. Introduced by the house manager with whom I had spoken over the phone, I stepped to the front of the room and told the assemblage that given my age and inexperience and the gravity of my situation, I felt more comfortable passing on the word game and would prefer simply to make my case. Though mildly disappointed, the room accepted this and heard me out.

I explained what my project was about, which other colleges I was visiting, and how I was willing to abide by various ground rules to cover whatever I might see or hear in the course of the week should, of course, they vote to take me in.

"Do we get to see what you write?" asked one student.

"Are you going to use our real names?" wondered another.

The consensus of the group was that I should either vet my material with them before publication or not identify the co-op or its members by name. In order to provide readers with a more accurate account, I opted to omit any further identification of the co-op or its members.

By voice vote, they approved me, though not unanimously. A couple of fellows sitting over on the side of the room said they didn't like the whole idea and thereafter steered clear of me. Most others were friendly enough, though for the most part they went about their business as Cal-Berkeley students.

A number of large universities have cooperatives and some smaller colleges allow one or two as pilot projects, but co-ops are not typical of college housing. In some ways they are a throwback to the early days of residential colleges—a step up from local boardinghouses and more like fraternities in the way they operate. While co-op residents as a Berkeley subculture despise fraternities and all they stand for, the place had the feel of a loosely knit coed fraternity, or perhaps more accurately a commune.

As part of their contract with the USCA, Berkeley co-op residents agree to put in five hours a week supporting the house by cooking, cleaning, washing dishes, gardening, or doing maintenance. In exchange they get a room and three meals a day for less than $2,600 a term, which in 2003 was about half what it cost to live and eat in university facilities. The USCA trains house managers in much the way the administration trains its RAs, the peer resident advisors most colleges recruit to proctor students. In exchange for keeping records, coping with resident conflicts, and dealing with the central office, managers get free room and board. But by tradition, co-op members are self-governed and have little to do with Berkeley's Res Life bureaucracy.

Obviously, an appreciation of the economics of cooperative living was one common denominator residents shared. There were a fair number of long-haired types and bearded young men in the place. I met premed students and engineers, classic nerds with pocket organizers, and others who looked like they had never cracked a book. Most were white, but a former manager assured me that they were actively recruiting from university residence halls, where they were passing out flyers specifically to attract more Asians. I asked one co-oper who had previously lived in university housing how dorm life compared. "No comparison," he said. "Living in a dorm, I felt like I was five years old and a criminal." As chaotic as life in a co-op might be, at least its residents feel free.

My fellow co-op residents were, if anything, a resilient lot. Their food was supplied in bulk through the central USCA office, but its quality hinged on who was assigned cooking duty. At mealtimes, vast trays of food—cornbread or pancakes in the morning, cold cuts at noon, and the likes of turkey cutlets or tetrazzini around six P.M.—were spread out on metal serving platforms in the outer kitchen. From there, diners would carry their plates to one of the twelve-foot Formica-topped tables in the adjacent dining room, which looked like a military mess hall, only not nearly as neat.

Beverages—mostly milk and "bug juice"—were pumped from stainless steel dispensers. If you wanted a soda or a beer, however, you could buy a can of either from a machine for seventy-five cents (no ID required). Regular mealtimes typically drew no more than two dozen out of well over a hundred residents. But since the kitchen was open 24/7, meals were less social gatherings than moving targets of opportunity. I learned that I could not count on the dining room as a reliable source of information.

Often, co-opers raced through the food line and then took their food-laden plates elsewhere to continue watching a movie in the smoke-infested air of the TV/video room, in the den, or outside. At suppertime one evening, I watched apprehensively as a young woman precariously balanced a plateful of an unidentifiable casserole concoction on one frayed arm of a lounge chair while poring over a thick chemistry text on the other. All around her, others watched *The Simpsons*. One or both of the two large-screen TV sets were on almost constantly.

I later caught up with her and asked what she was studying and if she had plans after college. "I'm hoping to go to medical school," she said. "But there are so many smart people here applying. I just don't know if I'm going to be able to get there."

As this was California, much of the co-op's social life, including meals, took place outside. The favored gathering spot was around the picnic table in the courtyard. Furniture clearly designed for the lounge had been dragged outside and left there. The table was often littered with leftover plates of food from dinners prepared easily two or three nights earlier. No one seemed to mind the mess, which I assumed for the first couple of days was a permanent part of the landscape.

One sunny afternoon in the courtyard, a group sat around watching a replay of the prior weekend's big house party displayed on a Sony laptop. A long-haired guy wearing a T-shirt emblazoned with "F.O.V.—Friends of Vaginas" offered wry commentary. A woman wearing a shirt that read "I wave my private parts at your aunties" stopped by to have a look. One guy with frizzy hair recounted for the group how he had been high on acid the night of the party. He said that being groped all night by strangers of both sexes—probably because he'd worn a tutu—added significantly to the surrealism of the experience.

Though there was a distinct chill in the November air, the outdoor hot tub got regular use at night, often by both sexes in the nude. "People are pretty casual about nudity here," an exchange student from Britain advised me.

From the clutter of liquor bottles and beer kegs, not to mention the beer sold out of the soda machine, I wondered momentarily if the twenty-one-year-old drinking age had been repealed in Berkeley. No one seemed to have qualms about smoking a joint in public either, and on a couple of occasions, a bong was passed around the picnic table late in the evening. While I was there only a week, I never saw anyone out of control or in danger, though on Sunday morning I saw two guys who had clearly ingested too much of one substance or another the night before. But that happens in heavily policed college dorms too.

On my first evening following my election as a guest, I was asked to join a small group going to another co-op to watch some movies and do some mushrooms. I had a hunch these were not going to be shiitakes and politely declined. Apparently assuming that my rejection was based on concerns about quality control, my prospective host said with assurance, "When we do drugs here, we know what we're doing." I had no doubt, I said, but suggested as politely as I could that I ought to settle in first. A couple of days later in the TV room, the same fellow came up to me holding a plastic jug filled with a liquid that looked like orange juice, only darker. "Have a whiff of this," he said. The overwhelming musky odor emanating from the jug made me wince.

"Stems and seeds," he explained. "They've been in there for about a week. Try some." I had no trouble declining this offer either.

Toward the end of my stay, one of his cohorts in the house took me aside. "Please don't assume that he is typical of what goes on here. Sure, there are drugs here. But it's not everybody, and it's not all the time." I assured him that I was not misled. While a little dope was clearly part of the scene, it was, as I had observed on most campuses, only marginally so.

Shortly past one o'clock on my first morning, heavy banging on the door of my second-floor room woke me. I threw on a robe and opened it to face four of my new housemates clustered around a half-empty bottle of Jack Daniel's, inviting me to join them. Again I declined—politely I hoped. Whether because of my failure to be sociable or just because I was the new kid on the block, I found myself on the butt end of a little college hazing later that morning. When I opened my door shortly past six on my way to the bathroom across the hall, I was facing a wall of metal beer kegs stacked over every inch of potential exit space.

Fortunately, the kegs were empty, and I was able to dismantle the blockade without waking the three women who lived next door. I never mentioned the episode, and no one made further reference to it during my stay, though the kegs remained in the hallway for the rest of the week.

What was I expecting? This was Berkeley, after all. Nothing I saw that week would have topped the sex, drugs, and rock 'n' roll that defined Berkeley in the sixties and seventies. While in some ways a time warp back to those anarchic days, when this brand of hippie libertarianism reigned on college campuses across the continent, the scene at the co-op was fairly contained. Despite the countercultural trappings and one inveterate dopehead, there was a sense of relative safety, sanity, and essential goodwill emanating from this motley crowd of undergrads. Scholars, radicals, and stoners of both sexes were all peaceably cohabiting, sharing duties, bathrooms, and sometimes beds with one another. Even the squalor turned out to be of limited duration. When I returned from campus late Wednesday afternoon midway through my stay, I was struck by a transformation: the plates were gone from the picnic table, as were the empty bourbon bottles and mattresses from the lobby. The cleaning crew was alive and well—just not operating on a daily basis. Once I got beyond the appearance of the place, I began to recognize that the principal business of going to classes, reading textbooks, and writing papers was getting done without a dean or an RA in sight.

Over the years, I have slept in many kinds of student housing, mostly when I was a student myself and in the period shortly thereafter, while I was still willing to settle for any surface that was dry and devoid of sharp objects and insects. I've slept on fraternity house futons, on lounge sofas, and in sleeping bags behind basement beer taps. Many of the settings I slept in while researching this book were very familiar to me: simple rectangular rooms with one or two single beds, shallow closets or clothes cabinets, plain wooden desks, some modest shelving, and maybe a mirror on the back of a door. At most places, beds consisted of thin institutional sheets and blankets spread over standard tick mattresses on box springs, usually set atop metal frames. Absent the stereo systems, posters, and other personal effects students use to transform these cells into homes away from home, my various digs were in their unadorned essences remarkably similar to each other and to what I remember from my own college years. We called the buildings we lived in dorms. Now, under threat of admonition from Res Life professionals, we must call them residence halls. Most students, I found, still call them dorms.

The biggest difference for me was the coed living arrangement. Occasionally, I was fortunate enough to have a private bathroom. But for the most part, the communal lavatories I shared with students were somewhere down long hallways and littered with the detritus of other people's personal care. I never quite mastered the protocol as to when a bathroom was open for my business and when I should return discreetly to my room and wait for the telltale sounds of departure.

Looking back on my other overnight experiences through the prism of co-op life at Berkeley, I realized that they had been somewhat sterile. One-on-one, I did pretty well talking to my various hall mates, some of whom were a third my age. But as a newcomer—and an older one at that—I was not automatically included in hallway conversations to the extent anyone these days even has them. Frequently, it took some urging by an RA to get students to come to me, after which things usually got easier.

Why it is that modern youth has a problem sharing bedrooms with members of their own sex struck me as odd, since few seem to have qualms about sharing bathrooms with members of the opposite sex. Yet fewer students today have roommates, and roommate issues are a big problem for Res Life administrators even though most colleges now use elaborate computerized matching systems to assure maximum roommate compatibility. One of the principal summer chores of junior Res Life staffers is to run the personal traits of each incoming frosh through a program that matches a nonsmoking, occasional beer-drinking white from the suburbs who wears Old Navy clothes and keeps a robust collection of Phish albums in his iPod with a cultural soul mate.

To be sure, certain unforeseeable incompatibilities can prove fatal to a rooming situation. A University of Maryland student put up with the inconvenience of having to sleep somewhere else ("sexiled," as they say) whenever her roommate brought her hookups (as many as twenty a semester) back to her room. But after she climbed into a pile of vomit on her bed late one evening, she was gone within the week. When Brad lent his erstwhile trusted roommate, Chris, his ATM card one night, he thought he was making a simple $60 emergency loan. Three weeks later, he discovered his entire account had been drained. At a southern school, an aspiring varsity golfer went to retrieve his clubs from the closet on the day of team tryouts to find that his roommate had peed all over them and down into the bag.

In each of these cases, I would have likely pulled out too. But by all reports, today's students seem to have considerably lower tolerance levels, and Res Life personnel seem predisposed to stepping in to resolve even mundane conflicts instead of leaving the parties to work it out for themselves. At some places, complaining about your roommate's penchant for playing video games at three A.M. can get you a hearing with an area coordinator or even a conflict resolution session with a counselor. The conflict may get resolved, but I wonder how that helps develop the practical coping mechanisms most of us need to get through life.

Across the twelve campuses, I saw a profusion of residential housing options—old and new, big and small, intimate and impersonal, specialized and all-purpose, substance-free and transgender-specific. At Stanford alone, students could live in lakeside townhouses, spacious singles off arched Spanish-style courtyards, or cozy bedrooms in rambling affinity houses along the Row. Some sought to gather students of the same foreign language and culture under one roof (Casa Italiana, Mittelhaus Europa). Others (including one called the Enchanted Broccoli Forest) shared a common interest in ecology.

The most difficult—or perhaps better said, exhausting—aspect of my campus stays was that I was often operating in a different time zone from most undergrads. To be honest, it was nice to have a bathroom to myself early in the morning, allowing me to avoid the discomfort of showering while a young woman brushed her teeth, or vice versa. I tried to stay up as late as I could, knowing that most students only began to hit their stride after eleven P.M. But whenever I did drift off to sleep, it was more often than not to the rising sounds of music and footsteps outside my room and the clear sense that the night had a ways to go.

The abiding feeling I had of nightlife in the residence halls was that with the exception of junior Res Life staffers living on the premises, I was the only adult around. Before the last of the supper trays got loaded onto the dining hall conveyor belt, most professors had gone home. Evenings brought a smooth and complete transfer of power.

The exceptions were the places where faculty stuck around because they lived there. Stanford has had professors serving as resident fellows for more than three decades. But their deployment is spotty, and it is getting harder and harder to recruit them to fill the available slots. Pomona also has around a dozen professors living in apartments embedded in dorms. McGill's hilltop houses have teaching faculty in residence. Harvard has had faculty in residence since the 1930s. Along with Yale, it stands as the granddaddy of the American residential college system. Based on the centuries-old housing model at Oxford and Cambridge Universities in England, Harvard's twelve houses were designed to subdivide the undergraduate population, numbering around thirty-five hundred when they were first built, into smaller, more cohesive social units. Along with these houses came masters, as well as tutors—faculty members and graduate teaching assistants who were assigned to one or another of the residential colleges within the larger university. Three-year Leverett House resident Mina Pell understood that her house master was a famous physicist, Howard Georgi, one of the pioneers of grand unified theories. But she knew him as the jolly bearded guy who brought doughnuts to students late at night. She relished the chance to eat dinner with Tal Ben-Shachar, an organizational behavior specialist with the psychology department and a nationally ranked squash player for Harvard as an undergraduate in the mid-nineties. Ben-Shachar lived with his wife and small children in one of Leverett's towers. His kids' swing set was in the house yard.

Being a master at Harvard is considered an honor. Built in the Depression-era 1930s, when a few million dollars went a long way, Harvard's original houses had spacious rooms for students and apartments for tutors. Masters were rewarded with rather grand attached houses that would have been suitable for any well-to-do Boston family had they stood alone elsewhere in Cambridge. Tutors, who had more modest apartments in the house, were expected to dine with undergraduates and to make themselves available for consultation not only on academic matters but on personal ones as well. While masters typically do not maintain the same level of personal contact expected of tutors, they periodically invite small groups of students to come around for dinner (which in the old days included sherry and a glass of wine with the meal). And they are expected to stay abreast of students' personal issues largely through their tutors.

The house, or college, system in and of itself cannot insulate Harvard from the larger trends that have been separating undergraduates from their professors. As Henry Rosovsky, former economics professor and dean of the Faculty of Arts and Sciences at Harvard, observed, professors these days dine less frequently in houses, in part because they live farther away from Cambridge. And students' personal issues have grown decidedly more complex. From what I learned of the fragile psychological nature of many students and the demands made by them and their parents, it seems unlikely that academics whose twin obligations are to teach and to pursue scholarship can also tend to every student's needs all the time. Most of that responsibility, of course, should be with the students themselves, but at least some require the watchful eye of professional counselors and other administrators.

Still, it appeared to me that the continued presence of teaching faculty in Harvard's houses through tutors and masters has preserved at least some level of intergenerational contact and, with it, a palpable air of civility around the houses that I found missing on other campuses. It wasn't simply a matter of having grown-ups around. It seemed to make a difference that these adults were often the same ones who were teaching students in the classroom. As Tom Dingman, Harvard's associate dean and senior tutor at Dudley House, put it, "There is a view that dorms are not meant to be a retreat from the intellectual life of the college."

More than two dozen colleges and universities nationwide have at least one residential college. At Yale, the University of California at Santa Cruz, Rice University, and most recently Middlebury College, they are the centerpiece of student housing. At others, including the University of Virginia and the University of Wisconsin, among those I visited, they are options for new students. My own exposure was at Chadbourne College, where I lived during my stay at the University of Wisconsin. Chad, as it is called by its inhabitants, was originally a women's dorm, but as such contains some of the key structural elements of a residential college: a live-in apartment for an adult, a dedicated dining room, and a large common area. Chad is not a pure replica of the Yale/Harvard residential college: students are assigned there for no more than a year or two; most are freshmen and almost all the rest are sophomores. There is no faculty master or teaching tutor living on the premises; the resident director is a Res Life person. But unlike at Wisconsin's conventional high-rise dorms, faculty members known as fac fellows are in and out of the place constantly. Almost every night, they could be seen eating alongside students in the dining hall. Almost every evening after dinner, there was some sort of academically oriented program run by a professor or notable visitor in the lounge. Attendance was not required, but events were well advertised over the house intercom. Sometime after supper, I would see anywhere from a few dozen to more than a hundred students spread out on lounge chairs listening to a lecture.

Joel Spiess was first impressed by Chadbourne College when he took the University of Wisconsin campus tour while a high school senior in Milwaukee. The idea of living in a place where it was more like having a room in a house than in a dorm appealed to him. The reality of living there as a freshman was even better, and he signed on again as a sophomore. "Other places have maybe one or two big events a semester," he said. "We have one or two a week. When I tell other students who live in big dorms about the amount of programming we have here, they're just floored, like, 'You mean this stuff is happening where you live?'" Chadbourne and other residential colleges physically bring people together over substantive issues. That's unusual for a generation whose principal form of communication is electronic.

Communications technology is now deeply embedded in campus culture as a way of extending and sometimes replacing the concept of community. While the information revolution has been under way for over two decades, the greatest changes have come since the new millennium. Information technology now infuses every aspect of campus life.

Technology has certainly been a boon to administration. Records are far easier to keep, though still more vulnerable to invasion, than metal file cabinets. New systems allow academic and student affairs deans at big universities to cross-check whether the student flunking two courses is the same one who has been written up three times in the past month for alcohol violations. "Technology has given us the ability to follow our students much better," said Connie Hanson, an academic advisor at Indiana. "We have the ability as never before to get information on our students and act on it."

It has also served as an effective investigative tool. A hate mail incident at Pomona was solved when IT (information technology) specialists were able to trace the messages to a remote location on campus and match their posting times to those when a certain student used his campus swipe card to get in and out of the same building.

Technology has replaced the letter home, the pay phone, the room key, the record store, the bull session, the *Penthouse* pinup, the personal diary, and even the Dear John letter. It is the alter ego, the introvert's entrée into the campus clique, the new gay bar, both a supplement to and a substitute for faculty office hours, the politician's soapbox, the bush behind which the stalker hides, and sometimes the mask behind which the race-baiter spews forth hatred. Wonderful and terrible things happen because of communications technology, and they happen with unparalleled velocity.

On move-in day at Middlebury, the corridors of Battel South residence hall were thick with duffel bags, crates, eighteen-year-old men checking out the new women, and dads serving as pack mules. As I sidled by the door of one room, I caught a glimpse of what has become the neoclassic first-day-of-college tableau: Mom was measuring the window for curtains; the kid sister was leafing through the face book checking out photos of her big brother's new classmates, and the young man of the hour was hunkered down at his new desk. His Dell laptop was already hooked up to the campus Ethernet server, and he was IM-ing (instant messaging) his high school buddies, many of whom were in virtually the same setting on some other campus.

Between classes at Indiana one day, I tried to count the number of students who did *not* have a cell phone flipped open and in use. From the snippets of conversation I picked up, there were students talking to a parent sometimes halfway across the country and students talking to other students less than a quarter of a mile away. They were giving glowing reports back home, commiserating over a little brother's loss in soccer, making a date or an excuse for not making one.

IM-ing is rapidly replacing the cell phone—in some cases commandeering the cell phone—as the means of electronic receipt and delivery. Most cells can handle any of the major messaging services such as AOL or MSN. Some students carry a PDA, such as a Blackberry or a Palm Pilot. But as more campuses are "WiFied" so that no physical connection is needed to get on the Internet, everyday laptops stored in a backpack and routinely used in classes become ever-present messengers.

Back in their dorms, students operate out of full-bore information centers in which the computer and the cell phone are supplemented by headsets for listening, an old-fashioned stereo system or a new-fashioned iPod or MP-3 player, and usually a TV set. It is not uncommon to walk into a room and find someone on the phone with Mom back home while IM-ing a buddy, Web-searching (Googling) a fact needed for a paper, and glancing occasionally at the TV set flickering in the background. Techies call it multitasking. To me it seems more like attention deficit fulfillment.

Instant messaging is only the newest addition to that information arsenal. "IM has really changed the place," Pomona senior Sam Glick told me. "It's gone from a convenient way to talk to friends around the country to the way to communicate on campus." Katie, a freshman at Indiana, who also talks to her mom in California daily by cell phone, said, "You meet someone and it's like, 'What's your screen name?'"

Two Hamilton students passing each other between classes held a brief conversation, which they promised to continue with a mutual waggling of the fingers on one hand at each other. I later learned this was the IM equivalent of holding up an extended thumb and pinkie to the ear to mimic use of a cell phone. The waggling fingers were meant to signify typing on a keyboard, as if to say, "Let's IM later."

Many campuses have had their own internal versions of IM for a decade or more. At Dartmouth, where cell phone service was limited, "Blitzmail," Dartmouth's internal computer messaging system, was the common means of communication and had been for so long that it was part of the Dartmouth vernacular. Only Dartmouth people understand that *Blitz me* is a request to get in touch.

"Men and women use Blitzmail differently," explained class of 2004 president Alexa Hansen. Within the "Men are from Mars/ Women are from Venus" dichotomy, she observed, "Guys tend to be much more utilitarian, nonchalant, whereas women tend to analyze the content and timing of responses." Hansen's classmate, Australian Catherine Dale, added, "If you Blitz someone and don't hear back within two hours, it's for one of three reasons: they're off campus, asleep, or they're being intentionally rude to you." Several students warned against using the system after partying too much. Drunk-Blitzing can get you in trouble for saying things you wouldn't otherwise. Before WiFi blanketed the campus, Dartmouth students relied on ubiquitous public terminals that they could log onto with a password to check their Blitz messages at any time of day or night. Turnover on these machines is so constant that when an outbreak of pinkeye swept the campus, it took little time to trace the spread to the communal keyboards. Warning signs to avoid eye contact placed next to public terminals kept students amused for months afterward.

On all campuses, servers manage multiple subgroups called Listservs for every imaginable configuration of community. Professors e-mail assignments via class Listservs. Clubs schedule meetings. The exclusive class Listserv is how Stanford seniors— not juniors or sophomores—learn where their ritual senior pub night is to be held each Thursday. Closed message boards and internal IM systems allow members of groups to discuss and debate anything, anytime, without the discomfort of personal confrontation. A Stanford RA awakened at two A.M. by the loud bass thump of a stereo coming from the room above her used the dorm e-mail Listserv to make her point:

To the boys in room 221,

In the future please keep in mind that quiet hours start at 11 on weekdays and 1 on weekends. Please come talk to me (room 121) if you have any questions or concerns, but otherwise I expect that I will not be hearing your music again after hours.

* * *

The same technology that has opened new worlds for students with hearing and speech impairments is also the perfect medium for social misfits. I heard of one campus stalker who had six different screen names with which to haunt the object of his obsession. Most uses are more benign. Their import is less criminal than simply harmful to ordinary face-to-face civil discourse. An arm's-length electronic message allows a student to tell his professor that he's going to be late with a paper and not have to undergo her careful scrutiny of his face for some clue as to why.

I heard of a guy who broke up with his girlfriend of several months in an IM exchange and finished his lunch at the same time. A college student in Pennsylvania admitted that she used e-mail and IM to break up with her boyfriend because she knew "if I did it in person, it would be ten times more emotional and I would cry, and I didn't want to give him that satisfaction." More out of whimsy than any real need to communicate, I suspect, a Harvard woman crept out of the bed of a guy she was hooking up with while he was in the bathroom. She logged onto her Hotmail account on his computer and messaged friends: "i'm in some guy's room getting ass, but he's in the bathroom. just wanted to take this time to say i love you guys." Her kiss-and-tell was interrupted when he returned to the room.

Steve Lustig, who directs Berkeley's student health center, detected a correlation between a growing student demand for the university's arbitration services and an atrophying of communication skills. Berkeley trains some three hundred students as peer facilitators who are available to work out "issues" (the all-encompassing substitute word for conflict) their fellow students might have with others. "We have a lot more student requests for facilitations at meetings," said Lustig. "It is very sophisticated. But the flip side is that they don't have the skills, so they come here a lot to use the student counseling facilities."

Stanford's residential computing department has studied student computer usage and concluded that instant messaging is more egalitarian than other forms of communication, including just plain talking. The Stanford studies also revealed that almost a third of Stanford students were spending thirty hours a week or more on the computer. Academics were the number-one topic, followed by social interaction as a close second. My guess is at academically less demanding colleges that order would be reversed. Generation Keyboard, as Stanford's residential computing director, Rich Holeton, labels this group, has adopted the computer not just as a means of communicating but as *the* means by which they communicate with one another.

Steve Friess, information culture columnist for *USA Today*, reported about one student who wrote on his application for a camp counseling job: "i want 2 b a counselor because i love 2 work with kids." Friess commented, "This informal instant communication lends itself to linguistic shortcuts, shoddy grammar and inappropriate or absent punctuation."

Beyond the shortcut substitution of numbers for letters and emoticons, there is an entire lexicon of acronyms to accelerate an already impatient mode of communication: "IYKWIM" (If You Know What I Mean), "YMMV" (Your Mileage May Vary, as in "it may be different for you"), and one that speaks volumes to me: "POS" (Parents Over Shoulder, so let's change the subject). IM-ese, if you will, is less about loose grammar and punctuation than it is a means by which a generation seeks to distinguish itself by intentionally using a language that adults simply don't understand.

There is a frenetic aspect to student life on these campuses that is both impressive and a little frightening. Other than one poor woman who was frozen in front of her TV set across the hall from me at Wisconsin, everyone I met seemed to be doing something all the time as if their futures depended on it. Fourth-year student Steve Ander told me he got on average four to five hours of sleep a night at U-VA, devoting his daylight hours to running the University Guides, serving as a prosecutor for the Honor

Committee, and going to classes. At night he went to meetings, then did his schoolwork: "I don't start my work until midnight, when I put in an hour and a half to two hours studying. I probably spend more time doing guide-related work than I do studying [twenty-five hours a week vs. twenty]. People want to make use of their time here and succeed."

One editor at the Duke *Chronicle* claimed to spend up to ninety hours a week at the newspaper's office, using it as a study hall some of the time but more often working on assignments for the paper. Her more concentrated study time was back in her room between eleven-thirty P.M. and two-thirty A.M. Her social life, she said, consisted of long dinners with friends.

For most students, participation in the vast array of extracurricular activities dictates their schedules. Wisconsin has over six hundred registered student organizations, including two daily newspapers. Choirs, bands, a capella groups, religious clubs, debating societies—all the usual suspects—beckon students from the day they arrive. At UW's Memorial Union, I dropped by the kickoff meeting of the group calling itself WHAM, an acronym for Women Happily Advocating Masturbation. Over strawberries dipped in chocolate (paid for with student activities funds), about a dozen students, half of them males, kicked around slogans for posters advertising the organization, whose purpose, according to one officer, was to "help people get in touch with themselves and be more comfortable with their sexuality."

Most college administrations not only tolerate these nonacademic enterprises, they nourish them—partly, I suspect, because they believe that busy students are less likely to get drunk, stoned, or depressed. Colleges and universities today are in the catering business literally and figuratively. In their effort to be all things to all of the best students, every college that can afford to is going out and buying expensive toys. The University of Houston has hot tubs and water slides; Ohio State has a new 657,000-square-foot complex with kayaks, canoes, and indoor batting cages; the University of Vermont spent $70 million on a resort that has a pub, a ballroom, and an artificial skating pond. Northwestern and Dartmouth, among others, are connecting twenty or so broadcast and cable stations to their high-speed Internet servers so that students can watch up to four TV channels at the same time on their laptops. While I was visiting the campus, Stanford's residential computing staff was considering installing two-way videoconferencing equipment in student housing so that Casa Italiana residents, for example, could do live exchanges with fellow Stanford students studying in Florence. When the class of 2008 arrived at Duke, each of them received an iPod engraved with the Duke crest and "Class of 2008" to use however they see fit.

I'm happy to report there are still the mindless activities college students have pursued for decades. Streaking is still big, for example. Hamilton has a streaking team that performs at major campus events, including graduation. In the fall of 2004, following a scrimmage with neighboring Colgate, the team went on a road trip to the college's New England athletic rivals. At Virginia, it is a rite of passage to streak the Lawn. Steve Ander said he and his Lawn neighbors keep spotlights handy, and at the first sound of a prestreak giggle outside, they flood the gauntlet with light. "I bet there's someone streaking every night," he said. "Some nights we get as many as twenty."

Staying up late has been part of the thrill of college life for generations. But over the past twenty years, students have succeeded in forcing college administrators to reset the campus clock to match their biological rhythms. Discouraged by low attendance at early morning classes, professors have largely given up on them. Students check off their academic requirements in the course of the afternoon and early evening, then launch their own agenda just as night falls. Following suit, Wisconsin keeps two of its big dining halls open until two A.M. daily. Pomona's late-night Snack is essentially a capitulation to students' nocturnal lifestyle. The Den on the Berkeley campus was designed as a "Grab 'n' Go" outlet that stays open until two A.M. Delis and cafes at Dartmouth and Duke are open twenty-four hours a day, and everywhere students are asking for more services later into the night. It is their time.

Dining hall service has become just one of several interchangeable eating options. With the advent of electronic debit cards—all-purpose plastic cards that in some cases are room key, ID, and e-cash rolled into one—students can drop by campus convenience stores or even order out. Aramark, which provides the food service at U-VA, Duke, and Yale, among hundreds of other colleges and universities, has a program called C-3, for "convenience to the third power," with stores that keep all the popular food items and stay open well past midnight. Wisconsin has late-night C-stores from which students can have pizzas and subs delivered to their rooms and debited from their dining cards, just as if they had gone to the cafeteria at six P.M.

Here and there, signs of passion over national or global issues popped up during my tour of campuses. A small group of Stanford students went on a hunger strike to promote "living wages" for university employees. A pro-Israeli Christian group planted the burnt-out remains of a suicide-bombed Jerusalem bus in front of the chapel to protest a pro-Palestinian conference at Duke. But such displays were rare.

On a weekday evening when George W. Bush was telling the nation about his plans to send U.S. troops after Saddam Hussein, I was in Indiana University's Student Recreational Sports Center, a fitness complex as big as a suburban high school. At nine o'clock, the place was packed with hundreds of students grunting and rotating across acres and acres of exercise equipment. Suspended above the treadmills and rowing machines were rows of television sets projecting images of Bush's grimacing face above the "Breaking News" banner. Yet hardly an eye lifted more than casually up toward the screens. When I later asked a student about what I'd seen, she replied, "There's not much debate among the general student population about Iraq. There are regular weekly protests in Bloomington in front of the Monroe County courthouse. But those are older folks from the sixties, not students. There was a lot of media attention during the aftermath of the Bush/Gore election, but it was interest, not activism. The last big protest here was when Bobby Knight was fired."

Policies that affect students' daily lives, not global history, stir the blood of today's undergraduates. The biggest crowd in years outside Parkhurst Hall, which houses Dartmouth's senior administrators, gathered to protest the elimination of the swimming team; the biggest at Hamilton was a town hall meeting on the college's alcohol policy. And yet an extraordinary number of college students participate in community service and enroll in academic courses that involve so-called service learning.

According to surveys, better than four out of every five undergraduates do some form of voluntary work for the less fortunate. But not all of it comes from the heart. Student clubs and Greek organizations often put in specific amounts of community service to meet recognition requirements. Res Life staffers use community service as a disciplinary tool. Judicial boards routinely sentence convicted offenders to a designated amount of hours coaching youth league soccer or volunteering at a local hospital. And not every collegiate act of charity involves personal sacrifice. At Wisconsin-Madison, Greek advisor Ed Mirecki remarked of the fraternities and sororities, "Every one of them talks a good community service game, but they're still focused on philanthropy and fund-raising, rather than real hands-on service." Marathon dance contests, cake sales, kickball tournaments, and events like the Indiana sorority midnight breakfast for drunks between parties are more representative of college charity than hands-on work with child cancer patients.

Some educators contend that community service is today's equivalent of student activism—that this generation has learned to think globally, act locally, observing a catchphrase that has spread from the environmental movement through the business world. I suspect it's more conventional than that. "It depends on what your definition of activism is," said Stanford student Jessie

Duncan, who spent most of her junior year in Morocco and Chile. "Lots of people do work/study stuff. But in terms of challenging the system, to be honest, I don't do it. Are you going to jeopardize a grade by missing a class in order to protest something? I don't think so."

Despite all their intentional acts of separation from the real world, students pay close attention to the standards by which they are judged as they amass the credentials needed to move on to the next rung of success. But there is something oddly compartmentalized about it. Classes have their place in the calendar of events, as well as some time allotted for preparation. As far as I could see, however, the drama of daily life revolves around clubs and teams and the getting and spending of social capital—the essence of the undergraduate experience.

2

Hooking Up:
Sex on Campus

I t is nine-thirty on a Wednesday night in a dorm room at Dartmouth, though it could be almost any North American college. A group of freshman women is getting ready to go out for the evening. Kay is excited because a guy across the hall has asked her to go to a movie. The rest of them figure on hanging out at one of the fraternities, playing a little Pong, drinking some beers, and, if all goes well, hooking up.

The women pregame with some vodka and tonics, lounging on big pillows that substitute for furniture, talking about which guys are promising, which ones are tools, about school, about plans for Thanksgiving break. Nicole wants to Blitz some guys to come over and join the preparty. But Lindsay quashes that idea: "What? Booty call?"

Even this early in their first year, they know that a guy on the receiving end of a Blitz message inviting him to a woman's room is likely to interpret it as an invitation to have sex. There are women who figure that a little gratification without the emotional baggage of a relationship is better than wasting a night making the rounds of the fraternities in another *schmob* (a derogatory term used to describe a wandering pack of first-years), getting drunk and hoping to end the evening with a decent hookup.

But hookups have their risks. Nicole is bothered by the blatantly transactional nature of the idea. "People just seem to go out with the express purpose of getting ass," she said. Her friends try to coach her into taking the attitude that "the guy means nothing to you. You're using him, and it doesn't matter if he's using you as well."

A couple of hours later, the women are in the basement of a fraternity house, sticking loosely together but hoping that one of the brothers will spot them and at least offer them a beer. As they approach the bar, one of the guys starts in: "I need a joke."

"It's common at many fraternities for brothers to ask for jokes or trivia answers as a trade for beer," one woman explained. It's a double power play: he's demonstrating his ownership as well as his role as the gatekeeper who decides who gets a beer and when. It's understood that the joke has to be either funny or dirty. The next logical step would be an invitation by one of the brothers into a game of Pong. Then the beer would come as naturally as the banter; one thing would lead to another. There would be a room somewhere, either up on one of the sleeping floors or back at a dorm, his or hers.

Though some traditional dating still goes on in college, the predominant pattern for the past decade or more has been for students to go to parties, or preparties, in packs of friends to hang out over drinks or drinking games and small talk until late in the evening, when they hook up with someone if the conditions are right. A hookup is vaguely defined—by intention. It could be limited to innocuous kissing, it could mean oral sex (most likely female on male), or it could mean intercourse and staying the night. Leaving the term ill defined implies choice and an absence of commitment, and it removes any need to explain to friends what actually happened. The more random a hookup appears, the less likely it will be interpreted as intentional or predatory—just the way the good times happened to roll that evening.

Today's students don't think twice about the hanging out scene; it's what they do. Many parents and even some college administrators welcome it as a healthier way for young people to socialize in the belief that it avoids the rush to commitment and sex implicit in old-fashioned dating. Because of its ambiguity, the hooking-up part leaves many adults confused, which is part of the point.

A study done by Norvall Glenn, a sociologist at the University of Texas, and Elizabeth Marquardt, a scholar at the Institute for American Values, put the new courtship ritual in perspective. Over eighteen months, their researchers held in-depth interviews with sixty-two women on eleven college campuses and separately conducted twenty-minute phone surveys with one thousand other college women nationwide. Through the interviews and surveys, they were able to identify some important changes in attitude among these young, educated women toward marriage and family as well as toward sex.

In the 1950s and 1960s, women tended to view college as a place to find a mate, which was the American standard of security and stability. There was little stigma attached to dropping out of school once a woman had found a suitable husband. While I was in Cambridge, I came upon an item in the Harvard digital archives reporting that in the early fifties an engaged Radcliffe senior would find a yellow rose at her place at the graduation luncheon.

Today's female undergraduate is more focused on career and fearful of letting a relationship interfere with her career trajectory. This commitment phobia is heightened by the widespread perception that early marriages are more likely to fail. And yet, said Glenn and Marquardt, marriage remains a major life goal for most college women; 63 percent said they would like to meet their future husband in college.

Another important change in the mating culture is a shift away from men as the initiators of relationships. "In an earlier time," wrote the researchers, "it was understood that it was the man's job to risk rejection first by asking the woman out on a date and seeking to impress her. It was then the woman's decision whether to pursue something with him." Nowadays, women "speak of feeling confused after the hookup because they do not know whether the guy will want a relationship, and most often it appears that he will not." Several of the interviewees described situations in which they or women they knew felt compelled to wheedle some clarification out of a man with whom they had had repeated hookups; otherwise the relationship would have gone on undefined indefinitely.

Even as students claimed to be inured to the nondating scene on campus, most said they were dissatisfied with it. Some—particularly women—said they plain hated it. Alexa Hansen said it was one of her biggest complaints about life at Dartmouth. Daisy Lundy, elected head of the Student Council at U-VA, called it flat-out dangerous. Men, however, were generally okay with it. From their perspective, the scene allowed them to evade the commitment implicit in dating while satisfying basic sexual needs. "By asking someone out on a date, you're showing your cards," reasoned Mike Wilson, a Stanford soccer player from New Zealand. "I'm happy the way it is."

On the flip side, while a lot of guys liked the idea of maximum access to physical gratification with a minimum of risk, others were vexed by the transactional nature of a mating ritual over which they seemed to have little control. They took little solace in the typical female response, which was that they were merely treating guys the same way guys have treated them for generations.

The result of these often conflicting role-reversing feelings is a macabre dance around the twin pyres of sexual intimacy and commitment. Commitment is out, but so is promiscuity. Hooking up is okay, up to a point. It's still important that a woman not be seen as hooking up *too* often. "Past a certain hour, like two A.M., it's sketchy to go talk to guys in frats because they think you are asking to hook up," reported a Dartmouth woman. "I just want to talk to people, but I feel sketchy just going up to them, so I don't. People, even guys, are judgmental. Either a girl is cold and a prude, frigid bitch, or a slut."

College couples do make commitments, according to Glenn and Marquardt's research. But when they do, they tend to move swiftly into a relationship that is everything short of marriage—

eating, partying, studying, and sleeping together. A student at Pomona told me of two couples who applied—male with male, female with female—for adjoining double rooms. When they got them, they simply swapped roommates and lived like two married couples.

In between these two extremes is a shrinking pool of couples who date, a situation representing the worst of both worlds to this generation: it requires work and commitment but brings no assurance of sexual favor. "It's easier to go out and get fucked up and hook up than be sober and ask a girl on a date and get nothing for it," one male Ivy League junior said. Better to have a "friend with privileges," a sexual license of convenience granted to a pal of the opposite sex who can be counted upon to provide sexual release without the emotional encumbrances. Close by in the lexicon of the hanging-out/hooking-up culture is the booty call, a more specific invitation than the ritualized random hookup. Booty calls are often issued electronically through the campus instant messaging system.

In the hanging-out/hooking-up culture, both men and women initiate. Contemporary feminist doctrine assumes equal rights in choosing sexual partners, as opposed to the ancient practice in which women waited to be chosen. Walking across Dartmouth's Green one day, I overheard a male student telling two friends about his weekend encounter: "So she has me backed up against the wall and she's grinding on me, and I'm thinking, Where is this going?" Those words would almost certainly have once come off as braggadocio, yet I had the distinct sense that this was less of a boast than an admission of a true dilemma. Ted, a student leader at Indiana, told me of an experience one day when he was sitting in a dining hall. He overheard a woman at a table behind him say to her friend, "I'm in a bad mood. I haven't had any ass in a while."

"And she was cute too," he added. "I was surprised."

All of this takes place in a residential environment no longer constrained by the parietal hours that the older set of today's parents will recall. One of the signature changes in the student revolt of the late sixties/early seventies was the end not only of curfew hours for residence halls but also of housing separated by sex. A survey of housing policies at forty-nine representative institutions taken in the early nineties found that nearly four out of five housed men and women in separate buildings during the 1969–1970 academic year. Twenty years later, that ratio was only one in ten. By now, it is smaller still. During my travels, I found two rare pieces of retro living: one at the University of Wisconsin, where one section of the 482-bed, all-women's Elizabeth Waters Hall actually has limited visiting hours for men; the other at the 266-bed Royal Victoria College for first- and second-year women at McGill, which has the look and feel—and some of the rules—of the girl's finishing school it once was. Some others, mostly the big state universities, continue to house the sexes on alternate floors. But on the majority of campuses today, they're all combined.

About the only backsliding from this otherwise inexorable roll toward unisex living I detected is that coed bathrooms appear to be falling out of favor. It is now becoming the custom to let students themselves decide whether they want to share their bathrooms with the opposite sex. When residents of mixed-gender corridors at Hamilton and Stanford voted to keep them separate, they tended to do so along bipartisan lines: ladies who like their toilet lids down sided with gentlemen who prefer to shower without tripping through fields of plastic shampoo containers.

I know plenty of parents, my wife and I included, who have dropped their children off in dorms with unisex bathrooms and left biting their tongues. Watching our daughters go in and out of bathrooms just ahead of some hulking, testosterone-saturated male brought out every protective instinct in us. Even more uncomfortable was when one of us adults had to pause from lifting heavy things and actually use a unisex bathroom. The acute anxiety that some eighteen-year-old in a bathrobe (or not) would walk through the door or out of a shower at any moment trumped longings for bodily relief. I confess that I felt those same anxieties return when I stayed in coed housing during my campus tour.

Even some recent graduates who experienced coed bathrooms have voiced unhappiness. Recounting her experiences as a student at Williams College in the mid-nineties, author Wendy Shalit described the reaction among women on campus in an article she published denouncing coed bathrooms:

> I was positively overwhelmed with letters and e-mail messages from female students. Each began a different way—some serious ("I had to share a bathroom with four football players my sophomore year, and it was the most horrible year of my life"), others gleeful ("Dear Sister Chastity: *I can't stand it either*"). But all eventually got to the same point, which was, I thought I was the only one who couldn't stand these bathrooms. One student confessed that her doctor said she had contracted a urinary infection because she wasn't going to the bathroom enough. "I was simply too embarrassed," she confided.

Perhaps college women confess such feelings only to other women. Most of those I spoke with brushed off the modesty issue and claimed to have grown inured both to the chronic lack of privacy and to more mundane inconveniences such as urine-splashed toilet seats or worse: vomit-filled sinks (more of a guy thing, apparently) on weekend mornings. They seemed nothing if not adaptable.

Dr. Pierre Tellier, director of Health Services at McGill, lectured resident fellows during their presemester training week on how to deal with issues ranging from eating disorders to psychotic breaks, drug overdoses, and other serious matters they could well face in the year ahead, acknowledging that he might sound obsessive on the subject of sex. "We talk to you about this all the time because we assume that you do it like rabbits," he confessed. "In fact, a lot of people of my generation fantasize about living in a residence hall."

To either the great relief or the great disappointment of older readers, I am here to report that coed dorm life is nowhere near as prurient as it's cracked up to be. Don't get me wrong: these students are having a lot of sex; surveys say that more than 80 percent of them engage in it during their undergraduate years. And I have no doubt that in some shared shower room somewhere in North America, a group of eighteen-, nineteen-, and twenty-year-olds has thrown caution to the wind and cooking oil onto the tiled floor in the wee hours of some weekend and engaged in wild sex. But mostly they slip discreetly in and out of their communal bathrooms—girls with their newly washed hair wrapped in towels, guys in sweatpants carrying Dopp kits. The sex happens furtively behind closed doors, under blankets and piles of laundry, with roommates sexiled to sleep elsewhere.

Instead, what coed living often renders is a kind of ersatz sibling environment in which proximate room-dwellers treat one another more like brothers and sisters than sex objects. Alexa Hansen has fond memories of what she described as a family atmosphere in her freshman dorm at Dartmouth. "Guys take care of you," she recalled. Dressed one evening in what must have been a rather revealing dress, she was on her way out when a male dorm mate stopped her. "Would your father let you go out looking like that?" he demanded archly.

"Well, actually yes," said Alexa sheepishly.

"Well, *I* wouldn't," he snapped and ordered her to go back to her room and change into something more modest.

There is linguistic evidence of anthropological change in the modern college lexicon: one of coed living's unwritten commandments is "Thou shalt not engage in dormcest," defined as any kind of sexual or romantic liaison with someone living on your corridor or entryway. The logic behind it is sound enough: the aftermath of a breakup with someone just down the hall and possibly sharing your bathroom can be uncomfortable, even nasty.

A new college ritual—an outgrowth of the Saturday and Sunday morning posthookup room resettlement process—is known everywhere as the Walk of Shame. The best place to watch the parade at Middlebury is in the dining room during Sunday brunch, advised Peter Yordan, class of 2004. Pomona students have been known to set up lawn chairs on Bixby Plaza late on a weekend morning to catch some southern California rays as well as a glimpse of underslept and overserved hookup migrants as they head for Frary dining hall or their own rooms. So universal is the Walk of Shame that a number of musical parodies celebrate it. The Williams Street Mix, a Connecticut College a capella group, got big laughs whenever it performed its rendition of "The Walk," sung to the tune of Simon & Garfunkel's "Sounds of Silence":

> Hello daylight, my old friend
> Oh God, I've done it yet again
> And by the early morning light I see
> The random stranger sleeping next to me.
> Last night he seemed cute
> But now he doesn't seem so cool;
> He slept in drool.
> It's time to take
> The Walk of Shame.

In many obvious ways, college women have made enormous strides over the last four decades. They demanded and won coeducation at formerly male sanctuaries during the late sixties and early seventies. Where there had already been women, which was in the majority of the schools I covered, coeducation expanded from the classroom into the dorms and then through Title IX into the athletic departments. Women also came into key campus leadership positions. Donna Shalala was chancellor at Wisconsin, later the University of Miami; Duke thrived for a decade under the strong leadership of Nan Keohane; Condoleezza Rice was provost at Stanford; and in 2003, Hamilton inaugurated its first women president, Joan Hinde Stewart, after almost two hundred years of men.

At the student level, leadership by women is much more widespread. Increasingly, they are making their marks as undergraduate scholars. Of the institutions I covered alone, women won valedictorian and/or salutatorian honors at Dartmouth and Hamilton in 2004; a woman won the prestigious University Scholar award at Berkeley, and roughly two-thirds of the Phi Beta Kappa memberships awarded at Wisconsin and Pomona were to women. I met women in key leadership positions on every campus I visited: class and student council presidents, judicial board chairs, and campus newspaper editors. At most colleges and universities today, women simply outnumber men. A recent study predicted that in the first decade of the century, the ratio of women to men in college would continue to rise from 128:100 in 2000 to 138:100 by 2010. It is a growing imbalance that has educators worried.

And yet with all these numerical advantages, titles, and honors has come less-welcome baggage: higher levels of stress associated with higher levels of achievement and expectation, the right for women to drink as much as men. By demanding equal access to sexual gratification and freedom from the bonds of commitment to a relationship, college women find themselves competing as men have for decades. Perhaps someday society will reach a higher plane of gender equality, but at this juncture of our cultural evolution young men and women remain caught between old traditions and new expectations. The tectonic plates are rubbing up against one another in ways that often make college a jarring experience.

Disturbed by persistent indications that women's experience at their institution was inferior to that of men, Duke administrators formed a commission that conducted in-depth surveys of female students, both graduate and undergraduate, alumnae, professors, and administrators from 2001 to 2003. The result was the Women's Initiative report, a forty-page psychosocial profile of women's life at Duke. Its most trenchant observations were about the lives and attitudes of Duke's undergraduate women. The report described a social environment encapsulated in the phrase "effortless perfection"—the expectation that a Duke woman would be "smart, accomplished, fit, beautiful and popular, and that all this would happen without visible effort."

> Both men and women expressed dissatisfaction with the dating scene at Duke. Students rarely go out on formal dates but instead attend parties in large groups, followed by "hook-ups"—

unplanned sexual encounters typically fueled by alcohol. Men and women agreed the double standard persists: men gain status through sexual activity while women lose status. Fraternities control the mainstream social scene to such an extent that women feel like they play by the men's rules.

The Women's Initiative also concluded that Duke men and women follow "opposite trajectories" over their four years, "with women losing status in the campus environment while men gain status." Because of their relative scarcity, "African-American men hold power over their female counterparts who vie for their attention." Women's relationships with other women too often revolve around their relationships with men, while relationships with men "are often sexually intimate but otherwise superficial."

The Duke report might well have described life at all of the other institutions I visited. The main difference would be in the relative impact of fraternities on social life, since the role of Greeks varied widely from one campus to another. Otherwise the profiles were identical: the unhappiness with the dating scene, the pressure to achieve and to do so with the appearance of effortlessness, and the fragility of self-esteem. The more prestigious and selective the school, the more pronounced the problem.

At first I was surprised by the ease and candor with which students, especially women, talked about sexual matters. Then I was reminded that this was a generation brought up on a steady diet of sex education. As kids they were taught safe sex years before algebra. They have also been trained in the general theory of tolerance that espouses acceptance of different lifestyles and beliefs and admonishes criticism of sexual orientation as much as any form of racism or sexism.

Gay students tend to maintain a separate culture on most campuses and are politically organized in ways they hardly dared to be when I was in college. And the wall separating them from mainstream heterosexuals is considerably lower than in the past.

To be sure, there are still students who don't want to even be seen in conversation with someone known to be gay. But the line has blurred and the change has no doubt been accelerated by the open discussion of sexual orientation.

Some colleges are known as gay-friendly. Some get labeled as gay schools, though such a sweeping label is usually meant as a pejorative. There are campuses and social circles within campuses where it is considered cool to be gay, or at least to have experimented with homosexuality. New York University is consistently on lists of gay-friendly schools, as are Smith and Mt. Holyoke, two of the remaining all-female Seven Sisters colleges, which were said to mirror the Ivy League in the years before coeducation. I often heard Yale mentioned as a place that in recent years has attracted gay students. Pitzer and Harvey Mudd, members of the Claremont consortium along with Pomona, have also been mentioned on lists of gay-friendly campuses, as has Reed College in Oregon—all schools with excellent academic reputations.

Soon after accepting its first men, Vassar College, another of the former Seven Sisters, became known as gay-friendly, in part thanks to its Homo Hop gay dance, which drew lots of gawking straight students as well. The Queer Student Union (QSU) at Williams College holds a similar Queer Bash every semester that is widely attended by straight students attracted by the overtly sexual atmosphere. "The themes of these parties are generally gender-bending," said Alex Golden, a former QSU cochair. "People are encouraged to come in drag or as little clothing as possible. Since gay people are far outnumbered at any sizable party at Williams, the QSU usually projects gay pornography throughout the party, reminding people that the party is a celebration of queerness. This obviously offends some people and keeps many away, including some gay students (though most will come anyway and then complain later). People like this party because it's sexy and naughty and fun—the music, decor, and lighting are much better than anything else on campus, and it's a nice change of scene from the typical Williams party."

Duke, though generally characterized by gays as inhospitable, has shown signs of change. "When I first got here," said Duke senior Christopher Scoville, "gays were complaining about how awful it was. Now I'm a senior and there's a lot more space for those kids. I'll go to straight parties with someone I'll hopefully be sleeping with later," said Scoville. "I rushed and pledged a fraternity and went to parties there with gay dates. But that's pretty rare here. Queer people are not allowed to be queer in those spaces. Others would do that only if they knew everyone in the group pretty well."

Gays generally see the apparent level of tolerance and support for their gayness as only skin deep, however. While almost everyone in this generation has been thoroughly coached in the importance of acceptance, says Alex Golden, "this sentiment is not necessarily born out of a genuine empathic concern for humanity. I think the tolerance of out LGBT [lesbian, gay, bisexual, and transgender] students actually stems from the importance that academic cultures place on political correctness. It is definitely uncool to be homophobic, much like it's uncool to be racist. The result is a somewhat artificial tolerance stemming from people's narcissistic need for approval rather than from a more empathic human connection. Thus, currents of homophobia are still prevalent beneath a facade of tolerance." At the more conservative schools like Williams, Hamilton, or Duke, the less visible gay people are, the more acceptable they are to the straight majority.

Young people who are aware of their homosexuality, even if they are not out, have the advantage of being able to check out the atmosphere and reputation of the schools they are applying to on lists such as *The Princeton Review*'s ranking of most and least friendly gay schools. That wasn't so for Thomas Acampora, who didn't come to terms with his sexual orientation until well into his senior year in high school in the Bronx. Accepted at Amherst and several other highly selective colleges, he chose Hamilton because it offered him the best scholarship package. But when he arrived, he found that life for a gay person was pretty lonely.

"I had a straight friend who told her roommates that she was going to a Rainbow meeting, and they asked, 'Why is there a Rainbow here? There aren't any gay people.'"

In fact, the Rainbow Alliance, the recognized campus gay organization, had about two dozen active members and about twice that number on its e-mail list. But Acampora said that he could count the number of datable gay students on his fingertips. Social life usually involved hanging out in one another's rooms or possibly going to gay clubs and bars in Utica or Syracuse, about 45 minutes away. Hamilton had a Rainbow variety show with performances by dancers and singing groups that attracted a crowd of nearly a hundred. But when the entertainment was over and the entertainers' straight friends left, the crowd quickly dwindled down to the same fifteen or twenty who usually showed up at Rainbow events.

Thomas thought of transferring, but scholarship money isn't portable. Besides, as a double major in history and English, he was intellectually challenged at Hamilton. He was devoting his senior year to an honor's thesis on homosexuality during the Imperial period in British history, when, he says many gay Britons went to the colonies, where they could express their sexuality more openly than in Victorian England.

Tamar Carmel didn't come to terms with her lesbianism until well into her first semester at Northwestern, where she was living in the so-called Virgin Vault, an all-female corridor in Allison Hall dominated by conservative Christian girls, including her roommate, who were more comfortable in the Vault than they would have been in coed housing. She spent almost all her time elsewhere, came out, and joined the Rainbow Alliance, whose Listserv of three hundred names drew heavily from Northwestern's music and drama programs. The university's south campus "tends to be where most liberals and countercultural types— artists and actors—live," she said. "The north campus is more traditional and fraternal. Gays there feel very uncomfortable." But there is, she said, a certain blurring of those lines not just in terms of where gays feel comfortable hanging out but in who is gay and who isn't.

There aren't many guys who call themselves bisexual, a term committed gays often see as a cop-out. "Women," said Tamar, "are more open about going both ways. It follows the feminist notion of a lesbian continuum, along which every woman falls someplace and shouldn't be afraid to acknowledge that part of her is attracted to other women."

Poet and essayist Adrienne Rich is said to have coined the phrase "lesbian continuum" in advocating a new approach to cultural feminism that rejects the radical separatist approach that dominated the women's movement in the 1970s. Physical attraction to women is not just an expression of political anti-patriarchalism, Rich posited, but rather a place along a spectrum of emotions shared by every woman. That concept effectively gives permission to a new generation of college women to experiment with lesbianism and bisexuality.

Even at macho Duke, there are circles in which experimentation is accepted. Pink Tower is not a building on campus, nor is it widely known. "It started as a wild party in someone's room in one of the nerdier SLGs [selective living groups, Duke's term for private societies, fraternities, and sororities]," recounted Christopher Scoville, a participant. That initial gathering, which came to be known as Freaky Friday, grew from around twenty to about eighty students drawn from different campus subcultures. "People were making out with everyone," recalled Scoville. "Two women were kissing each other, then they'd be off with guys." The same crowd reconvened in other locales, at one point migrating into one of the quads where several fraternity parties were under way. "Some of the frat guys got curious," said Scoville. "They'd look over at this group, and then some of them would wander over and join in.

Over the year, Freaky Friday evolved into a regular thing, acquired the name Pink Tower, and began functioning as a student organization with clothing exchanges, an ice cream "antisocial," and scheduled bar nights. "It's not a gay group; it's just really progressive," he said. "It is sort of becoming cool but only among the people who do it. Greeks will show up but won't talk about it back in their world."

While the openness and official endorsement of queer culture on campus has allowed students who have doubts about their own sexuality to experiment in ways few would have dared several generations ago, it has in other ways made it harder to cross the line. "Here at Harvard," said Carol, a lesbian student, "being queer has become more political. An us-versus-them mentality discourages testing sexual boundaries. Gay women are wary of relationships with bisexual women because they fear they will be deserted in favor of some man," she said. Conversely, she allowed, "I don't date guys largely because it would betray my political views." Her lesbian sisters, she said, would accuse her of "giving in to the patriarchy."

The college years have been and always will be a time of sexual experimentation—a lot of it good old trial and error. Colleges can do no more and probably a lot less than parents to keep the errors at a minimum and prevent heartache. The culture we live in has given the current generation unprecedented permission to test and talk about their sexuality. Colleges have come to feel obliged largely for their own protection to provide graphic lectures on safe sex practices, hand out free condoms and dental dams in their health centers, and provide other clinical supports that amount to an elaborate safety net for those who fall victim to the physical risks inherent in sexual experimentation. But in doing so, they may also be granting their students a kind of tacit permission to test the limits of their own sexuality and endorsing what has become a tyranny of the majority that all but demands students to become sexually active, in some cases before they are psychologically ready.

3

How Hard Are Students Studying?

S eeing the number of parties on campuses, the local bars jammed to the rafters on weekday nights, and the incredible amounts of time students spend on extracurricular activities, I wondered how much time these students were devoting to their studies, which were, after all, why they were in college in the first place. Data from the National Survey of Student Engagement (NSSE) indicate that only 11 percent of college students spend 25 or more hours a week studying, reading, writing, and doing other activities for their classes; 40 percent spend 10 hours or less out of the 168 that make up a week. Those numbers have been steadily trending downward since the NSSE surveys began in the mid-1980s.

There are and always have been college students who grind out their degrees, students who are diligent, students who dabble, and students who really shouldn't be in college. The true scholars, the professors' dreams who devour knowledge like a feast and virtually frolic in the life of the mind, are rare birds. But I managed to meet one: Javier, as I'll call him, a sociology and economics major at Duke from Europe. At the end of his sophomore year, he had a GPA of 3.985, which put him eleventh in his class of some fifteen hundred. He had been number one until he blew off a course in multivariable calculus. It wasn't that difficult a subject, he said, which was part of the problem. He didn't put much into it, made some "stupid mistakes" on the exam, and only got an A-minus.

While he found himself bemused by the antics of his beer-swilling American schoolmates, Javier really didn't have time to waste. He did more than prepare for class. He was guilty, he confessed, of "overkill. . . . I sometimes solve problems that are not required for class." Academics took up so much of his time that he was barely able to fulfill his duties as the floor representative to his dorm council, which amounted to organizing a lecture, a film night, and some sort of community service activity. What turned Javier on were the minds of his professors and the knowledge available in the books he pored over daily. He not only knew his professors; he knew their scholarly strengths and weaknesses relative to colleagues at, say, the University of Chicago. Naturally enough, he was a teaching assistant, lecturing to and grading his peers. When we last spoke, Javier said he was going to Paris in his junior year to brush up on his French, then hoping for a summer internship with McKinsey & Co. in Montreal. I said I thought he had a good chance of getting it or something just as interesting.

More typical than Javier but still highly respectable are the so-called vocationals who are there to get what they need in order to succeed in careers ranging from accounting to brain surgery, and the collegiates, who work in order to get respectable grades but who thrive on extracurriculars. They have in fact become the model modern college students—the ones who win scholarships and prizes not simply because they do well in class but because they throw themselves into every aspect of campus life.

Anthony Vitarelli, president for two years of Duke's campus council, an officer in his fraternity, and a man well known and liked on campus, was a poster child collegiate. But like many of the student leaders I met, Anthony admitted that he spent more time studying in high school than he does in college. Speaking for himself and many fellow students, he observed that the average course load at Duke is ten hours a week, for which he said, "Believe me, you're not filling up thirty-five hours doing homework for that."

"The people I see being successful in life are also some of the more social people on campus," he observed. They're the class presidents, club leaders, BMOCs (big man on campus), and BMOC wannabes. And in the current campus environment, they do well. Vitarelli was awarded a prestigious Truman scholarship in his junior year as a political science major and was looking forward to law school. His classmate Jen Hasvold, another poli sci major, with a 3.77 GPA and carrying a premed load as well, said she put in about four hours of studying a day for four courses and in preparation for the MCATs, the medical school entrance exams. "I know people who don't work nearly as much as I do," said Jen. "But unless you were born knowing what a benzene ring is, you're probably going to have to put in some time."

Holly Johnson, who graduated with high distinction from Indiana University in 2004, also said she worked hard—she was the recipient of a Herbert B. Wells scholarship, which paid "full freight," as they say, over four years at IU. "But I really didn't work my ass off or anything," she confessed, comparing her several hours a day of studying to her boyfriend's regimen as an engineering student at Purdue, where he put in six or seven hours every day outside of class.

There are people who put in very little time and still do fine. I was fascinated by how many students at good schools managed not only to get by but also to earn what were once considered impressive grades—B's and B-pluses. A Harvard junior, a varsity athlete with a B average, took me through her typical weeknight routine:

6:00	Dinner in the house dining room
6:30–9:00	Hang out, study
9:00–11:00	Pregame in someone's room (a few beers, a gin and tonic)
11:00	Head out to a bar or club nearby in Cambridge
2:00 A.M.	Drop by a final club briefly after the bars close

Even though the ceiling for achievement at these top schools remains very high, the floor—the minimum level of achievement necessary to stay at them—is surprisingly low. "You can work as hard as you want to," is how a Middlebury senior put it. And riding on the momentum of achievement that got them there in the first place, many do work hard at least part of the time they're in college. But as a Harvard history major explained, "It's very hard to get a bad grade [which she classified as anything lower than a B or a B-plus] assuming you're smart and clever enough to get into Harvard in the first place. But for many classes, the cut between a B-plus and an A or an A-minus and an A is much greater. If you want a straight A, it's almost impossible to get one without going to all the sections and doing all the reading."

The popular term for what has happened is *grade inflation*, although professors much prefer the term *grade compression*, which subtly removes the suggestion that their standards have fallen. Much has been written about grade inflation, mostly by those responsible for it in the first place. But none refute that there has been an increase in the overall grades of college students, particularly at the most selective institutions.

The latest surge in discussion was triggered by a report that 91 percent of Harvard's class of 2001 graduated summa, magna, or plain vanilla cum laude. Patrick Healy of the *Boston Globe* wrote that Harvard has become the laughingstock of the other Ivies—"the Lake Wobegon of higher education, where all the students, being above average, can take honors for granted. It takes just a B-minus average in the major subject to earn *cum laude*—no sweat at a school where 51% of the grades last year were A's and A-minuses." To be sure, Harvard students seem to get brighter every year, according to their admissions dossiers. But many educational observers find in those statistics confirmation of a widespread belief in the college world that the hardest thing about Harvard is getting in.

Laugh as they might at their rivals in Cambridge, Princetonians have a similar grade inflation problem. The median graduating grade-point average of Princeton's class of 2002 was 3.46, or between a B-plus and an A-minus. According to a report to the faculty in the winter of 2003, a senior with a solid B average at

Princeton graduated 973rd out of 1,079th, which is to say in the bottom 10 percent of the class.

When I was at Hamilton, a C was average because it was more or less the mean grade of the entire student body. Last I checked, the college average was hovering around 86—a solid B. I suspect this degree of inflation is fairly typical at selective schools across North America.

Stuart Rojstaczer, a professor of environmental science at Duke, did a study of thirty-four colleges and universities including big and small, public and private, gathering grades from as far back as the 1960s. His Web site, www.gradeinflation.com, documents a steady and significant rise in grade averages across the spectrum, albeit less so at the less selective institutions. His data also undercut assertions that affirmative action has contributed to the rise: during the period in the late eighties and early nineties when there were significant increases in minority enrollment at the schools he surveyed, there was actually a dip in the grade inflation rate. If there is a correlation, said Rojstaczer, it is with the advent of policies that reflect a view of college as a consumer enterprise.

That view would comport with those of his Duke colleague Larry Evans, who documented and published Duke's record of grade inflation, department by department. He found it everywhere, though less pronounced in the quantitative courses (like his, physics), where answers tend to be either right or wrong. His numbers were much like those for other selective schools. His blunt conclusion: "They're not getting A's and B's because they're working harder than [their counterparts] thirty years ago. They're getting A's and B's because they're being graded more lightly."

Professor Evans's personal solution was simply to stop giving C's—a grade rendered meaningless by compression. But many of his colleagues argue it's not that simple; that with the greater array of course offerings and specialization, students (in upper-level courses, anyway) are flat-out more competent in subjects they choose to take and are motivated to do well. Evans thinks it has more to do with consumerism: the growing attitude among students and their families that the purpose of college is to provide a service, which includes the awarding of marks high enough to gain entry to the next level on the ladder to success, whether it's graduate school or a high-paying job. "Beginning in the early nineties," Evans told me, "I began to notice a pattern where students were coming in with a fixed notion of an upper limit on how much they were willing to do." Rather than hold them to traditional standards, he posited, most professors simply acquiesced. I heard an echo of that at Berkeley, where history professor Paula Fass told me that she assigns her undergraduate students far fewer pages to read these days than in years past. It would be futile: "They won't read them," she said.

Paralleling both the rise in grades and the retreat from students' lives beyond the classroom has been the institutionalization of student evaluations as a piece of tenure and promotion decisions. It's not a big part, to be sure; student evaluations pale in comparison to a professor's scholarly publishing record. But it is indicative of a larger cultural shift. Student evaluations of professors were originally devised as a grassroots service to help steer incoming students toward and away from professors who were respectively good or bad, entertaining or dull, fair or unfair. But like everything else in the post-1968 revolutionary period, evaluations metamorphosed. "As long as they were subterranean documents among students, it was okay," said Larry Evans. "Then the faculty devised a form of our own. Now it's completely reversed— it's a grading system. The administration has decided these are good enough to make statistics out of. Originally they were strictly within departments. Now we are required to submit all of them for tenure review." Each Duke professor is rated on a 1-to-5 scale on forms handed out before final exams. Ironically, the students never learn the results of their own surveys and have taken to resurrecting their old grassroots system on a Web site.

It makes sense that students will do better in courses they are interested in, so perhaps one of the reasons grades are higher these days is that students have so many more courses from which to choose. To be sure, part of the course proliferation comes from the rapidly growing body of knowledge out there to be absorbed, especially in the sciences. Any student intent on getting the most out of the vast troves of information and the thinking of great minds at a prestigious institution would surely be daunted at the prospect of covering even a modest sample of what is available. But much of the profusion is an outgrowth of the collapse of curricular structures—the end of core requirements in many of the most prestigious colleges and a newfound ability of individual professors to create courses that reflect their particular academic specialty.

The overthrow of traditional curricular requirements followed the rise in feminism and civil rights in North America. The establishment of women's, African American, Hispanic, Asian, and queer studies programs on many campuses was accompanied by an expansion in the number of courses based less on traditional disciplines than on popular culture. By the 1990s, some college students were graduating with the help of credits for courses such as Principles of Recreation at Auburn, Dance Roller Skating at Kent State, Ultimate Frisbee at the University of Massachusetts–Amherst, and Music Video 454, a course at the University of Michigan whose sole text was *The Rolling Stone Book of Rock Video*.

The trend has not abated. Professors frequently build courses around popular cultural icons such as *The Simpsons*. Muhlenberg College professor Susan Schwartz uses the TV series *Star Trek* as the basis for a religion course. "Popular culture courses help us teach liberal arts skills using subject matter that's more accessible to students," St. Joseph's University history professor Jeffrey Hyson told the *Philadelphia Inquirer*.

Lynne Cheney, chair of the National Endowment for the Humanities during the Reagan and George H. W. Bush administrations, coauthored with former Colorado governor Richard Lamm a study of curricula at fifty leading American colleges and universities, concluding that because of the lack of curricular cohesiveness and rigor, "many students graduate from college with less knowledge about the world, our nation, and our culture than would have been expected of high schoolers of fifty years ago. Our current college graduates often have only a thin and patchy education, with enormous gaps of knowledge in fields such as history, economics and literature." Among the examples of less traditional offerings found in current catalogs: History of Comic Book Art, an arts and humanities requirement at Indiana University; History and Philosophy of Dress, taught in the department of humanities at Texas Tech; Rock Music from 1970 to the Present, an arts and humanities requirement at the University of Minnesota; and Campus Culture and Drinking, taught by the Duke social sciences department.

Defenders of the more fluid curricula counter that most of the criticism is ideologically based; that the plaintiffs are almost always political conservatives whose beef is less with the use of popular culture as a medium than with the leftist or progressive thrust of the topic selection. For me, the issue is less the content than whether the course advances the cause of critical thinking and whether the content contributes to students' general understanding of what makes the world work. More often, I fear, these courses simply restate in some quasiacademic jargon what students already know.

The other danger of curriculum inflation is that it weakens the common bond college graduates have with one another—what it is they have mutually learned in the course of four years of study. Cheney and Lamm cite a claim by Cornell University's bulletin that "there is no course that all students must take, and there are nearly 2,000 from which they may choose." So what does it mean to have a degree from Cornell? In the nineteenth century, having a college degree at the very least meant that you could read and write in Latin and Greek. Graduating from St. John's College in Maryland at any time in the last fifty years meant that you had read a specified canon of great books in philosophy, religion, literature, and science. It is now likely that two students can obtain bachelor of arts degrees from the same highly selective

American college over the exact same four years and not have shared a single course.

Harvard professor of government Harvey Mansfield took his fellow professors to task for their failure to challenge Harvard's brilliant students, who were collectively, he declared, the best of any college in the country. "Today, what I see occurring on the campus signals the damage that may result when higher-education institutions compromise their virtue to minister to the self-esteem of students," wrote Mansfield. Grade inflation, course evaluations, a hollowing out of core curriculum that allows professors to "teach what they have chosen as their own research," in Mansfield's words, have advanced a culture of self-esteem that ultimately diminishes the value of a Harvard education.

"What happens at Harvard sometimes presages, sometimes reflects, what happens at other colleges and universities," wrote Mansfield. Indeed, what appears to be happening over the years is that except for the most highly motivated, students and their professors seem to have grown apart from one another as increasingly distinct elements of campus culture. As the distance separating their lives has grown, the roles of studying and teaching as the principal facets of campus life have begun to fade.

One of the first casualties was the Friday class. Class schedules, which at many colleges used to include Saturday mornings, started to be compressed as a fuel-saving device during the oil embargo of 1973–1974. But when the supply lines opened up again, the class week did not. Friday became institutionalized as a writing day for the pure scholars, a consulting day for the more entrepreneurial faculty. (When Donna Shalala was chancellor of the University of Wisconsin, she was heard to have referred to them as "private practitioners.") Students were delighted, as it made Friday the first day of a long weekend. When I was at Hamilton, I asked my housemates if my last Friday evening would be a good time to throw a wine and cheese party for them. The consensus around the dinner table was immediate: "Thursday would be much better," they chorused. "That's when the weekend starts."

In some places, even Mondays have been softening. "We've run out of classroom space between ten A.M. and two-thirty P.M. Tuesday through Thursday," a Duke administrator acknowledged. "There is an unwritten contract between students and faculty," Larry Evans told me, "that we won't bother you if you don't bother us."

At Indiana University, an admissions officer showering after exercise asked a group in the faculty/staff locker room why faculty members hate Wednesday meetings so much. "Because it ruins two weekends," was the punch line. The quip drew knowing laughter from the group, which included a number of professors. When I asked an Indiana University history professor, who was an engaged and popular teacher by reputation, if she had any Friday classes, her response was reflexive: "Oh God, never!" she said, rolling her eyes upward.

Other faculty vehemently defend themselves on the grounds that too many students don't care enough to warrant the attention. They don't show up at an early Friday morning class anyway. Too many of them take courses because they think they're easy A's or because they have to as a degree requirement, or because they must in order to maintain NCAA (National Collegiate Athletic Association) eligibility to do what they're really there for, which is to play a sport. Why waste time and energy on these students, goes the argument, when there's valuable research waiting to be done?

Others blame the significant erosion in preparation for college—an indictment of the American high school system—claiming that faculty must spend more time doing remediation in class and less time teaching the substance of the course as a result. This is a far bigger problem for the less selective state institutions than it is for most of the schools I visited.

Whether underprepared, indifferent, or just overwhelmed, some students seeking refuge from the demands of school have for centuries turned to cheating. To an extent, the level of cheating that goes on at any given point in history reflects the moral climate of the times. By that measure, particularly in the high-stakes climate of campus life, where cutting corners often no longer seems to shock the conscience, it should be no surprise to anyone that cheating is on the rise.

A recent study by psychologist Augustus Jordan of Middlebury College found that when asked anonymously, an outright majority of college students acknowledge cheating by one means or another. A big chunk of it—more than a third, according to faculty member Donald McCabe of Rutgers—is Internet-based cut-and-paste plagiarism.

The Internet has made it much easier to cheat but also much easier to catch cheaters. Finding fodder to fill term papers became a whole lot easier with the arrival of search engines such as Yahoo and Google. Finding whole essays—the modern equivalent of the old frat house term paper archive—is now a thriving e-business. Sites such as www.termpapersonfile.com and www.papertopics.com offer surefire A papers for $9.95—surefire, that is, if you don't get caught.

On the other side of the ethical battlefield is a growing arsenal of plagiarism detection programs such as www.turnitin.com. Many professors say Google is all they need to search the Web for hauntingly familiar phrases or paragraphs or even whole papers lurking out there in cyberspace.

Where does the attainment of real knowledge fit in? The research indicates a clear difference in ethical behavior between those who actually need to know things in order to succeed and those who just want a degree. The biochemistry student en route to a medical career or the computer science major for whom a thorough understanding of Boolean logic is essential if he's to launch the next killer-ap dot.com is less likely to cheat than the student who feels all he needs from a course is a passing grade. The credential seekers come up with the most amazing repertoire of rationalizations for their dishonesty. One excuse, according to McCabe, is that everything on the Internet is ipso facto public knowledge and therefore doesn't need to be cited. More wide-spread is a twisted logic that runs like this: Everyone around me is cheating, which means the system is unfair, which means the only effective way to get a fair shake is to cheat too. I'm not being dishonest; I am just playing by the rules.

Such thinking is stunningly pervasive. When I met with Berkeley professor Robert Jacobsen in his physics department office, he had already served on many judicial panels. Three involved potential expulsions. He recalled one case involving a student who felt no remorse for cheating. "He looked me straight in the eye and said, 'I got into Berkeley by copying other people's homework. Why should I stop now?'"

Overhearing this, a senior faculty member on the panel let out an audible gasp but regained enough composure to ask the student, "And how do you expect to survive in the real world after college?"

The young man turned to him and said with casual self-assurance, "Same way."

"Almost at any time, the human condition is a tapestry of good and evil," observed Tom Morris, former Notre Dame professor, author, and self-styled public philosopher whose lectures and consulting assignments on ethics got a big boost during the Enron and Worldcom corporate scandals. Sometimes, he said, there's more evil evident than good. "The ratio is worse today," he explained, "because there has been a fracturing of the institutions of our society—the family, cultural institutions, religious institutions." Combined with the extraordinary pressures young adults feel they are under these days from their parents, their peers, and themselves, this drives them to scratch around for any means to achieve their goals: getting into the best colleges and graduate schools and having lucrative careers.

"The ancients saw ethics as a source of strength," said Morris. "Nowadays, 'excellence' is so much more important to many than ethics. I think the ancients understood that ethics was the basis of excellence. We seem to have lost sight of the link between the two." Little wonder then that many kids gravitate toward an ends-justify-the-means approach.

Because so many colleges and universities are facing the same ethical erosion, many have been reforming their judicial codes. Stanford underwent a major change in 1997, granting more judicial authority to students and clarifying the rules of due process. Hamilton tightened up its rules in 2003, aiming to make the system better understood and more consistent over its three separate bodies: a judicial board, an honor court, and a third body to handle sexual harassment and assault cases. Both schools have enlarged the pool of students trained to serve as panel judges.

A number of students on different campuses told me they felt that their school's systems of punishment were internally inconsistent. "Sometimes someone convicted of rape goes away for a semester while an honor code violator goes for a whole year," said Isabel Carriego at Dartmouth. Claire Bourne, editor of the Middlebury student newspaper, admitted she couldn't tell me what her college's honor code actually said, but every professor seemed to assume every student knew it and would consistently obey it. Unmonitored or take-home exams are normal procedure at Middlebury. "It's all nice and idealistic to think that someone's not going to look at the material," she said. But people take advantage of the privilege regularly.

A Dartmouth student I'll call Paul was serving a two-term suspension from the college when I met him in Hanover. His story of being prosecuted for failing to correctly document what was his work and what was his partner's in a collaborative engineering assignment left me confused as to why he had been accused at all and what criteria Dartmouth's Committee on Standards (COS) used to convict him. Because he requested anonymity and because the Dartmouth administration would never give me its side of the story, there was no way for me to check his story out. Paul believed that he was guilty only of a technical oversight and told the COS panel that he honestly did not believe he had violated Dartmouth's honor code. He took the fact that they handed him only a two-term suspension versus the standard four for cheating as evidence that they weren't very sure he had either.

Charged with presenting another student's work as his own during his required sophomore summer term, Paul was not tried until the following winter. His appeal was denied, and he was given forty-eight hours to pack his things and get off campus. He remained in Hanover during his suspension, however, working a couple of jobs to keep afloat and living in his fraternity house, though it was technically in violation of the rules to do so. Dartmouth, he explained, took a sort of don't ask/don't tell attitude toward such violations. A buddy of Paul's had been doing the same thing, but his unauthorized presence was exposed after he was cited by campus Safety & Security for public intoxication. Paul, whom I met in a restaurant in downtown Hanover, was being careful, as they say in the military, to fly under the radar.

Biding his time before he could return and finish his degree, Paul reflected on the Dartmouth judicial system he had run afoul of. He complained about the backlog of COS cases. "It could be six or eight weeks between the time you're charged with something and when a decision is rendered. Your stomach is tied up in knots. You can't concentrate on anything." But mostly he complained about the inconsistency. Intentional cheaters seldom got caught, he told me, only the inept ones. In Paul's mind, he made a procedural error, whereas "a guy who gets drunk and kicks in a vending machine gets a slap on the wrist." Paul had only contempt for those underage drinkers on campus who when caught by Safety & Security were quick to reveal where they were served alcohol—usually in a fraternity. "My word isn't good enough to keep me from being suspended, but the word of one drunk kid will put a whole house on probation," Paul observed. "That sends a message." The message he got from the fickle world he depicted was: Do what you need to do to survive and move on.

In the spring of 2002, another Dartmouth student, Roger Brown, was called in by his computer science professor and informed that the code he had written for an assignment to create a blackjack game was identical to a code turned in by another student in the class. The professor said he couldn't be sure which of them had stolen from the other, so he was reporting both. The Committee on Standards charged both with the same honor code violation and left it to the panel to decide which one was lying.

As is customary, Roger received a packet from COS containing all the evidence. "When I had the time and sat down and looked at it," he recalled, "it was a big relief. I could see that he had stolen my entire code." But he had to convince the panel. Given the option of an open or a closed hearing, he chose open. Roger didn't know the other suspect and had no idea what defense he had planned. "I feared he would claim that I had given it to him," said Roger.

Reconstructing events with the evidence at hand, Roger figured out that the other guy had picked up an earlier version of his code from the trash icon of one of the public terminals in the computer lab. From the time stamp he could tell that the other guy had printed out his paper at seven o'clock on the morning it was due, suggesting a last-minute act of desperation.

Roger was exonerated; his digital doppelganger was suspended for six full terms. "I think if he had 'fessed up, it would have been much less severe," Roger said.

I wondered why computer science departments seemed to be such cheating hotbeds. Stanford's computer science department, which represents only 10 percent of undergraduates, accounts for more than half the cheating cases that come before the Board on Judicial Affairs. The social scientists' theory—that the students less likely to cheat are those who believe mastering a body of knowledge is key to success in life—would suggest the opposite. But cyberspace is the new frontier and the stakes are enormously high. At Stanford, all students need to do is crane their necks and look down into neighboring Silicon Valley to see the potential payoff. The most talked-about IPO (initial public offering) on Wall Street in 2004 was Google, the invention of two Stanford computer science graduates.

Maybe part of it is that in the vast frontier of cyberspace it is an easy step from the hippie libertarian mantra claiming all information is free to the even more anarchic notion that all information is up for grabs, whatever the source. The same rationale that blurs the line between plagiarism and Internet resource mining helps computer code writers justify plucking someone else's work off the Web, or, for that matter, the desktop trash bin of a public terminal. Code is also terribly hard to get right, observed Stanford computer scientist Eric Roberts, a guiding force behind the university's 1997 judicial reforms. Enter just one backslash in the wrong place and a whole line of logic collapses. The tight assignment schedule imposed by Stanford's ten-week semester is yet another excuse to take shortcuts. But, like Internet plagiarism, code copying is as easy to trace as it is to accomplish—another big reason why Stanford tries so many cases.

Faced with this palpable erosion of values, a lot of people look to honor codes as a panacea. Schools that have them tout them among their strongest assets. Yet Donald McCabe's research suggests that having an honor code doesn't guarantee a campus will see less cheating. What is key, he found, is not the code but the culture in which it operates.

The University of Virginia's honor code, the oldest in the United States, posits a social and academic environment that is a seamless community of trust. It was designed to pervade every aspect of life on the Grounds in Charlottesville—from the so-called honor debts students accrue with local merchants to the unproctored exams professors routinely allow students to take in the classroom, at the library, in their room, or even at a tavern down at the Corner. Alumni cite it as a signature piece of their U-VA experience. Many current students say it was an important reason why they came to Virginia. Nicole Eramo, who was secretary for the Honor Committee in 2003, said that she transferred to Charlottesville from another college after administrators there deeply offended her by asking for proof of her father's death before granting her an exam postponement. She assured me that would never happen at U-VA.

Maintaining such tradition, however, requires vigilance and consistency in a world that is constantly changing. Virginia's honor court trials were at different times in the university's history open to the community. FERPA, the Federal Educational Right to Privacy Act of 1974, ended that. While students still have the right to an open hearing, few are willing to have their ethical laundry aired in public. As a result, most trials are held in total secrecy: no names or details are revealed; verdicts are published in the student newspaper, the *Cavalier Daily*, but with the names stripped out.

At the heart of the Virginia code is the Single Sanction, an all-or-nothing penalty of permanent banishment from the Grounds for any student who lies, cheats, or steals. There are no gradations, no gray areas in an increasingly nuanced world—just black or white justice. Talk about high stakes.

Its critics say that the Single Sanction, like everything in life, is too inflexible and that as a result its excesses have begun to outweigh its successes. "One former student's degree had been revoked eight years after he graduated, following a trial held in his absence," reported Erich Wasserman, a former U-VA court defense counselor and now executive director of the campus civil liberties watchdog FIRE (Foundation for Individual Rights in Education). "Another former student lost her diploma three years after graduation. Her crime: writing five bad checks totaling $150 while a student."

To guard against such apparent miscarriages, the Honor Committee relies on a loophole: a so-called seriousness clause that allows members to determine whether a given act of dishonesty rises to the level of prosecution in the first place. In the age of computer programs capable of determining precisely how many borrowed words or phrases are repeated in a paper, a couple of degrees of plagiarism one way or the other could determine whether someone gets off the hook completely or is banished from the Grounds forever.

Opposition to the Single Sanction and a subordinate debate over the efficacy of the seriousness clause have been running at a low fever grade in Charlottesville for decades. About every five or six years, there is a serious campaign to end or at least modify the sanction. When I visited U-VA, a new challenge was in its incipient stages. Many faculty have grown increasingly weary of bearing the entire burden of bringing honor cases forward—a commitment that guarantees hundreds of hours of additional time, writing up charges, backing them with evidence, presenting them, and living with the consequences. It is, said physics professor Louis Bloomfield, "a time sink."

Bloomfield was leading this latest charge against the honor code. Two years earlier, he had stunned the U-VA community by bringing 158 separate charges against students for plagiarizing material used in their final papers for Physics 105: How Things Work. Though not exactly a gut, the course is widely viewed as a safe way for nonscience majors to get credit for a science course. The final grade is based largely on a student's ability to demonstrate in a paper an understanding of the underlying principles of physics at work in everyday items—whether the zap in microwave ovens is really radiation, how electronic listening devices work, and so on. Since the course has been around quite a while, there is a substantial bank of papers floating around the Grounds and probably floating around in cyberspace as well. I was told the frequency of plagiarism on How Things Work term papers has been notoriously high for years.

Professor Bloomfield was not deaf to recurring themes, not to mention recurring phrases and paragraphs. He fashioned a search program that uncovers these often egregious similarities and decided to bring the hammer down. The ensuing honor court caseload was staggering. In the end, however, forty-eight students—less than a third of those charged—received the Single Sanction of banishment from the university. Ten were referred to psychological counseling on a verdict that some form of mental disorder contributed to their cheating. The rest got off—many of them weeded out as trivial before trial.

Most people at Virginia believe that had permanent expulsion not been the only penalty available, it's likely that more would have been punished. The all-or-nothing stakes forced both the committee members and the students on trial to extremes—the committee toward arbitrary conclusions about the gravity of charges and the students who were tried toward desperate means of defense. "Once a student gets caught up in the process," said Nicole Eramo, "there's no benefit to being honest."

Bloomfield and his faculty colleagues see the Single Sanction as just one of the code's shortcomings. Equally corrosive, they believe, is a student culture that accepts looking the other way when someone else cheats. Historically, the honor code's principal enforcement mechanism was a nontoleration clause that held all students responsible for maintaining the community of trust. If you saw a fellow student cheat, you were obliged to turn him in not just by whispering to the professor and letting him or her carry the burden of prosecution but by bringing formal charges directly to the committee. Bloomfield wanted a return to a system that held each and every student responsible and one that also punished those who knowingly looked the other way. In the meantime, he has said he would never again try to do what he did with 158 students in 2001. "It took too much out of my life," he said. "It was two years that came out of my research, my writing, and my family, not in that order. . . . It was a total loss."

As Honor Committee chair, Carey Mignery understood that, but he also understood the mood of his fellow students. Too few were willing to step forward and accuse a peer, to risk the ostracism that would surely follow such a bold breach of that unwritten code, a code of silence. They wouldn't phrase it that way, of course. They would simply claim they couldn't know all the facts and were thus not in a position to make such a charge.

To be fair, no matter who does the judging, college rules and standards should be clear and concise but also widely understood. I liked the fact that Middlebury was moving acknowledgment of its honor code from an afterthought enclosure in its freshman registration packet to a public signing ceremony in the college chapel and that the Indiana Promise, an articulation of Indiana University's basic standard of ethical expectation, is now recited as part of freshman convocation.

With a qualified exception for victims of sexual assault, students ought to be willing as part of a contract with their college to sign a general waiver of their right to privacy in a judicial hearing. Louis Bloomfield is right: enforcement of campus rules is meant to be more than just a method of keeping order; it is an opportunity to educate students. If the lessons are heard by only a handful of students—the ones who are in trouble—they've badly missed the mark. Everyone should learn from the process.

Coming up with a list of such structural recommendations is the easier part. Much harder is figuring out how to reinstill a sense of personal and social integrity in the culture as a whole. College life happens inside a protective bubble. But it is hardly immune from the ethical lapses so evident in the surrounding world.

The cause of intellectual honesty might also be furthered if students had more contact with the men and women who teach them. The conscience of a student is more easily pricked if he has a personal relationship with the professor in whose course he is considering cheating. I have a hunch, for example, that fewer students cheat on people like Luis Fraga, associate professor of political science at Stanford.

Fraga is unusual for a big university faculty member: he not only enjoys being with undergraduates, he actually devotes a considerable amount of time to them. He teaches three courses plus a graduate-level course and advises as many as forty undergrads.

Students like him. At the close of the 2002–2003 academic year, the student government presented him with its annual teaching award.

It's not always easy to get office time with Fraga, but students feel it's worth it. "Generally speaking, if I want to meet with him, I have to plan it two or three weeks in advance," said one student, a double major in political science and economics who chose Fraga as his advisor. "However, I feel that I do get enough time to talk with him. I see him often for both a directed reading class and personal advising. I've met with him perhaps six times this year regarding personal advice." The student praised Fraga's teaching style as well, crediting his efforts to be innovative in class and to arrange local internships for his undergraduate students.

Fraga and his wife, a college counselor at a private school in Palo Alto, spent ten years as resident fellows in several undergraduate residence halls at Stanford, running a network of undergraduate residential advisors and occasionally inviting groups of students into their apartment for food and conversation. They moved out only after their third child was born and time demands just got too great. With an infant in their home, Fraga found the additional duties of being an adult presence in the lives of a hundred or so college students were even beyond his abilities. Fraga is in the classroom most days from ten A.M. to five P.M. He goes home for dinner and time with his family before working on lectures, doing research, and answering e-mails, often until two A.M.

Fraga took his role as a resident fellow seriously. "We chose to be very actively engaged with our students," he said. The role of resident fellows, which Stanford has had for more than three decades, is loosely defined by intention. Often filled by junior faculty in need of subsidized housing, resident fellowships demand at minimum the oversight of half a dozen or so selected and trained upper-class staffers who deal directly with the students. Beyond that, it's up to the individual fellow to decide how often or intensely to interact with his or her charges. Some get deeply involved in everything from organizing parties to dealing with a student struggling with anorexia or one in need of time management skills. Above all, Stanford wants residence fellows to be role models. The Fragas tended to leave the details to their RAs and concentrate on promoting the right overall environment.

It has become less common to see a student and a professor engaged in conversation outside of office hours or just after class. "We have graduates who don't know a single professor well," a senior administration official at Stanford acknowledged. I heard a number of tales about juniors and seniors writing applications for internships and graduate schools that required a letter of personal recommendation from a professor. The stories had a common theme with a few variations: either they couldn't think of a single teacher they knew well enough to count on getting a favorable recommendation or they ended up having to remind the professor who they were.

Some of the disengagement, to be sure, comes from students preoccupied with other aspects of their collegiate life. But a lot reflects a long-term shift in faculty priorities. The percentage of Stanford faculty who serve as undergraduate academic advisors fell from 45 to 15 during the 1990s. For some professors, distance from undergraduates has become a reflection of their academic status. "I've heard senior faculty members boast that they have not had an undergraduate advisee in ten years," Fraga told me. "That sends a message."

The message is that while good teaching, good advising, and mentoring are commendable skills, they don't count for much in the academic culture. What does matter is publication of research and reputation in a particular field of scholarship. "Publish or perish" has always been the academy's admonition to its junior scholars, but it appears to have narrowed from being a necessary condition for faculty advancement to a nearly exclusive one.

John Gardner, founder of the National Resource Center for the First-Year Experience and Students in Transition, put the trend in perspective for me: "Eisenhower's military-industrial complex was really a military-industrial-academic complex. It insinuated what [social commentator and economist] Thorstein Veblen referred to as a 'pecuniary emulation' system that worked its way down from the big research universities and into small college culture. Every faculty member now wants to become a university research professor."

Indeed, most of the major growth in universities in the post–World War II era came from research contracts and grants that filled the coffers of places like Harvard, MIT, Wisconsin, and Berkeley and provided the single greatest source for new faculty hiring. Paul Barrows, the vice chancellor at the University of Wisconsin in Madison, told me that more than a third of UW's operating budget comes from research grants. The faculty members know who butters their bread. "Their allegiances have shifted from the campus to their disciplines," said Barrows.

The professorial vanishing act is not universal. At virtually every institution, there are teachers like Luis Fraga for whom the mentoring aspect of the job remains paramount. And there are small liberal arts colleges and community colleges where teaching is the only thing professors do. The irony is often that the bigger and more prestigious the school, the less teaching appears to be rewarded.

"Good teaching is commended and appreciated," Fraga acknowledged, "but it is not rewarded. Many faculty members choose to work primarily with graduate students in order to spend more time with people who will contribute directly to their research." As much as he values his contact with students, Fraga admitted that he couldn't in good conscience advise his younger, untenured colleagues to do the same. "My advice to junior faculty members is to focus on their research. I tell them that once they have tenure, they will have more independence and more time to modify their responsibilities and time management, including having the ability to focus more on teaching. But before the guarantee of the tenure position, they have to be very focused."

The costs of this reward system are many. It discourages young, energetic professors closer in age and culture to the students from playing an active role in their lives. Academics who might not be first-tier scholars but are excellent classroom teachers are less likely to be promoted. Every task asked of them—from committee work to advising students to taking on an extra course—is viewed as a zero-sum loss of time otherwise devoted to research and publication. Professors are, said Fraga, driven toward a "free-agent mentality" that fosters loyalty to their academic specialty rather than to the institution or the teaching profession.

To be sure, there are other factors contributing to this disconnect. Three or four decades ago, most professors were male; their wives were stay-at-home moms. At rural institutions such as Dartmouth, Hamilton, and Middlebury, they also tended to live close to campus where it was convenient to invite students over for social occasions or ask them to babysit. For better or for worse, they tended to know more about students than just their performance in class. They often knew when their students had a role in a campus play or whether they'd scored in the weekend's soccer game.

Harvard's veteran Henry Rosovsky told me that when he was a young professor in the mid-sixties, "There was a tremendous amount of interaction [between students and faculty]. Then the houses became very crowded. Second, the sixties created antagonism between students and faculty. Thirdly, there was the 'me' thing: I could have lunch with students who would not only ignore me, they'd ignore each other. And finally, faculty have come to live less and less in Cambridge. Their involvement here is more of a nine-to-five situation."

One other small but ironic factor mentioned by several veteran college teachers: the change in the national laws regarding the legal drinking age in the late eighties put an end to a common custom at a lot of places where a professor would join a group of students at a local bar or campus pub. Often, they brought with them the topics of the classroom. "When I first came here, every Friday afternoon we'd go to the Rosebud to have a beer with students," recalled Middlebury physics professor Jeffrey Dunham. Now liability concerns conspire with the broader cultural gap between students and faculty to make that unlikely if not often illegal. Within a year of the change in the law, both the Rosebud and the Alibi, the other big student hangout in downtown Middlebury, went out of business.

Indiana history professor David Pace acknowledges the distance that has come to separate professors from their students: "When I came here, teaching was a charismatic exercise," he said. "Now, there's a kind of learned helplessness on both sides."

Fueling that sense of helplessness is a growth in the complexity and specialization of nonteaching roles on campus. Academic types understandably feel increasingly out of their element handling delicate issues such as depression, eating disorders, and date rape and even advising students on how to choose from the dizzying array of course offerings far afield from their own scholarly interests. As trained administrators took charge of admissions and judicial systems, once-engaged professors retreated to adjunct roles as mere committee members rather than practitioners. "As faculty, we stopped managing residential halls; we stopped overseeing judicial processes," John Gardner noted. "We took ourselves out of Greek affairs. Increasingly, we're taking ourselves out of the advising process. For three hundred years, we faculty gave students advice on their careers. Now we have career centers."

Being stripped of responsibility does not have the same career implications it might in the business world, however. The less time spent on student problems, the more time is available for research. Students with whom I spoke treasured their contact with their professors. Those who were most pleased with their college experience often cited their relationships with their professors as a highlight. As Anthony Vitarelli observed, time spent with his Duke professors out of class is always an unexpected bonus. "Professors are exceedingly interesting people," he said.

Personal exchanges with teachers made Duke senior Jen Hasvold feel that "I'm being treated as a peer, not just as a student."

Harvard's new president, Lawrence H. Summers, has made grade inflation a target of reform. In the spring of 2004, Princeton's dean of the faculty announced a proposal to limit A's to 35 percent of all grades awarded. That figure had been 47 percent. Naturally enough, there have been protests from students who fear that graduate school admissions officers and employers won't understand the change, leaving them handicapped against all those other thousands of institutions that don't make the adjustment.

Far more significant than capping A's and B's, however, is a movement by many colleges and universities to reinsert faculty into students' lives beyond the classroom. It is a movement that is long overdue. If a decoupling of faculty and students has marked the last twenty years, the next may well be noted as the era of reconnection. One popular new way to improve relations is by offering interesting courses taught by senior faculty members to first- and second-year students. In the fall of 2003, for example, first-year Stanford students could sign up for a course entitled Reflections on the American Condition: American History through Literature, taught by Pulitzer Prize–winning historian David Kennedy, or Technological Visions of Utopia with Eric Roberts, head of undergraduate computer science. The idea of the program, which listed more than seventy seminars for the 2003–2004 year, is to develop long-term mentoring relationships with some of the university's most distinguished professors.

At Dartmouth, the Res Life staff has been charged with coming up with effective strategies to draw professors into the residence halls for informal gatherings where they might give talks on subjects that interest them and might offer students more excitement than one of their standard course lectures. At the suggestion of the student affairs staff at the University of Wisconsin's

Chadbourne College, physics professor Don McCammon spent hours one night early in the fall semester of 2003, while Mars was in its closest proximity to Earth in sixty thousand years, showing interested students what the red planet looked like through the giant telescope in the campus observatory. He stayed there until one o'clock in the morning.

Growing in popularity among top liberal arts colleges is the idea of undergraduate research associates. More than a hundred students each at Hamilton, Middlebury, and Pomona no longer go home with their classmates in the summer; they stay at school to work one-on-one with their professors on projects directly related to the professors' research. Abby Markeson did it twice at Hamilton—the first time during the summer before she had even enrolled as a freshman. Her work with chemistry professor George Shields on solvation energy established a personal relationship not only with the department chair but also with the entire department. Besides working together every day, summer researchers and their faculty mentors often socialize in the evenings, having barbecues at professors' houses and even taking a road trip all the way to Boston to see a Red Sox game.

George Shields, who helped Abby get the scholarship she needed to attend Hamilton, extolled the benefits of the summer research program: "You can just see their self-confidence rise. Students really like to talk to professors outside the classroom in part because it makes it so much easier for them to approach them later when they have an academic problem," or any problem, for that matter. One student came to Shields when the college reduced his scholarship package without explanation. The professor was in a position to go to bat for him and get the money restored.

One big reason collaborative research programs are popular with faculty is that they don't get in the way of a professor's scholarship; indeed, they contribute to it. Students have been listed as coauthors of studies published in academic journals—a feather in their caps and also a bonus point for the professor, who gets credit both for the scholarship and for working directly with an undergraduate.

If more colleges rewarded the twin notions of students as apprentices to professors and professors as mentors to students, the prevailing view of teaching as a requisite appendage to scholarship might promote a healthier view that teaching is a calling.

4

Emotional Troubles

When she arrived for our meeting in the atrium of the Garage, a mini-mall cum food court in Cambridge, Kristin Waller looked delicate and thin. Unlike many Harvard students who exude a confidence forged over a young lifetime of unbroken successes, she seemed vulnerable, cautious, and self-protective. Or perhaps I projected that from what I had learned about her through a series of e-mail exchanges and a brief mention of her in the Harvard *Crimson*.

I knew Kristin had spent half her life dealing with crushing bouts of depression, her parents were divorced, and the father who raised her had been jobless for ten years and lived in his car back in Oklahoma. Her mother was working in the same coffee shop chain as Kristin's sister, and an older brother was serving jail time. Kristin was able to attend Harvard only because a full scholarship and a work-study job provided her with enough money to get by. Under normal circumstances, she would have been a candidate to take time off from her studies in order to get a grip on her psyche. But Kristin could not take time off the way most college students might: she had no place to go. For most breaks, she stayed in her Harvard room; over the summers she found work and a place to live in Cambridge. Only over winter break of her junior year was she able to leave: she accompanied her boyfriend to his family's house in San Diego. For all practical purposes, Harvard was her home.

Kristin's depression and a compulsion to cut herself had been with her since the seventh grade, though she did not come to

85

recognize it as a problem until her sophomore year in high school. By then she was using a pocketknife she'd stolen from her father to cut gouges into her arms. By covering her wounds, she managed to elude detection. Even the high school counselor in whom she once confided told her that if she were really depressed, she wouldn't be able to get out of bed in the morning. Without health insurance, she was unable to afford even so much as a diagnosis. Certainly Harvard knew nothing of her mental state when they admitted her to the class of 2005.

Kristin arrived at college with every intention of being a typical student. She joined Harvard's notoriously sassy marching band, playing the French horn. But some early relationship problems, bouts of loneliness, and the psychological pall that descended over campus life in the aftermath of 9/11 summoned depression from where she had hoped she had permanently left it. "Over spring break, I started cutting myself again," she told me. "Someone took note and told my freshman advisor, who was also the assistant dean of freshmen, and he advised me to go to University Health Services."

She took occasional advantage of college-offered therapy in her sophomore year but also continued to cut herself. "For me—and for all the other cutters I know—cutting isn't about self-esteem, it's about control," Kristin explained. "Much like an eating disorder, self-injury lets you express the internal anguish that seems unceasing by making it an outward pain that's so much easier to deal with. Cutting can be—and was for me—a cry for help: 'Look at me—I hurt so much I'm bleeding—*help me stop this pain!*'"

Kristin's cries for help were apparently so clear in November of her sophomore year that when she failed to answer her phone for an entire evening, two friends rushed to her room along with her senior tutor and a member of the campus police force. She was all right—at least physically. Thereafter, Kristin went to therapy weekly. She went on Zoloft, and following a second cutting crisis in December, Harvard's psychiatrists added lithium carbonate to the Zoloft, with good effect. "I've found that they've made an enormous difference in my life," she was able to say of the drugs a little over a year later. "My mood is more stable—a thousand times more stable. I haven't had another serious crisis since the meds took effect. I still see my therapist at UHS, . . . but now I actually have the energy and ability to get out of my room and go to appointments!"

For this she said she had Harvard to thank. "If I were going to the University of Oklahoma, which is pretty likely had I not gotten into Harvard, I think administrators there would have reacted like my high school teachers by not noticing at all," she said. "They take every pain to make sure we know the option is available," she said, crediting Harvard's efforts to advertise its mental health services. "Whenever I found something situational that triggered my depression, the pressure was personal. It was me, not the college."

In many ways, Kristin Waller is a success story both for her and for Harvard. In other situations, those suffering as intensely as she was might be encouraged to go home until they can gain sufficient control over their lives to return to their studies. This issue captured the interest of Anne Kofol, editor of the *Crimson*, and Katharine Kaplan, a sophomore reporter from Bethesda, Maryland. During the spring term of 2003, Kofol and Kaplan were sharing their mutual amazement at how many of their friends and fellow students seemed to be on antidepressants. That conversation led to Kofol's suggestion that Kaplan might want to look into a story on depression for the special commencement issue of the newspaper in May. How prevalent was it at Harvard? Who was suffering? Who was seeking help? How good was the help?

Katie Kaplan proceeded to take on what a college reporter in an earlier generation might have viewed as the daunting task of searching for people who were in psychological trouble—and seeking them within a population of students who were at Harvard in the first place because they had succeeded in selling themselves as capable and effective people. Constrained not just by the delicacy of the subject but also by federal and state privacy laws that protected individuals' medical and psychological histories, she decided to go fishing.

Kaplan put together a formal letter and e-mailed it to all undergraduates, inviting anyone living with depression to write back. It was like fishing in a stocked pond: she heard back from thirty fellow students, each willing to talk about his or her struggles and experiences with University Health Services, Harvard's student medical center, which provides counseling and often doles out medication. Many willingly spoke on the record.

The five-part series on depression at Harvard eventually ran in January 2004 at more than fourteen thousand words, quoting dozens of students, many of them speaking on the record and some even permitting their pictures to be printed in the paper. Its overarching premise was that Harvard was dealing with a mental health epidemic that it was not adequately equipped to manage. Unable to handle the volume of requests for counseling and medication and fearful of the consequences of inadequate treatment, especially suicide, the administration was quick to encourage troubled students to withdraw rather than to burden the institution with their problems, the *Crimson* series maintained.

The reporting, most of it Kaplan's work, quoted students who felt they had been pressured to leave as well as students who felt their medically untrained house tutors were insensitive to the urgency of their needs. One article quoted a junior as saying her senior tutor hastily encouraged her to deal with her depression elsewhere. "As soon as I suggested I wanted to leave, she was like, 'Go!' . . . She didn't give it a second thought. . . . I feel like they're really fast to have you leave if you're going to be a problem." After a tutor allegedly dismissed his pleas for counseling, another student placed his laptop with a suicide message on its screen in front of a friend in the Winthrop House dining hall. The friend took him to the University Health Services, from which he was taken immediately to a Boston-area psychiatric hospital.

The series also contained testimony that at least Harvard had helped salvage students' college careers, if not outright saved their lives, including quite possibly Kristin Waller's. Harvard usually meant well but did not always do well, the *Crimson* suggested. The consistent message throughout the series was that the university's handling of its massive mental health workload was inconsistent.

Reacting quickly to the *Crimson* series, the administration distributed a mental health fact sheet: two single-spaced pages of bullet points acknowledging the volume of mental health cases but also citing the considerable human and monetary resources deployed to deal with the onslaught as well as the protocols employed to ensure prompt treatment in critical situations. House tutors were summoned to a meeting with health services staff members and college administrators to review procedures. The chair of the University Student Health Coordinating Board, professor Jennifer Leaning of the Harvard School of Public Health, was recruited to write an op-ed piece for the *Crimson* that both outlined the reasons for the growth in demand for services and touted the progress Harvard had made in delivering effective and confidential treatment.

Harvard conceded that its nine psychiatrists, eight psychologists, six nurse practitioners, and nine licensed social workers were in constant demand. Over a mere two-year span from 2001 to 2003, visits by undergraduates had increased 30 percent to 4,871 students. But officials hastened to add that Harvard was up to the task, providing follow-up care and preparing for emergencies around the clock with supplemental access to the many first-rate medical facilities in the Boston area. It was a message designed in part to soothe an anxious parent's heart and I suspect in part to insulate Harvard from future litigation.

It was both tragic and inopportune when twenty-one-year-old Anthony "Deuce" Fonseca, a junior economics student from Lawton, Oklahoma, was found dead in his Winthrop House room, an apparent suicide, within a month of the *Crimson* series' publication. It had been only fourteen months since another Winthrop House resident, Marian Smith, had killed herself. Fonseca's was the fourteenth Harvard suicide in fourteen years.

Deuce Fonseca's sudden death was particularly unnerving because he seemed to be okay. A neighbor in his house entry had seen him that evening and "had the impression that he had things under control." His colleagues at HRTV, the Harvard-Radcliffe television station where he was vice president of the executive board and director of the station's student-produced soap opera, *Ivory Tower*, expressed shock at the news. "None of us thought he was troubled," the station president told the *Crimson*. Others described him variously as outgoing, laid-back, devil-may-care. Members of his family whom Katie Kaplan contacted as part of her mental health beat reporting were even more shocked by the news. A cousin voiced doubt that he had actually killed himself. But while they would not say how they knew, Cambridge police were confident that Deuce brought about his own death.

Only a couple of bends farther down the Charles River, the problem seemed just as pronounced. In early March 2004, less than a week after the last part of the *Crimson* series was published, Boston fire department members hauled the body of MIT (Massachusetts Institute of Technology) junior Daniel Mun, wearing in-line skates, from the Charles. He had been missing since the beginning of the winter break in early December 2003, when he had left a note on his computer admitting his despondency.

Mun's suicide was the first at MIT in almost three years. The previous two had spawned highly visible wrongful death suits filed by the families of the deceased students. One, asking for $20 million in damages, faulted MIT for not protecting sophomore and chemistry major Julie Carpenter from an alleged stalker. Frustrated by the inability of the dean's office to prevent a fellow student from harassing her—the suit claimed the man broke into her room, installed tracking software on her computer so that he could monitor her, then slept on a couch down the hall from her room—Carpenter killed herself with cyanide she ordered over the Internet.

When Julie Carpenter died in April 2001, she was the sixth suicide at MIT in four years. She lived in Random Hall, the same dorm in which Elizabeth Shin had burned herself to death a year earlier after a long bout with severe depression. The Shin family sued MIT for $27 million in a case widely and warily watched by higher education lawyers and psychiatric counselors who were anxious to see what implications the decision might have for the level of oversight and preventive response they might be required to maintain, as well as for what it says about students' rights to privacy.

However much more visible they might have been, the mental health and suicide issues faced by Harvard and MIT were similar to those faced by almost every institution. Suicide is the second leading cause of death among North Americans of college age. It occurs at an annual rate of one per ten thousand nationwide. By the late 1990s, "college lawyers discussed among themselves perhaps one or two pending suicide cases at any given moment," according to Ann Franke, former legal counsel to the American Association of University Professors. By 2004, there were about ten, "with the prospect that many more suicides could, over time, move into the courts."

While the prospect of litigation spawned some welcome suicide prevention programs, it also created a hair-trigger mentality among campus health and Res Life officials. David Weigel was a sophomore at Northwestern when a computer crash that destroyed a major term paper prompted him to pick up his phone and call a campus mental health hotline to vent his frustrations. "I felt really doomed," he recalled. "I guess I ranted a bit about my computer, the pressure, my general unhappiness." After getting it off his chest, he thanked the person and was about to hang up when he was advised that he really shouldn't be alone at that point. Next thing he knew, the campus police were at his door. He was taken first to a hospital, then to a mental health facility in Chicago, where he was kept for three days. "I was told to sign these papers and that if I refused, I would have to go through a lengthy process of challenging them. Mostly I was angry that I'd had what I thought was a private conversation with this person that turned into this whole thing." Thereafter, Weigel began to view North-western's efforts to control student behavior with a more jaun-diced eye.

Suicide gets people's attention, but it is only the tip of a massive mental health iceberg. For every successful suicide, there are forty failed attempts. Nine times again as many college students seri-ously think about killing themselves. According to a study of college mental health led by Dr. Sherry Benton of Kansas State University, reported incidents of depression and suicidal thoughts doubled during the nineties. The average age of depression's onset dropped from twenty-eight to twenty in just two decades. And according to the study, the percentage of students seeking psy-chological help rises steadily from freshman through senior year.

"For a couple of decades now, two large national surveys have asked college counseling centers to tell them how many people they are seeing and what for," said Jim Clack, who runs the Counseling and Psychological Services (CAPS) center at Duke. "Every year, the number goes up, the severity goes up, and the chronicity goes up. It's not just a money-grabbing exercise by col-lege counselors. Each year, the *Diagnostic and Statistical Manual* comes out with new labels for new disorders. The book just keeps getting bigger."

Depression remains the leading reason why students seek help, but college counselors and psychiatrists are treating the full palette of mental illnesses from attention deficit disorder to obsessive-compulsiveness to dysmorphia (body image problems that typi-cally manifest themselves through eating disorders among women and obsessive bodybuilding among men), from bipolar depression to borderline personality disorder on up to full-blown psychosis.

Why this is happening continues to puzzle experts. Are there more disturbed people in college today than twenty or thirty years ago? Have all the new psychotropic medications simply made it possible for people with psychological disorders to get into college—people who otherwise wouldn't have bothered to even apply? Has the stigma associated with mental illness dissipated to the point where more young people are willing to speak openly about their problems? Or is there something about contemporary North American culture that is feeding more anxiety to its youth so that by the time they get to college they are on a steady diet of doubt, fear, and sadness? I believe the answer to all of these questions is yes.

Since the Food and Drug Administration (FDA) approval of Prozac in 1987, the use of psychotropic antidepressants has exploded, and college students are one of the biggest markets. "When I arrived here in '96, 3 to 5 percent of the students were using psychotropic drugs," said Jim Clack at Duke in the fall of 2003. "Now 26 percent do." Fully a third of Harvard University's Health Services pharmacy budget in 2003 was for antidepressants, meted out by the equivalent of ten full-time prescription fillers. Nationally the number of students on such medications nearly tripled in the decade leading up to 2004.

Many students are arriving at college already on meds. McGill conducted a survey of new students at the beginning of the decade and found that 10 percent of them had already been given prescriptions for psychotropic drugs; among the American students at McGill that figure was 15 percent.

Overprescribing is part of the problem. Young people, charged Dr. Norm Hoffman of McGill's Mental Health Service, "are being way overdiagnosed. They have been put on medication in very inappropriate ways. During high school, if their parents get divorced, or they break up with a boyfriend, they're brought to a doctor and given an antidepressant. By the way, there's very little evidence that these drugs ever work at a young age." Indeed, recent studies have indicated that use of antidepressants in young people may actually lead to more depression and suicidal thoughts.

"We have kids who have been medicated and don't even know why," said Dr. Eric Heiligenstein, the chief psychiatrist at the University of Wisconsin. "I call it McMedicine." Beginning with

Ritalin as a treatment for attention deficit disorder (ADD) and on up through anxiety control drugs like Xanax, hometown GPs have been using drugs as chemical babysitters, often with parental encouragement. By the time they get to college, students are well versed. "They say, 'I know what I want,'" Heiligenstein said. "They are consumer sophisticated, medically naive."

As dangerous as overprescription is a growing tendency among college students to go off their meds unilaterally. Most of these medications work in part by dulling feelings—by leveling off the emotional peaks and valleys. Every place I went, doctors and deans spoke of troubled young people who decided to go cold turkey upon arriving on campus because they believed medication was preventing them from experiencing the full impact of college life.

Predictably, when they did, the results were bad. Outside the Collis Student Center at Dartmouth at lunchtime in May, I overheard a group exchanging accounts of a fellow student stalking a girl on campus, both in person and on Blitzmail. He even attached photos of himself in his messages to her. When he confronted her in the library, however, he was apprehended by Safety & Security. "He was apparently off his meds," said a participant in the conversation somewhat offhandedly, as if she expected everyone else in the gathering to understand immediately what that meant. Apparently they did.

That so many students actively seek help for any psychological reason seemed news in itself to me. I would observe to counselors as I met them that when I went to college very few people would admit to feeling depressed, let alone helplessly so. Acknowledging that, Harvard's head of counseling services, Richard Kadison, recalled how when he was an undergraduate at Brown in the seventies, he was not even aware that help was available. "I was pretty depressed and probably drank too much. But I just got through it," he recalled. At Middlebury, Karl Lindholm, who was dean of students for many years and a member of the class of

1967, believes the difference lies almost entirely in recognition and treatment. "We had all these kids here who were untreated," he said, speaking of the days when the parents of today's students were in college. "They flunked out. In the sixties, they killed themselves—in Vietnam. The difference today is that we lay more people on."

Now students who feel troubled or unhappy come to their health centers for help in droves. "Society has given us permission to talk about these things," said Dr. Vincenzo DiNicola, a McGill University psychiatry professor who was also the resident director of Molson Hall, a first-year dorm. On several occasions, I heard groups of students unabashedly debating which antidepressant combinations and dosages are the most effective, or the relative effectiveness of Prozac versus Zoloft—the way my generation weighed the musical merits of the Beatles versus the Stones.

"A number of students who might have not been able to attend college because of their psychological problems now can because of the advances in psychiatric medication," wrote Robert P. Gallagher, former vice chancellor for student affairs and director of the counseling center at the University of Pittsburgh, during an online colloquy conducted by the *Chronicle of Higher Education*. "Similarly, other students who develop serious problems while in school are often able to remain in school because these drugs are available to them." Most educators not only endorse that view, they are proud that drugs have made college attainable for people who in previous generations would have never made it there in the first place.

But there are costs. The financial price tag has been enormous. From 2002 to 2004, Harvard's mental health budget went up 15 percent in a single year. Kathy Poi, director of health services at the University of Wisconsin, told me that her department, which used to have one psychiatrist working half-time, now has the equivalent of four full-time psychiatrists plus three psychiatric nurses and eleven psychologists. This was the trend at college after college I looked at.

The other cost, though it has financial implications, is measured in human capital. When a student flips out or attempts suicide, it triggers all kinds of emergency protocols and locks legions of deans and counselors into literally hundreds of hours of meetings and internal memo writing. Especially with the Shin verdict pending in Massachusetts, no one in higher education is going to risk missing a procedural step that might prevent both personal and institutional disaster.

To make matters more confusing, there appears to be no fixed relationship between mental disorders and academic performance. Administrators report an increase in the number of failing students who appeal their dismissals on the grounds that their poor performance is the result of psychological problems. Counselors can count on a crowd of students at their doorsteps late in the term. Whether these students are in genuine need or are simply creating a paper trail to cover a semester's worth of indolence or intense partying can be hard even for the pros to discern.

In contrast, some of the brightest students with the highest GPAs are socially dysfunctional. An emerging diagnosis on campus is Asperger's syndrome, a form of autism characterized by a strong intellect often combined with severe social ineptitude. Because they typically get good grades and test well, some Asperger's sufferers can slip through the admissions process unrecognized. But in the socially intense residential college environment, they often fall apart at the seams.

Asperger's was only defined and labeled in 1994. Before that, people who displayed its symptoms were vaguely classified as learning disabled. According to Dr. Linda Geller, a psychologist and Asperger's specialist at the Cody Center on the Stonybrook campus of the State University of New York (SUNY), one out of every four hundred or five hundred people suffers from it to some degree. Asperger's is not just a temporary psychological problem. If you have it, she said, "you're wired differently."

With care, some Asperger's patients are able to make it in a residential college setting. Brian Previtt's family was willing to allow him to give residential college a try. So were the deans and counseling staff at St. Norbert's, a small Catholic college in De Pere, Wisconsin. Given a single, Brian had no roommate problems. He did complain that the noise in the dorm often went on until one or two in the morning, but he got a white noise machine to block it out so that he could sleep. A double major in computer science and Japanese, Brian was also president of the Japan club and founder of an anime club. But he said he was having trouble getting people to show up for meetings.

He also confessed that he didn't have many friends at St. Norbert's. "I try to talk to people, but they generally don't talk back to me," he said without any noticeable sense of anguish. At least it was better than it had been back in middle and high school in Waukesha, where, he said, "Everybody hated me." He added, "I didn't have to do anything to be hated." Other students would regularly taunt him and occasionally beat him up in high school. He would fight back. "I had to or else I'd get the crap beaten out of me." Like many Asperger's sufferers, Brian assumed it was somehow his fault. "If the entire school thinks you're worthless," he asked rhetorically, "how could they be wrong?"

Despite all this, Brian was holding his own in college. His family has taken a gamble every family must face in deciding whether they want to subject a child with psychological problems to a culture where failure carries so much weight. So far, it has paid off.

Parents are almost always a piece of the puzzle—more often than not a complicating one. In the best of circumstances, they have raised their children well, instilling in them a strong work ethic and good study habits, imbuing them with a sense of self-confidence. In many instances, parents are able to spot their children's weaknesses and disabilities early enough to help them so that they can succeed in life. Good parents are there for their children as study counselors, moral guides, and predawn chauffeurs to hockey games, after-school ballet or violin lessons, and some-times psychological counseling sessions.

But they can be obstacles to their children's success as well—coconspirators along with a lazy doctor too quick to diagnose ADD and "fix" rambunctious behavior with medication. Once their child is enrolled in college, they can serve as a cooperative resource who works with college counselors and deans to come up with a strategy to work through psychological episodes, or they can stand in the way of their child's recovery or even survival.

Rena Fonseca, a senior tutor at Harvard, told me several hor-ror stories involving the parents of troubled students. In spite of the legal risks inherent in calling a student's family, Fonseca has on several occasions picked up the phone when she thought a stu-dent was endangering him- or herself or other students. The father of one girl who was clearly suicidal chided Fonseca for her interference: "What's the matter with you?" he said. "Our daugh-ter is fine. So what if she slashes her wrist once?"

Another, when informed that his child apparently believed he was a famous artist—a likely symptom of schizophrenia—reacted to the news by offering to sign any letter Harvard wanted to absolve the institution of responsibility for keeping the boy in school. "We are not taking our son out of Harvard," he told Fon-seca. "We have worked too hard to get this far."

Parents can be hindrances in other ways as well. There are cases, as with child abuse, where they are the source of trouble in the first place. In addition to the liability risk under federal pri-vacy laws, college counselors and deans must consider whether calling home might make matters worse. "In the old days we used to call the parents," said Eric Heiligenstein at Wisconsin. "Now we go through a second step where we ask ourselves, 'Are the parents going to help or hurt?'"

Bad parenting? Less stigma? More medicine? Russell Federman, CAPS director at the University of Virginia, rubbed his eyes at these questions about the underlying causes of psychological problems among college students. "I don't know; I don't know; I don't know," he confessed. "But there is, I can tell you, a widening pool of anxiety and depression which is not just because of better diagnosis."

At every campus I visited, deans and counseling directors spoke of a palpable level of stress among students, of an emotional fragility and inflexibility that provided no cushion for those who suffer setbacks, even seemingly minor ones. "There is a feeling that if they stray at all from a perfect record, their chances of success will completely disappear," said Dr. Rebecca Kornbluh, director of CAPS at Pomona. "There is a sense that 'If I drop this class, I'm going to be homeless!' "

It is not just the daunting height of their life goals that unsettles them—it is their perception of where they are in the great scheme of things as they look upward. Nancy Buckles, director of CAPS at Indiana, where the demand for psych services doubled between 1998 and 2003, said that she heard students echo the sentiment captured in Michael Moore's *Bowling for Columbine*. "Even though they are safer," she said, "they don't feel safer." Swipe key lock systems, video monitors, and nighttime campus escorts help ensure their physical security, but they can't overcome a haunting, unspecific anxiety that the earth beneath their feet is shaky.

From her perspective as the mental health reporter at Harvard, Katharine Kaplan saw control and the loss of control as key factors. "Harvard students are uniquely self-motivated and think they can handle things themselves," she told me. When they find out that they cannot or that someone for the first time in their competitive lives is better at something than they are, they are rattled, sometimes to the core. Dr. Norm Hoffman, who has been treating students at McGill for more than two decades, noted the change there as well. "In the late eighties, students saw themselves in a broader context," he said. "Now they are labeled. They see themselves as products, not people." But products that have not yet achieved their market potential just might be defective and therefore in need of fixing.

It is a logic that might help explain the prevalence on campuses of eating disorders, which were hardly mentioned when I was a student. The vast majority of cases are women, but not all. Walk through a college fitness center (almost every campus has a fully equipped one with all the latest machinery) on a weekday evening between eight o'clock and ten o'clock and you'll see at least one manifestation of the disease at work. Females occupy almost every stair and elliptical machine, working themselves from the waist down. On the other side of the room, guys grunt and grimace over free weights and Nautilus equipment, then linger between rep sets in front of the vast sidewall mirrors to check out bulging biceps, pecs, and other visible indicators of physical prowess from the waist up. Most of these spandex-clad women and sweat-soaked men keep their exercise in perspective. But others use the ostensibly healthy setting of a fitness center to disguise an illness. "Go back there at different times of the same day," said a senior administrator at one college, "and you'll see the same ones coming back, sometimes three or four times every day."

These are often the same ones who vomit after meals or don't eat meals at all. Some start in junior high school, others in college after putting on the freshman fifteen, the extra pounds that often creep on in the first year, when all the tightly imposed constraints of adolescence are off. Suddenly, eating, sleeping, drinking, and daily schedules are unregulated. Some laugh it off; others get a grip and work it off slowly. And some are undone by it.

For too long, Mary Adkins was undone. "I felt lost in the world," she told me as we sat outside a coffeehouse on 9th Street in Durham, North Carolina, on a warm October evening. Three years earlier, a freshman weight gain made her realize that looking good—being thin—had become her guiding philosophy. The seeds had been planted back in high school. Being thin "was a palpable way of showing that you're winning the game, that your body is completely within the realm of your control. I wanted to do everything well, but I didn't have a filter, an ideology to figure my life out. So I got skinny. I became thinner and I *was* happier."

Mary's social life was good, she was doing well academically, her life was in order—under control. "Then," she recalled, "there's an invisible line you cross. It had become an obsession and I was miserable."

At the end of freshman year, Mary went home for the summer and told her mom about her affliction. She started seeing a therapist and searching for a new ideology to replace her eating disorder, which she began to realize was the means by which she had been measuring her life.

When she returned to Duke in the fall, she thought she had it figured out. But she was wrong. In late October, she sat down and wrote, "I sit here facing a blank screen with swollen eyes and a half-eaten jar of peanut butter on my desk, and I am as unhappy as I've ever been." Mary meant those words to be as much a battle cry as a confession. And so she wrote on, in what would become a column in the Duke *Chronicle*, reaching out to her fellow students to help her break the silence about a disorder that afflicted so many:

> Food has a grip on my mood, self-worth and schedule. Every day I move with this little monster on my shoulder reminding me constantly of the standards I'm meeting or not meeting. Some days it takes all the energy I have to shut him up.
>
> For those of you who don't understand, I'm right with you. It never ceases to baffle me how in a culture as advanced as ours, at the top of the "needs triangle" way above water and shelter, we somehow work our way back around to struggling with the most basic necessity of survival: food. But we do. And as illogical, shallow and limited in scope as it may seem, it is an epidemic that is bringing pain to many, many people. It's complicated by the fact that it is multifaceted, this voluntary starvation: a physical and psychological plague.
>
> There are obvious reasons why it manifests itself so successfully at Duke. We are success-driven people-pleasers and control-experts. We've made it to this point by our own initiative and see it as our logical responsibility to continue climbing.

We are tomorrow's senators, BMEs, CEOs, success stories. We can control life. We can control. Control.

In her own way, Mary Adkins was trying to regain control. "As long as people who've conquered the problem of disordered eating aren't talking to the people who have potential for it, the same battle is being fought over and over again unnecessarily," she wrote. She issued an invitation to send her e-mails, diary entries, anything that would help build an inventory of common emotions about an all-too common problem. It worked. Within a week of publication, she had received over a hundred messages. She used them to produce a play, *The Perks of Disordered Eating*, which was ultimately produced in a campus theater before a packed house. She felt she had helped to bring the issue out of the closet at Duke.

Like Kristin Waller's tale at Harvard and Brian Previtt's at St. Norberts's, Mary Adkins's is a success story. No college administrator minds helping a handful of promising students work through their issues. And while it is nearly impossible to predict whose psychological problems can be resolved or at least managed and whose will hopelessly entangle the institution in disruption, surely there are ways to filter out at least some of the trouble.

Part of that can happen during the admissions process. These days, professional file readers pore over transcripts, test scores, essays, and letters of recommendation in what has become a highly sophisticated art form of predicting college success. The good ones can pretty much tell which applicants will do well, academically at least. If it were so inclined, Harvard could probably put together an entire freshman class of students with combined SAT scores of 1600. But the most selective private schools sculpt classes made up of a careful balance of disparate specialists: a chemist/flutist here, a soccer goalie who writes computer code there, and so on. There is room in that mix for the psychologically vulnerable but otherwise promising student who might go on to become a great painter or a software tycoon.

Under current practices, screening college applicants to weed out the incorrigibly troubled is probably illegal and for most institutions impractical. Privacy laws forbid high schools to divulge and colleges to demand a student's psychological or medical records. And any attempt to screen is bound to yield both false positives and false negatives—those on the one hand who would eventually succeed in college by overcoming or at least managing their psychological disabilities and those on the other hand whose symptoms might not appear until after enrollment.

But if the heart of the selective admissions process lies in its ability to predict success, knowledge of a candidate's psychological condition seems to me to be as critical a factor as his or her intellectual capacity or work ethic. The risks of erring in these kinds of judgments seems no greater than those inherent in relying on SAT scores or the recommendation of a high school counselor. The more an admissions committee knows about an applicant, the wiser its decision is likely to be.

The smaller and more selective schools find ways to learn what they need to know about their applicants, though the knowledge is never uniform. Personal interviews and direct contact with high school guidance counselors give admissions officers at places such as Hamilton, Middlebury, and Pomona the opportunity to see past the paperwork and learn about the whole person. Depending on how forthcoming the students and the high school counselors are willing to be, admissions counselors can learn a lot besides what's written on the uniform application form. "Kids have a lot of issues," acknowledged Bruce Poch, head of admissions at Pomona. "But if something in the application doesn't align properly, we'll pick up the phone and call."

Every college has at least one tale of an admitted student who wasn't all he or she was cracked up to be in the application file. One prestigious mid-Atlantic university admitted a student who was eventually thrown out for making bombs and threatening to blow up college buildings. Tracing back through his application file after the fact, administrators were able to detect anomalies in his record that should have triggered inquiries back to the high school. Alas, only later did they learn that the high school was well aware of his problems.

Most cases involve behaviors that are less dangerous to the community but still potentially tragic. One woman with combined SAT scores of 1390, impressive grades, captaincy of a major sports team, and a slew of other extracurricular and curricular honors at a private school in Connecticut earned admission to an Ivy League college but made it less than halfway through her first semester. By the end, which was in October, she had isolated herself to one of two places: the classroom or her dorm room, in which she locked herself each night until she could venture out to classes the next morning. Her parents had to bring her home. They should have known better than anyone whether their child could hack it in college. But too often, parents' need to create and share in their children's success blinds them.

The harsh truth is that residential college is not for everyone even if they are academically qualified to do the work. Fortunately, the North American system of higher education offers an impressive menu of alternate routes to a baccalaureate degree. Students who function well in the structured comfort of home might fare much better at a local college to which they can commute. The University of Phoenix and other online programs have expanded access to a wide array of baccalaureate programs not only for older, working, nontraditional students but also for those traditionally aged students who have trouble coping with the vicissitudes of campus social life.

There are residential options as well—even for those with severe disabilities. Some mainstream colleges are more accommodating and better equipped to deal with mentally disabled students; all of the institutions I covered, including Harvard, have both the capacity and the willingness to take on the challenge. But every school has its limit.

There are plenty of people out there who can give advice as to whether sending a student off to a mainstream residential college is worth the risk. But it will take a major shift in public attitudes as well as changes in the law to allow college admissions offices, high school guidance counselors, doctors, and psychologists to share information. Of course, there's no guarantee they will always use that information wisely. But the alternative is to continue to operate in the dark and to diminish the quality and value of the college experience for everyone.

5

The College Alcohol Crisis

It's usually fairly easy to spot someone who has been drinking: the loud voice, glazed eyes, elided consonants, reckless gestures. It's a bit more difficult to tell if someone has drunk so much that he or she is in danger of dying.

Fortunately for Jessica, a first-year student at Hamilton, her friends could tell. At around two-fifteen on an October Sunday morning, one of them called the campus emergency medical technicians (EMTs) to come and get her. I was on campus that weekend traveling with Wayne Gentile, the college's senior uniformed safety officer, as he made his evening rounds. We were sitting in his dark blue van watching students move about from one party to the next when his radio crackled with news that a girl had OD'd in North Hall. By the time we got there, two student EMTs, sadly but reassuringly well schooled in such matters, had ascertained that Jessica was no longer in mortal danger but still in need of medical attention. As they carted her down the stairs to an awaiting ambulance, the driver loudly complained for my benefit about what a waste of time and resources it was for her to be taking this drunken college kid to the ER while something serious might be happening in the community. I got the message that this was a regular occurrence.

Jessica's Saturday night had started out calmly enough. Neither fond of the taste of beer nor willing to join friends who planned to smoke weed, Jessica nonetheless wanted to get high. She started the evening with a few hits of vodka in her room. "Then around ten P.M.," she recalled in a conversation we had a year later, "we got invited by a guy to a party in another dorm where couples were sitting around in a circle. You drink a shot as a couple when it's your turn—sort of a drinking game but not as organized as most drinking games. We took shots of vodka—vodka limone. I felt normal. It just wasn't hitting me. Two people who weren't drinking but who were sitting next to me later said that I seemed fine. I made it to round sixteen. Others were getting pretty drunk or getting sick in the bathroom. We were the last ones still drinking; then my friend stopped. We later calculated that all together I had the equivalent of twenty-two one-ounce shots."

Strong and in good health, Jessica survived. By the time she got to the Utica hospital, she was conscious enough to apologize to the doctor and nurses for imposing on them. Rehydrated, she was released around five A.M. Because of her good behavior in the aftermath of her incident and because she had had no previous violations of the college's rules against underage drinking, she received the minimum penalty of one evening of alcohol abuse education. Typically, transports (those who require hospitalization for alcohol poisoning) are required to take a six-week course.

I drank when I was at Hamilton—I still do. But until that incident, I had never seen anyone so drunk that they needed to be hospitalized. Indeed, in the four years I was in college, only once did a student go to the hospital for alcohol poisoning. That was a pledge in my own fraternity who had gone temporarily blind (literally blind drunk) after consuming a lot of rotgut red wine in an initiation ritual—a ritual that would draw criminal charges today. He recovered. But the incident was the talk of the campus for weeks to come. Despite all the boasting we did about how many kegs of beer we could knock off over a house party weekend, we were generally not lethal drinkers.

That's no longer the case. Unless you are actually there, you're not likely to see just how differently—just how intensely and purposefully—some of today's students go about consuming alcohol. When they come home for Thanksgiving or winter break, they are likely to moderate their behavior. But when they are away at school among friends, on any given night they have a shot at winding up in an emergency room.

Hospitalization for alcohol overdoses has become a regular feature of weekend life at even the best colleges. By winter break in 2003, more than twenty Hamilton students had been carted off to area hospitals for treatment of alcohol overdoses—seven in one weekend alone. Dartmouth, with forty-four hundred undergraduates, was admitting on average about two hundred alcohol emergencies a year to Dicks House, the campus health center. Middlebury, with twenty-three hundred students, had about a hundred transports in the 2002–2003 academic year. Before Thanksgiving of the following year, cozy, cerebral Pomona College had sent nine to the ER—more than twice its total alcohol hospitalizations the entire previous year and the highest number in eleven years. And these were the lucky ones.

According to a 2002 report issued by the National Institute on Alcohol Abuse and Alcoholism (NIAAA), alcohol accounts for the deaths of fourteen hundred college students a year. The majority of the deaths calculated by the NIAAA—about eleven hundred annually—still occur on the roadways as they did in my day. But highway deaths have actually fallen well off their heights of a couple of decades ago. What's different is the number of college students getting too drunk to even climb behind the wheel of a car, let alone crash it.

When people speak of someone drinking himself to death, they usually mean the long, slow way, wherein the liver is overworked and falls prey to cirrhosis. What's happening to these college students is a far more acute process: After a few drinks, the speech slurs and muscle coordination starts to go, followed by conscious memory. And after many, many more drinks, the central nervous system is overwhelmed. Ultimately, the brain suppresses natural functions such as breathing, and coma ensues. Absent heroic intervention, death follows—death by poison.

That apparently is what happened over the 2004 Labor Day weekend to nineteen-year-old Samantha Spady, a sophomore at Colorado State University. A former honor student, homecoming queen, senior class president, and captain of the cheerleading squad at her high school back in Beatrice, Nebraska, Samantha had told a friend in an IM exchange that she planned on "getting extremely wasted this weekend, not just because it's Labor Day, but because Colorado State plays Colorado in football tomorrow."

Colorado State lost the football game; Samantha lost her life. In the company of a few friends throughout Saturday, Spady knocked back enough beer and later vodka—roughly the equivalent of thirty shots—over eleven hours to bring her blood alcohol concentration (BAC) up to 0.43. Early Sunday morning, Samantha was wandering around the Sigma Pi fraternity house, her eyes glazed, her speech slurred. When last seen alive just before dawn, she was unable to stand on her own. Two friends carried her to a second-floor lounge to sleep it off. It was not until Sunday evening that a Sigma Pi brother who was taking his mother on a tour of the house found her body.

Samantha apparently drank of her own accord. Not so for Daniel Reardon, who was allegedly forced to consume a 40-ounce bottle of Hurricane malt liquor, followed by multiple slugs of Jim Beam bourbon, all of which were thrust upon him and his fellow fraternity pledges in a hazing ritual at the University of Maryland. It was not until the following day that Reardon was taken to the hospital with a BAC of 0.579—enough to kill a horse. He died a week later, having never regained consciousness.

Earlier in the same school year in which Reardon died, another Maryland student in another fraternity succumbed to an alcohol overdose. In the case of Alexander Klochkoff, the booze was supplemented by GHB, or gamma hydroxybutyrate, a designer drug often involved in so-called date rape cases. Though a few drops of it in a cocktail will render a woman helplessly pliant, some guys perversely use GHB to get themselves drunker quicker. For Alexander, the quick became the dead, as often happens when drugs and alcohol are mixed.

More often these days, college kids die from drinking's secondary effects. Drowning in one's own vomit, for example. According to official records, Duke University junior Raheem Bath died of pneumonia on the Saturday night of Thanksgiving break in 1999. But the root cause of his deadly infection was vomit inhaled after he had puked up a night's worth of drinks. Owen Smith, a senior at Vermont's Champlain College, froze to death in a snowbank on his way home from a party at which he was reported to have had a sizable amount of alcohol. A snowplow driver discovered Smith's body on a Sunday afternoon in December 2003 along the side of a road outside Burlington, Vermont. Last seen at a party the night before, Owen apparently wandered off, drunk and disoriented, and eventually fell victim to hypothermia. "You get lethargic, you get sleepy, and you start to make bad decisions," Dr. Steve Leffler, an emergency room physician, told the Associated Press.

Freshman Jeffrey Shank, age eighteen, plunged from a fourth-floor balcony of his Dickinson College dorm in February 2003. Four Dickinson seniors were subsequently charged with providing alcohol to Shank, a minor. The offense carries a $1,000 fine in Pennsylvania. Brett Jensen, age nineteen, fell off the deck of the Pi Kappa Phi house at the University of Washington and cracked his head open after playing a round of Century Club, a drinking game that calls for knocking back a hundred shots of beer in as many minutes. Indiana University sophomore Seth Korona died after performing a "keg-stand." Korona was suspended over the beer tap at the Theta Chi house at IU, inhaling as much beer as gravity and air pressure would permit, when he lost his balance, fell, and sustained a fatal concussion. University of Virginia student Leslie Ann Baltz also died from head injuries received in a fall down stairs in 1997 after she drank her fourth-year fifth—allegedly a U-VA tradition in which seniors consume a fifth of a gallon of hard liquor on the day of the last home football game.

Much of the difficulty in assessing the seriousness of today's college drinking scene is due to the fact that college drinking is hardly a new phenomenon. Historical and cultural twins, drinking and college are jointly celebrated in song, lore, and literature. Stories about college drinking date back to the origins of the modern Western university in twelfth- and thirteenth-century France and Italy. In his autobiography, Henry Adams recalls that his mid–nineteenth-century Harvard classmates drank so much that they had bouts of delirium tremens. F. Scott Fitzgerald's *This Side of Paradise* includes a classic college drunk driving accident at Princeton, the likes of which would be repeated in real life hundreds of thousands of times over the ensuing decades.

Yes, we drank when we were in college—sometimes a lot. Which is why those of us with memories of Sunday morning gin-and-juice parties (and for those who matriculated in the late sixties and seventies, a few other mind-altering substances as well) tend to dismiss the hand-wringing and apocalyptic warnings of Mothers Against Drunk Driving and other neoprohibitionists as old whines in new bottles. How different, we ask, could it be?

I pursued that question on every campus I visited, seeking out veteran professors and administrators who had witnessed student behaviors both then and now. John Bravman, a vice provost at Stanford University and a Stanford undergraduate from 1975 to 1979, recalled that there was drinking—"in some cases heavy drinking. But it was mainly about beer. Over time, there has been a clear shift to hard liquor."

"There were also drugs floating through the sixties and seventies," Richard Fass, Pomona's dean of students for part of that time, reminded me. "The irony is that the drug scene then was tame compared to the alcohol scene we're dealing with today."

My attempts to find objective data to back these anecdotal recollections proved futile. Tracking studies don't go back far enough to pick up the behavioral trails of the two relevant groups of parents spanning the sixties and the seventies. The University of Michigan's Monitoring the Future survey, which tracks the use of all drugs among teens, including alcohol, suggests that the *percentage* of young people who drink actually peaked in the mid-1980s and has decreased slightly since. However, that does not indicate how much individuals consume when they drink.

Measuring hospitalizations for alcohol overdoses would provide a useful comparison. But Linda Degutis, associate professor of emergency medicine at Yale Medical School and an authority on the subject, told me there really isn't any reliable way to compare. "We're not able to find any good longitudinal data—even for five years," she said. Hospital ERs are able to report only their own admitted alcohol-afflicted patients, not those of college health centers, which she noted are often reluctant to share such information. Even the broader figures on alcohol-related mortality would not help in identifying college students who overconsume.

But like many who have worked in and around higher education for a long time, Degutis believes college drinking has indeed worsened since she began a career in emergency medicine in the early seventies. "I don't remember seeing people coming in with alcohol overdoses the way we do now," she said. Victims of drunk driving accidents were commonplace then, but not as common as the alcohol ODs showing up from college campuses today.

If there has been any recent change, it has been for the worse. In the fall of 2003, there was an apparent spike in alcohol-related hospitalizations across the United States. The first two weekends of George Washington University's first semester saw a doubling of hospitalizations. An autumn surge of ER visits that year was leading Williams College "closer and closer to a major catastrophe," in the estimation of associate dean of students Dave Johnson. At Harvard, the number of undergraduates carried into University Health Services' ER on Massachusetts Avenue nearly

doubled during October and November from the previous year—
to a total of forty-four. Until then, Harvard health officials might
have expected twenty-five in a year, and as recently as 1997–
1998, only eighteen were hospitalized during the entire academic
year.

There are still parties on college campuses that look and sound
like the ones I remember: the sweat-inducing, amp-throbbing
eighties party I dropped in on at Hamilton's Bundy Commons
on the same night Jessica went to the hospital; the more mellow,
fraternity-sponsored Tuesday-night keg party held in the basement of Clark III on Pomona's North Campus; and a cleverly con-
ceived P party at Stanford, where everyone dressed up as something beginning with the letter P (as in Playboy bunny) and
danced until they shut the music down at two A.M.

A real college party these days usually starts with a pre-, as in
prepartying or pregaming. Another aptly descriptive term is
frontloading. Because of tight rules governing access to alcohol
on most campuses, students who want to drink tend to gather in
their rooms. There, typically in small groups, they consume
whatever amount of alcohol it takes to sustain a buzz for the rest
of an evening in which they expect to be deprived of alcohol. Parties sanctioned by college authorities either have no alcohol or
have alcohol limited by the estimated number of legal-aged students—typically 25 percent. If they're only eighteen, nineteen, or
twenty, as are roughly 75 percent of students at the institutions I
visited, odds are good to excellent that they won't get another
drink in public for a while.

There might or might not be music or even much conversation at a pregaming session. The focus is on drinking. Hard
liquor in whatever form is most available is the poison of choice.
As one U-VA student explained, "You drink hard liquor because
it's easier to hide." Largely because of a perceived tightening in
the enforcement of drinking regulations at Stanford, "there's a lot
smaller window in which to drink now," reasoned one senior in
Palo Alto, "so you drink a lot faster, and you drink it all rather

than waste it." Back East, a Dartmouth student set a dorm room scene in Hanover:

> There were about ten of us sitting on the floor, the bed, and the futon in what approximated a circle. There were several conversations going on at a time. On the floor in the corner were several bottles of alcohol (Pucker, vodka, tequila, vanilla liqueur) and mixers (Sprite, Coke, orange juice, lime juice) along with an assortment of plastic, paper, and solid plastic cups. Most everyone had a cup with some mixture or another, and those who ran out would pass their cup to the person sitting closest to the alcohol and request a drink mixture. Also in the room was a pumpkin, a four-way bong used for smoking marijuana. Entry into the room is carefully monitored. One girl was passed out on the bed. Fear of Safety & Security coming is limited, as the expectation is that if you are quiet and not visible, you're okay.

Why college kids drink at all is essentially no different from the way it's always been. In the microcosm of college life, the need for friendship, support, recognition, and some respite from the perceived tensions of academic, athletic, social, and sexual competition is palpable. To drink is to break the ice, to oil the engines of sociability, to enhance confidence, and to stifle inhibitions. Especially in the uncertain first few days and weeks on campus, as Middlebury counseling director Gary Margolis wrote in the early nineties, "Students can feel anxious saying hello, sharing things about themselves, showing interest in another and managing their aggressive and sexual feelings." By getting buzzed, wasted, or hammered, explained Margolis, they can "go beyond the limits of their personalities, competence, and experience." That struck me as logical but rather timeless. The question I was interested in was why today's students seem so unwilling or unable to stop drinking.

Drinking games have always been a way to break the ice. They weren't all that popular in my circle of friends, but I do remember occasional games of Beer-Pong, in which cups of beer are placed on a Ping-Pong table where they serve as both obstacles and receptacles: land a shot in one and your opponent has to chug the contents. There were a few others, like Thumper, which is essentially a test of keeping your wits in a word game while drinking—and since drinking is the penalty for messing up, you risk getting sucked into a downward spiral.

We might have played a few others but nothing like the array of games now deeply embedded in campus culture. Run a Google search for college drinking games and you will encounter a rich menu of sites. Most promote one or more of the many different games. Some include enthusiastic testimonials. Others warn darkly of their dangers.

There are at least nineteen versions of Beer-Pong, with West Coast rules, Virginia rules, and several specific to one campus or another. At Dartmouth, Pong is arguably more popular than the Outing Club, its rules more familiar to most students than the words to "Dear Old Dartmouth." Virtually every fraternity and even some sororities have at least one Pong table in the basement. At Chi Heurot, home to many of the Big Green's ice hockey players, three well-worn tables made from reinforced plywood form the centerpiece of the basement. Indeed, they were just about the only pieces of furniture below the sleeping floors when I visited the house one afternoon.

It always amused me when students would inform me that "at [fill in the name of the college], we work hard and we play hard," as if they had coined the phrase. We used that cliché at Hamilton in the sixties. But my recollection is that we really did work most of the week, occasionally drifting out on a couple of nights to one of the local bars to shoot a game of pool and have a couple of beers. Then on weekends, we partied pretty purposefully. But everywhere I traveled in 2003–2004, the weekend had grown. With few if any Friday classes, most college weekends begin on Thursday afternoon. There are variations: Dartmouth favors a Monday–Wednesday–Friday class schedule, which leaves Wednesday night in particular free for fraternity "meetings." While there no doubt was some discussion of house business at these regular gatherings of fraternity men, the main activities seemed to be the singing of chapter songs, the bonding of brothers, the playing of Pong, and the drinking of beer—all of which was merely a prelude to the postmeeting open house that began sometime after eleven P.M. At that point, women usually arrived and the Pong mating ritual began. There was "little guilt attached to drinking," declared one Dartmouth undergrad, "since it is part of the established norm."

On most other campuses, Thursday nights are now so universally accepted as part of the weekend that they often feature well-organized, well-advertised parties. At Stanford, Thursday is senior pub night, when members of the senior class are notified during the day through a class-restricted Listserv as to which of Palo Alto's watering holes has been designated as that week's meeting place. Starting around ten P.M., seniors (and some underclass hangers-on) pile onto the Marguerite, the campus shuttle bus, and head downtown. Obviously the entire 1,700-member senior class does not participate, but by midnight on the pub night I attended, the Nut House, with a legal capacity of maybe four hundred, was chock-full of Stanford students shouting orders at a frantically overworked bar staff.

All manner of college traditions that might have started out benignly have been sliding toward incivility. At Indiana University's annual spring Little 500, centerpiece of the Academy Award–winning 1979 film *Breaking Away*, what was once an almost family-style bicycle race has gradually deteriorated into a three- to four-day college-town drunk for which the Bloomington and IU police routinely cancel all departmental leaves and run overtime shifts to handle what now averages over a hundred arrests, mostly for underage drinking, public intoxication, and illegal drug use.

While Harvard's twice-annual Primal Scream, a naked run through the Yard on the eve of semester exams, has not yet produced any catastrophes, a similar Naked Quad Run each December at Tufts University across the Charles River has been progressively infused with booze, to the point where President Larry Bacow condemned the 2003 running in a campus-wide e-mail message. When students fired back at him for being, in effect, an uptight killjoy, Bacow retorted, "Should we wait until a student dies before we do something?" With the same fears in mind, Princeton administrators shut down the annual Nude Olympics after the 1999 event disintegrated into mayhem. "Seven students required treatment at Princeton Medical Center and there were numerous reports of sexual assaults on women," read a local Princeton *Packet* account of that year's event. "Reports involved students trampling on each other, excessive groping and bathrooms covered with urine, vomit and feces."

Such mayhem is not confined to the East. For an indeterminate number of years, Stanford students have celebrated the first full moon of the fall by gathering on the broad plaza of the Main Quad at midnight. According to the somewhat murky tradition, if a senior male kisses a first-year coed, she becomes "a Stanford woman." When Laura Wilson, now director of public safety at the university, was a Stanford frosh herself, she remembers taking a bottle of champagne with a group of friends to mark the occasion—"kind of like Valentine's Day." There were no police present, because the event was unofficial.

Now, Wilson said, Full Moon on the Quad has devolved into a "group grope-a-thon." A columnist for the Stanford *Daily* called it an "annual festival of spit-swapping and nudity." After eight students were carted from the Quad with alcohol poisoning and two women were sexually assaulted in 2002, campus police officers made their presence felt the following fall by conspicuously lining the entrances to the Quad and checking for open containers. Even so, four students had to be transported to the hospital and several women complained of being groped. "It was a more innocent thing when people just lined up and kissed," lamented Carole Pertofsky, who ran Stanford's alcohol education program. "Now it's edgy."

When an alcohol-related death or serious injury strikes, odds are excellent to overwhelming that it will be followed by a campus-wide crackdown on underage drinking. The pattern is a familiar one: a task force is convened, experts are brought in, souls are searched, and inevitably reforms are initiated. In fact, there probably isn't an American residential college that has not at least once during the decade surrounding the millennium undergone a residential life review with a specific focus on alcohol policy. In the immediate aftermath of Samantha Spady's death, Colorado State derecognized the Sigma Pi chapter where her body was found, declared all remaining fraternities alcohol-free, and formed a committee to explore the roots of binge drinking. After MIT freshman Scott Krueger died following a fraternity initiation (he was among six undergraduate deaths, including two suicides and a drug overdose, during a four-year period in the late nineties), MIT restructured its entire residential life system.

Leslie Ann Baltz's death prompted University of Virginia president John Casteen to convene a campus-wide task force that recommended sweeping changes designed to wipe out not just the insane practice of the fourth-year fifth but the culture behind it. Embracing a new tradition dreamed up by undergrads of running a fourth-year 5 K race for seniors that ended in a prize ceremony during halftime of the last home football game was an easy step for the president to take. Stopping the Valediction Day tradition of filling the 1912 Tiffany loving cup with mint juleps for the communal sipping pleasure of fourth-years on the eve of graduation drew some grudging complaints from traditionalists. Postponing fraternity and sorority rush from the spring of first year to the fall of second in an effort to stave off new students' introduction to the drinking culture met with outright resistance from a Greek community that represents nearly a third of U-VA students.

Under Casteen's leadership, U-VA made alcohol education a prominent piece of the first-year orientation program not only for new students but also for their families. The dean of students office began notifying parents when their sons or daughters were written up for violating alcohol rules or otherwise accumulating four V-SOCs (U-VA parlance for violation of standards of conduct). Campus cops are quicker now than they might have been five years ago to write up anyone under twenty-one who shows signs of inebriation, even when there's no physical evidence in sight. While I was there, one unfortunate second-year resident of Lambeth Commons got busted for sleeping through a fire alarm that had inexplicably gone off sometime after two A.M. He had committed no overt violation of U-VA rules except not to wake up and join several hundred other scantily clad, shivering students in the Commons courtyard on a frigid October night. In the estimation of the U-VA police officer present, excess drink had caused him to miss the wakeup call. The result was a V-SOC and an unwelcome letter home to Mom and Dad.

Virginia also launched an on-campus education campaign based on a relatively new theory called *social norming*. Developed by a Hobart–William Smith College sociology professor named H. Wesley Perkins, social norming takes a kind of cognitive dissonance approach to student perceptions about how their peers behave and how those perceptions influence their own behavior. Perkins and colleagues have analyzed data showing that individual students often believe a lot more drinking goes on than actually does, and in reaction those individuals tend to drink more in order to fit in. Social norming posits that if you can correct that misperception, students will readjust their behavior accordingly.

When asked what percentage of his schoolmates drink and with what frequency, for example, Kevin may report that he believes 60 percent have at least ten drinks every week. To his surprise, when he learns that in fact only 30 percent drink ten drinks a week and that the majority of his fellow students have between zero and four drinks, he will adjust his own drinking over time to his new perception of conventional behavior. Some two hundred colleges and universities have adopted social norming in recent years with varying degrees of success. Whether because of its campaign or because of other steps, Virginia's drinking measures improved in sixteen of seventeen categories since the social norming campaign started three years earlier.

Other colleges and universities have also taken comprehensive steps following tragedies. In the aftermath of two student deaths, including that of Seth Korona, Indiana University officially declared its Bloomington campus dry. By the hand of either the IU administration or their own nationals, six fraternity chapters were shut down for alcohol policy violations in an eighteen-month period beginning in January 2001. During that same period, campus alcohol busts quadrupled. Just when IU president A. Miles Brand (subsequently named president of the NCAA) thought his university had a handle on things—after *Time* magazine named Indiana one of its four Colleges of the Year for its programs to ease the transition of first-year students into university life—it was handed another more dubious media honor. *The Princeton Review*, best known for its SAT preparation course but also a publisher of various college guidebooks and surveys, named IU its number-one party school for the 2002–2003 academic year.

Indiana students reveled in their *Princeton Review* ranking. In the stores and taverns along Kirkwood Avenue, the student bar strip outside university gates, T-shirts celebrated IU's new national status. My favorite one was a send-up of a MasterCard television ad campaign of the time: the last item on a price list of several popular beverages and activities was: "Being Named #1 Party School: Priceless!"

Brand and other administrators were not amused. Campus police stepped up surveillance of student drinking and the frequency of arrests. Students chafed under the whip. Complained Bill Gray, a criminal justice major and president of Indiana's student government, "The worst part is that they arrest students who are just walking home. They tell us we're not supposed to drink and drive," he argued like the lawyer he was studying to become. "So when guys choose to be safer and walk, why arrest them?"

The Princeton Review's party ranking is one top-ten list college presidents pray not to make. At the University of Colorado, insult was added to injury after its 2003 #1 Party School ranking triggered an NBC *Dateline* piece featuring footage of relentless partying on the Boulder campus. The sad irony for CU was that the university had just come off a six-year program aimed at stemming the avalanche of parties in Boulder. Funded with nearly $1 million by the Robert Wood Johnson Foundation, the nation's single most generous supporter of efforts to combat alcohol abuse, the Matter of Degree Program, which enlisted the cooperation of area bar owners, established a three-strikes-and-you're-suspended policy, and promoted responsible drinking and driving through poster campaigns, ended in a total wash. At the end of the six years, Colorado's binge drinking rate was just where it was when the program started, which was almost 50 percent higher than the national average.

Frustration with the inability of college administrators to dent their drinking problems has often led local and state lawmakers to intervene. In January 2002, the Indiana legislature passed a law requiring that any beer keg sold in the state—there are about seven hundred thousand of them purchased each year—must be tagged with the buyer's name and address so that if that keg ends up someplace where there are underage drinkers, police can identify the source. Connecticut, Pennsylvania, and Georgia had recently passed similar so-called keg-tagging laws, and legislatures in Texas, Maryland, Wyoming, Minnesota, and New York would follow suit.

Incited by the violent hockey riots at the University of New Hampshire in Durham, the state legislature passed a law banning open containers of alcoholic beverages. In advance of the annual

Green Key weekend in May, State Liquor Authority Commissioner Anthony Maiola warned Dartmouth's fraternities that he would have undercover agents all over campus ready to hand out $250 fines. "We will be bearing down and bearing down hard," he told a reporter from the *Dartmouth*, the school paper. Maiola said the parent of a Dartmouth student had alerted him that there would be no school Friday on the Hanover campus, which he took as a clear hint that trouble was in the offing.

As it turned out, the Green Key scene was much more benign than Maiola or the anxious parent might have anticipated. At the AD house, which has had a beer-and-band party on its lawn off East Wheelock Street over Green Key weekend for generations, the brothers set up a fence of plastic tape—the kind used by police to block off crime scenes—as a barrier to underage drinkers. Bouncers checked students' IDs as they came through a narrow break in the fence to drink beer and watch warily to see who among them might be working for the state. Nobody got busted.

Across the border in Vermont, state liquor agents went after underage drinkers with no less zeal. A week before the 2003 Thanksgiving break, undercover agents raided a Kappa Delta Phi fraternity party just off the campus of Castleton State College near Burlington and charged forty-one minor-aged students and three adults who by providing alcohol illegally each faced a possible eighty-four years in jail and $84,000 in fines.

Officials at Middlebury College have in recent years had to cope with an unusually diligent Vermont liquor inspector known to show up unannounced at college functions to ensure enforcement of the law to the letter. It is illegal in Vermont for a bartender to serve more than one drink at a time per customer. The law is intended to prevent majority-aged drinkers from supplying their underage friends with alcohol. The inspector so intimidated bartenders at Middlebury's 2002 reunion weekend that one of them refused to give Lynne Bruhn, a member of the class of 1947, a second cocktail to take back to a wheelchair-bound classmate.

* * *

In the course of two decades, Americans have gone from being generally blasé about underage drinking to being obsessed with it. Amid all the challenges that higher education in North America faced at the turn of the twenty-first century—from controlling costs, making diversity work, and modernizing the curriculum to revitalizing teaching and rebalancing the role of athletics—it was the drinking issue that dominated the conversation around the tables of academia.

6

The Date Rape Dilemma

O ne sight I did not expect as I walked through Harvard
Yard on a windy April afternoon was a clothesline. Yet
right in front of stately Widener Library was a triangle
of ropes strung from the trees festooned with robin's-egg-blue
T-shirts, each bearing the phrase: "Our Clothesline Project: Take
Back the Night."

The shirts said much more than that—some in carefully
blocked letters written in neat rows, others scribbled angrily in
slashes of magic marker. Some were poems, some screeds, some
about fathers or older cousins or high school jocks. Written by
Harvard women, most of the messages appeared to be about Harvard men. The pictures they painted were dark and ugly: "I was a
freshman," read one, "and I was raped on the slimy bathroom
floor in the club."

"I woke up next to my ex-boyfriend—bottles and beer cans,
words of denial coming from his mouth," read another. "But I
wouldn't believe him. I knew what had happened, and he just kept
denying it. Fuck U!"

Later, well after dark in raw, rainy weather, I joined 187 other
people (we counted)—almost all of them women—gathered in a
straggly, silent circle in front of Widener's steps. Each guarded
a lit candle against the wind and listened as victims of rape

individually stepped into the center and struggled to tell a story. One was a male student, but most were undergraduate women who disgorged bitter accounts of unwanted sex. Journalists covering the vigil were asked not to publish details of these stories. But in general I can say there was a recurring theme of betrayal by classmates and trusted friends who took advantage of weakness or stupor invariably brought on by too much alcohol.

I am the father of three daughters not a lot older than the young women who spoke that night, and I knew how outraged I would have been if I discovered that one of them had been forced to endure such emotional pain. As each woman told her story and returned sobbing to the arms of others, my heart reached out to them.

But there were other times when as the same father I wanted to reach out, grab one by the arm, and ask, "What were you *thinking*? What did you expect would happen when you went out and got drunk, came back to his room, and lay down on his bed?"

I suppressed that urge, knowing that I would have been accused of blaming the victim, which in the zero-sum calculus of date rape activism is seen as the only way to characterize any reaction other than full support for those who have been sexually assaulted. To suggest otherwise is to say they were asking for it and to refute the irrefutable tautology: that no means no.

There were a handful of other men at the vigil in Harvard Yard that night. But none stepped forward to tell the other side of the story—to have the temerity to suggest perhaps that it wasn't that simple; that she sure seemed like she wanted to have sex; and that there really was never anything like an unambiguous no in the slurred and limited conversation that preceded the act. No one stood up and cried, "I am not a rapist, for God's sake! Do you really think I'd do something like that?"

I have by now heard a dozen or so date rape stories—several in gruesome detail. There is a numbing sameness to most of them. Give or take a detail, they are the same stories heard on college campuses all over North America by roommates and friends in the tearful aftermath, by deans and judicial boards struggling to assign responsibility, and sometimes (though not often) by district attorneys, judges, and juries in felony trials. Sexual assault by someone known by the victim—more commonly referred to as acquaintance or date rape—remains one of the most divisive, vexing, and seemingly intractable issues on campuses. In a cover story on date rape in 1991, *Time* used statistics that have been repeated thousands of times since then: "that while 1 in 4 women will be raped in her lifetime, less than 10% will report the assault, and less than 5% of the rapists will go to jail." Activists say it is the most underreported of campus crimes, and it isn't just a by-product of the macho culture of the Air Force Academy. One student leader at a liberal arts college told me that every woman she knows on campus either had been sexually assaulted or knew someone who had. "When I first started here and we had a sexual assault," said Captain Pat Connell, a twenty-five-year veteran of the Cal-Berkeley police, "it was almost always a guy jumping out of the bushes. Now what we get are date rape cases. It's the biggest problem we have here."

Campus date rape is such a big problem not because thousands of these rapes are reported and investigated but because those that are reported almost always depend on the testimony of one man and one woman with two very different accounts of what happened. During the 2002–2003 academic year, Harvard had nine cases adjudicated, only one of which resulted in a conviction. At Duke, says dean of students Sue Wasiolek, "we have one or two a year that come up for a judicial hearing, but we have yet to find someone truly responsible for a sexual assault."

One of the more heart-wrenching and detailed accounts I heard came from a woman at the University of Wisconsin with whom I had met to talk about an entirely different subject. In the course of the conversation, however, she revealed that as a UW student she had been a victim of sexual assault. In that meeting and through a number of subsequent exchanges, she recounted to me the events that changed her life.

It was a warm August evening in Madison when Melissa went off to Wando's on University Avenue with five guys. Four of them were friends. The fifth, a guy named Eric, she didn't know. He was sharing an apartment with her friends in the same off-campus complex where she lived. He kept buying rounds of Wando's drink special that night—the Fishbowl. While expensive at $20 a pop, the Fishbowl gives a lot of bang for the buck: a 100-ounce (about three-fourths of a gallon) snifter contains gin, rum, vodka, Triple Sec, and peach schnapps blended with various fruit juices, depending on whether you want a red Fishbowl, or a blue, green, or orange one. House rules are that you must have three willing drinkers present to order one. There were six willing drinkers that night, including Eric, Melissa, and her good friend Kurt.

Probably only Eric's credit-card company knows for sure how many Fishbowls they had before heading back to Eric's and Kurt's apartment. Melissa was pretty drunk. She remembers kissing Eric. But she was in control—at least able to walk on her own. Otherwise, Kurt said later, "It would have been a different story."

Back at the guys' apartment, where she planned to have a beer and go home to her place just two minutes away, she found the party was breaking up . . . except for Eric. At one point, Kurt took Melissa by the arm and asked, "Are you sure you want to do this?"

What Kurt meant, he told me later, was that he could see where Melissa and Eric were headed. He knew that Melissa had had a boyfriend on and off for most of the last year at Wisconsin. He assumed that they were still together. Otherwise, Melissa's apparent attraction to Eric looked, as he said, "like just the random college hookup mainly to have sex."

Melissa said she never saw it coming and thus didn't understand that Kurt was warning her: "It seemed like everyone was in on it except me." Next thing she knew, Eric had her in his room of the apartment, where he shut and locked the door behind him. "Don't tell anyone," he instructed her. Then he raped her without a condom.

Afterward, she found her shirt and pants and worked her way toward Kurt's room. Shaking and crying silently, she crawled into his bunk bed. "What's wrong?" asked Kurt. "Why are you shaking?" She just passed out.

The next morning, Melissa got up, inexplicably loaded the guys' dishwasher without saying much to anyone, and went home. The first person she told was her on-again, now off-again boyfriend, Dave. He reacted swiftly and violently. Dragging Melissa down the street, he called Kurt on his cell phone and demanded that Eric be brought over. "He's going to jail," Dave bellowed. He stopped a passing UW police patrol car on the street and screamed to the officer, "My girlfriend's been raped!" He even called Melissa's parents back East.

"It was very disempowering," Melissa recalled later. "I had no choice in what had happened the evening before, and I had no choice when and how I told the police because Dave told them for me." It didn't help that she was having a panic attack during the police questioning.

When Dave first called Kurt, the other apartment mates, including Eric, were out. When they returned around midnight, Kurt told them about the call. Eric denied he had raped Melissa, claiming the sex they had the night before was consensual. Kurt had no reason at that point to disbelieve him. He assumed that Dave was acting out of his jealous rage, and he sought to keep Eric away from him. Leaving Eric in the apartment, the other four went down to the street where four cops were waiting.

In the end, the case against Eric disappeared. The police said they didn't have enough evidence to charge him, and thoroughly unraveled by the ordeal, Melissa decided not to pursue it.

Kurt and Melissa had known each other before going to Wisconsin but as acquaintances more than friends. After the incident with Eric, they started to talk more in earnest and became close as a result. In the heat of the moment, Kurt had been inclined to believe Eric. The more he and Melissa talked, the more he believed her account. Over time, Melissa confided her worst fear: that as she changed student housing in future years, Eric could end up living near her, where she'd have to see him every day, feel his presence.

At one point while Melissa was recounting her ordeal for me, I asked her if she felt any responsibility for what had happened to her. The question chilled her. But in time, she responded: "Yes, I have responsibility in this situation. I chose to drink alcohol that evening. But that isn't the only responsibility I hold. For the rest of my life, I will remember this event and live in its shadow. I am the one who has to tell each partner about it. I am the one who contemplated suicide, who went through severe depression, who suffered from PTSD [posttraumatic stress disorder], who almost dropped out of school. He gets to move on and never tell a soul, and I get to live with it every day."

Most cases of campus date rape involve two people who each believe themselves to be accurate in their accounts of what happened. "I have sat in hearings and listened to her version and believed every word she said," said Sue Wasiolek at Duke. "And then I have listened to his version and believed every word he said."

Alcohol explains much of the confusion. "Alcohol and date rape are almost inseparable," said Isabel Carriego, who served as a student representative on Dartmouth's judicial board. And it is not just the guys who are doing the drinking. "Women are not just drinking more," Patrick Kilcarr, director of Georgetown University's Center for Personal Development, told *Time* in 2002, "they're drinking ferociously."

"Women didn't used to drink as much," confirmed Wasiolek. "Now they're catching up." She paused and with a wry smile and added, "You gotta love the feminist movement."

Indeed, many of the women *Time* talked to in the spring of 2002 as well as many I spoke with during my campus tours a year later saw drinking as a gender equity issue; they have as much right as the next guy to belly up to the bar. The trouble is, as a number of recent studies have shown, women's bodies don't handle liquor as efficiently as men's, not just because they tend to be smaller but because they have lower levels of the enzymes needed to break down alcohol.

The price for this physical inequity can be emotionally devastating. After being raped at an off-campus party at the start of her freshman year, one Indiana University victim was incapable of accurately identifying her attacker, whose upstairs bedroom she had inadvertently wandered into while looking for a girlfriend. Armed only with a fuzzy memory and a few random details, she initially brought charges against the wrong guy. Eventually, she found the right one and won her case. Throughout the ordeal, women friends regularly berated her for ruining the guy's life.

In a conversation I had with three juniors at Indiana, each of the women said she knew someone on campus who at one point or another had been forced to have sex. One confusing tale involved a woman whose roommate's boyfriend's roommate said she could sleep in his bed while he slept on the couch. (Her roommate and his roommate were in the other bed.) But while she slept, he got into bed with her. Another woman was so drunk she started to get sick while having sex. When she warned that she was going to throw up, the guy just handed her a pillowcase to use as a barf bag. Later, the woman told friends that the sex was unwanted but she was too embarrassed to pursue the matter.

The typical male response whenever I raised the subject of date rape was an awkward silence. Few of those I tried to engage in conversation were comfortable talking about it. But when they did, they usually offered a variation of one of three generic responses: (1) "None of *my* friends would ever do something like that, and if one did, I'd kick his ass" (a Dartmouth fraternity member). (2) "I heard about this guy who was accused of date rape by a girl he hooked up with. He was convicted, thrown out of school—his life was ruined; and then a year later she writes him and confesses that she made the whole thing up because he dumped her" (a McGill sophomore). (3) "Girls today are sexually aggressive, and when you hook up with one, you really can't be sure what you're getting yourself into" (a student at Indiana).

That there is some mystery in accounting for all the reported incidents of date rape is understandable. The widely quoted one-in-four statistic on sexual assaults is not based on any direct polling or police record but rather extrapolated from other data. Its presumption of vast underreporting is bolstered by another recent survey that calculated only 40 percent of U.S. colleges and universities have been meeting the requirements of the Clery Act in their reporting of campus crime, especially sexual assaults.

But even if this widely cited statistic is exaggerated, the smaller, harder numbers of sexual assaults are still disturbing and indicative of significant underreporting. A National Institute of Justice study in 2002 found that 3 percent (which translates to about a quarter of a million) of the nation's college women in the previous academic year had been victims of rape or attempted rape but that only 5 percent of them actually reported it.

Because most guys don't hear about rape or see it, they are even skeptical of these numbers. As one male actively concerned about the issue, Janos Marton, Dartmouth class of 2004, described the difficulty in ascertaining facts from the occasional date rape stories swirling through the campus rumor mill, "A girl will say, 'I had three of my friends assaulted in a fraternity basement last month,' and I'm like, 'Well, who?'" Marton's classmate, rugby player Michael Curley, offered his likely reaction to an unfolding date rape scenario at his fraternity: "If I saw a brother getting into a dangerous situation with a woman, I'd advise him to e-mail her the next day and try to hang out another time."

There is no doubt that certain young men, however well educated and polished on the surface, take a predatory approach to women. I don't know how else to explain the use of Rohypnol (known on the street as roofies) or gamma hydroxybutyrate (GHB, often called G), the best known of the so-called date rape drugs. Between 1998 and 2000, emergency room admissions in the United States for GHB quadrupled. To be sure, usage is not rampant; government officials say these drugs figure in only about 3 percent of the reported date rape cases. But evidence of their use ripples quickly through residential campuses. Many students who were on the Dartmouth campus when I was there in spring 2003 were aware of a woman who thought she'd been knocked out by a roofie pill. Just about that same time, a Hamilton woman tested positive for Rohypnol, news of which made the front page of the college newspaper. After a fraternity party at McGill, a number of first-year students, including one man I talked to about the incident, struggled to get back to their rooms. "I had no more than a couple of beers," he said. "I don't know how we could have gotten so disoriented without somebody having dropped something into our cups."

Feminist groups tout another statistic that claims less than 2 percent of sexual assault cases are based on false charges. While I am skeptical of the validity of that number, I also doubt that instances of blatantly false charges are commonplace. Still, there are a variety of apocryphal stories floating around in which some poor college Joe hooks up with a woman and has consensual sex only to be charged later with rape. Sometimes it's a one-night stand; sometimes they date for as long as three months; often there is just a hint that he might have been gentler or more chivalrous in breaking off the relationship. But the ending is pretty much the same: he is dragged through a college judicial process heavily biased in favor of the accuser, whom he is not allowed to face, and where it's his word against hers, and only hers is heeded. He is convicted, suspended, or expelled from college only to have her write a letter—sometimes years later—confessing that she made it up; that she was just angry at the way he treated her.

There are vigilante variations of the false charge story: in each case, a woman accused a fellow student of date rape only to watch as the system let him off. At Berkeley, a woman broadcast her alleged assailant's name over the loudspeaker during a Take Back the Night rally in Sproul Plaza. At Duke, a woman who felt frustrated by the judicial process created photo blowups of the man she accused, labeled them with "rapist," and plastered them around campus the day before graduation.

The threat of false accusation and the more frightening prospect of a conviction on false charges was at the heart of a debate in 2002 and 2003 over how sexual assault cases are adjudicated at Harvard. Following a year in which seven cases were brought before the university's administrative board, only one of which resulted in conviction and suspension from the college, the faculty approved a revision that required "sufficient independent corroboration" before a sex assault case could come before the board. Civil libertarians applauded it as a necessary correction to what they saw as an undermining of due process by those who wished to make proceedings less hostile for women. Some women were outraged, however, and appealed to the Department of Education on grounds that the new rule was discriminatory under Title IX's equal opportunity provisions. In April 2003, the department affirmed the legality of the new screening mechanism—but only after Harvard had lowered the standard from "sufficient independent corroboration" to "corroborating information."

Students continued to argue with one another over how date rape was prosecuted at Harvard, albeit less often in person than online or in print. Acknowledging a female housemate's position that tougher screening could have a chilling effect, one Harvard man reasoned in a lengthy post on his house open message board that while sexual assault by its very nature is unlikely to yield a lot of corroborating evidence, "that does not mean we should abandon fair jurisprudence." More publicly, Zachary Podolsky, class of 2004, wrote an opinion piece in the *Crimson* in defense of the falsely accused. "False accusations of rape do happen—and happen all too often," he asserted, adding that the "victims of false accusations of such a heinous crime are just that—victims. As such, their rights and interests must be vigorously protected."

As the controversy raged through spring 2003, a campus-wide committee that had been studying sexual assault procedures came forth with a set of sweeping recommendations that would separate sexual assault cases altogether from the administrative board's jurisdiction. Instead, they would be tried by a new Office of Sexual Assault Prevention and Response that would combine education, treatment, peer-to-peer training, counseling, investigation, and trial all under one roof. The office would have a full-time staff of three.

Over the past decade, most colleges have moved away from the strict evidentiary requirements of the court system in sexual assault cases. Offended and intimidated by the rough treatment of accusers in highly publicized cases ranging from the 1991 William Kennedy Smith case in Florida to the aborted Kobe Bryant trial in Colorado, victims' advocates pressed for and won reforms designed to encourage women to step forward. Long before Harvard did so, many student affairs administrators had separated sexual assault cases from general student judicial bodies. Many moved to keep the accuser and the accused in separate rooms or behind screens to relieve the accuser of the burden of facing someone whom she might well fear. To better ensure confidentiality, Duke reduced the hearing panel from five to three members: one student and two faculty or staff employees trained specifically for such cases. Adopted in the fall of 2003, Duke's new rules demand that consent must be mutual and clearly articulated. Middlebury grants the accuser the same privacy and confidentiality afforded a medical patient. And if the accused wishes to have an open hearing, the accuser must consent. Hamilton, which broadly streamlined its judicial process during the 2003–2004 year, opted to continue to try its sexual assault cases before a separate panel also used for sexual harassment cases.

As an assistant provost, Marsha Semuels oversaw sexual assault/harassment issues at Harvard until the end of 2003. "We *want* the numbers [of reported sexual assault cases] to be higher," she told me, "because that means people feel more comfortable coming forward." My clear impression from many conversations on a dozen campuses about date rape procedures is that most student affairs professionals share Semuels's conviction that because they believe the scales of campus justice remain tilted in favor of men, they will continue to look for ways to redress that perceived imbalance. Their default position is that even if the rights of the accused are diluted, the mere experience of a formal hearing offers accused males an "educational opportunity."

Not everybody agrees. Boston attorney Harvey Silverglate, codirector of the free speech group FIRE (Foundation for Individual Rights in Education), believes that midlevel Res Life administrators, "stoked by national conferences and burgeoning literature (including much faux science)," have made date rape "*the* signature gender-wars issue of our age." Their success, he said, has bred silence among men who "fear being dubbed sexist or worse" if they protest.

Elizabeth Nuss, formerly dean of students at Maryland's Goucher College, recalls battles with feminist faculty members who were outraged by any suggestion that a woman might have contributed to a date rape situation—a suggestion that was, in their view, "totally antifeminist and politically incorrect."

"I was always annoyed by women who could sit there and refuse to contemplate that they had any responsibility," said Nuss. To those who feel that all of a college's support systems should be employed in defense of the woman, she replied, "I am the dean of all students, males included."

* * *

In recent years, there appears to have been a break in the wall of silence behind which college men usually hide whenever the subject of forced sex comes up. While every campus has a robust support system for female victims, some have begun to organize men's groups that work to educate their peers about sexual aggression and the protocols of consent. Each year, Dartmouth's Center for Women and Gender deploys two male undergraduates to go out and proselytize to fraternities and sports teams. The Men's Project, as it is called, was inspired by a West Coast program called No Zebras, No Excuses. The name was inspired by a less-than-admirable trait of zebras, which tend to stand by silently and look the other way when one of their own is under attack by a lion near a watering hole, anxious not to invite attention to themselves.

Brian Greenough was one of the two Dartmouth Men's Project students devoting seven and a half hours each week to the enlightenment of his gender mates. The summer before we met, he had given nine presentations to Dartmouth sophomores who are required to be on campus for the summer term preceding their junior year. With training from the Mentors in Violence Prevention (MVP) program run out of Northeastern University, Greenough employed scenario-based techniques to drive home the lessons about sexual etiquette. One of his techniques was to ask groups of men and women to list the various things they do every day to ensure their personal safety. Invariably, he said, the men write down "next to nothing," while the women come up with long lists—little things, like going out at night in groups, never leaving a drink unattended at a party, keeping a small canister of mace or pepper spray in their purse. "The idea is to sensitize guys to the threat they pose as a group."

Keeping some of the fraternity groups on message is not always easy, Greenough allowed. Meetings can easily deteriorate into gripe sessions about false charge anecdotes, sexually aggressive women, and angry feminists. These complaints usually come from "two or three guys who will dominate the conversation."

Sometimes, he said, "The most I can hope for is that guys will think about it for an hour and a half."

Because this is a generation that takes readily to infotainment, many colleges put on some sort of a skit or dramatization on sexual assault. Tapping into what has become a cottage industry of at least a dozen touring companies, colleges pay for professional actors to drive the message home. Harvard was using "Sex Signals" from Catharsis Productions out of Chicago. Two actors play out a series of miscommunications in a bar pickup scene that starts out funny and ends up disturbing. The players later quiz students in the audience about their views of whether it was just a bad hookup or a rape.

Pomona has had a contract with Outspoken Productions to stage a four-act playlet entitled "Drawing the Shades" for incoming freshmen. It presents four scenarios covering each of the permutations: male on female, female on male, gay, and lesbian. The female-on-male plot posits a girl coming on to a guy in a hot tub, eventually performing oral sex on him. He succumbs but doesn't feel good about it, and they talk about why. Watching it can make eighteen-year-olds feel awkward, acknowledged Frank Bedoya, Pomona's assistant dean of campus life, "but a moment of awkwardness is worth preventing a lifetime of misery."

Engagement in the process doesn't always take hold, even for empathetic males. Paul Hohag, University of Wisconsin class of 2004, signed up for a date rape prevention group called PAVE (Promoting Awareness, Victim Empowerment) during his sophomore year in Madison. But before long, he gave up because of the approach. One PAVE tactic that rubbed Hohag the wrong way was chalking images of a female on campus sidewalks with a target centered on her genital area with a caption that read, "Is this what we look like to you?"

"If I get defensive, I know my guys [fraternity brothers] get defensive. If you're going to get men involved," Hohag advised, "you have to be careful how you do it." The refusal on the part of many of the women involved in the antirape program to accept any responsibility ultimately turned him off. When they vehemently defended a woman's right to dress provocatively and to go drink for drink with the guys at the bar, Hohag became disillusioned with their tactics and left the group.

While Melissa, the Wisconsin date rape victim, was back home in the East, she, her best friend, and her mother were talking in the kitchen about the Kobe Bryant case. When her friend and her mother both agreed that Bryant's accuser should have known better than to put herself into such a risky situation, Melissa reacted sharply: "You're blaming the victim!" she cried.

"When I was in college," replied her mother, "we didn't call it rape."

Between generations of women, there is indeed a definition gap when it comes to sexual assault—a gap that has only widened by changes in the dating culture and by the removal of such obstacles to intimacy as separate dorms, parietal hours, and other rules of etiquette that simply aren't observed on most campuses today. The term *date rape* was not even part of our vocabulary until the 1980s. It emerged from a feminist culture that was in the throes of wrestling with denunciations of patriarchal power and coercion, for which rape had become a metaphor. In her hotly debated book, *Against Our Will: Men, Women and Rape*, Susan Brownmiller called rape "nothing more or less than a conscious process of intimidation by which all men keep all women in a state of fear." But many men, myself among them, feel that the metaphor has been stretched to the point where it has become an unhelpful repository of definitions ranging from the clearly criminal to the vaguely sociopolitical.

Even when strictly limited to acts involving sexual penetration, however, date rape in early generations of college students is impossible to quantify. Women in the fifties and sixties who experienced what Melissa did would have been more likely to say they had been taken advantage of rather than raped. And because there was a powerful stigma associated with getting oneself into such a predicament (that is, drunk and in a man's room), a college woman then would have been far less likely to make a public accusation.

Because of the very real regulatory impediments to sexual intimacy back when dorms were separated and parietal hours were in effect, couples intent on having sex had to take overt and mutual steps such as breaking curfew and going to a motel. Those steps weren't signals of consent per se, but they had a lot more clarity to them than anything in the hanging-out/hooking-up culture of today.

Most of those who have researched sexual assault believe that little has changed over the years beyond a broadening of the definition of rape and a newfound willingness of its victims to come forward. "I strongly believe that it was prevalent in the good old days more than most people realize," said Bernice Sandler, senior scholar at the Women's Research and Educational Institute in Washington, D.C., and someone who has written about date rape for as long as the term has been in use. "It was easy for individuals to see such an event as a single happening—a bad thing that happened to them—and not something that was part of a larger pattern."

Perhaps so. But as someone who was part of those good old days as a male, who has now explored this issue with dozens of contemporary students and the administrators who try to cope with the aftermaths of their unhappy encounters, I believe college date rape is a bigger problem now than ever. It is worse today not because the numbers are higher but because young men and women, despite relentless efforts to teach them otherwise, seem no closer to understanding either the unwritten rules or the clearly foreseeable risks of sexual intimacy with people they don't really know.

Hooking up is all about sex—and anything but risk-free. It is an intricate negotiation conducted by two people who speak different languages. In his language, an invitation to her room, a deep kiss, or some pelvic pressure is an open-ended invitation. In hers, they are nothing of the sort . . . necessarily. By her rules, she can stop the train whenever she wants. By his, the train has left the station. It is a disaster waiting to happen.

7

Is Diversity Working?

T he meeting was one the editors of Indiana University's
Daily Student newspaper weren't exactly looking forward
to, but it was one they knew they must attend. A dozen
or so of them filed into the formal lounge on the ground floor of
Teter Residence Hall promptly at six P.M. They were there at the
behest of the university's Black Student Union (BSU), which had
called a town hall meeting to discuss what they viewed as an
offensive editorial cartoon the paper had run a week earlier. The
subject of the nationally syndicated cartoon was affirmative
action—a hot topic in the winter of 2003 as the United States
awaited the Supreme Court's decision on the University of Michigan's admissions policies. It was not the content of the cartoon
that had offended black students, however; it was the drawing.
The head of the black man depicted was disproportionately small
for his body; his lips were thick; he had bug eyes and long simian
arms hanging down at his sides.

The editors were all white, though ironically the one who
selected the cartoon was of Hispanic descent. Most of the rest of
about a hundred people in Teter's lounge were students of color.
There were also a few representatives of the administration,
including IU's vice president for diversity, Charlie Nelms, an
African American who served as point man for minority students
in Bloomington.

Carolyn Randolph, BSU's political action chair, set the ground
rules for the meeting: speakers had to identify themselves; no

insults. Then, somewhat incongruously, she added, "I am not a box that can be categorized. We are all different."

No one felt more different at that moment than the newspaper staffers, all of them white-skinned, sitting uncomfortably along a row of chairs, their backs to the wall. Gerald Mitchell, BSU's president, opened the questioning. "What," he asked the editors, "was the point of the cartoon?" JP Benitez, the *Daily Student* editor who chose the offending cartoon, attempted to explain the process whereby he and his colleagues pick cartoons and other artwork. They were trying, he said, to reflect issues people are talking about. But, he confessed, "I didn't envision such an immediate response."

From then on, the town meeting became something of a one-sided lecture on race conducted by various members of the Black Student Union and other African Americans in the audience. One stressed that the cartoon said a lot more about race than it did about affirmative action. Another opined that the entire staff of the *IDS*, as the paper is known on campus, should go through diversity training. A former editor interjected that they had. Nonetheless, admitted another of the journalists quickly, "We didn't notice the stereotypes. That speaks to our need for sensitivity."

Amy Orringer, class of 2004, the paper's assistant managing editor, cited some statistics in defense of the *Daily Student*. "Forty-one percent of our issues included coverage of major black issues," she noted, but without effect. "I hate it when everything gets reduced to a black-white thing," called out an African American student. Besides, offered another, the *IDS*'s idea of coverage is to write stories about the Hip Hop Congress (a national black student cultural organization with a chapter at IU) and to print stereotypical cartoons like this one, not to publicize black scholars at Indiana.

The tone of the exchange was civil, if laced with barely contained anger on the part of the black students in the room, until one white student in the audience—someone unaffiliated with the

IDS—stood up and pronounced that 41 percent coverage was, if anything, a bias *toward* blacks, since African Americans comprise only 3 percent of Indiana University's student body. Besides, he went on, he knew through his studies that African American males *were* somewhat larger than their white counterparts.

The room itself seemed to seethe. A black male in rimless spectacles standing in the back stepped forward. "What you just said goes back to nineteenth-century thinking and is what led to the Holocaust," he charged. "What you just said just makes me want to slap you."

But there was no violence. Instead, the news people conceded their insensitivity, promised to do better in the future, and urged black students to provide them with more positive story ideas and to write for the paper themselves. The *IDS* had had some black reporters over the past year, but few stayed.

At the end of the ninety-minute session, Charlie Nelms congratulated everyone for having come and contributed. In his view, the *IDS* coverage of racial issues had improved a lot in the five years he had been in Bloomington. Their ordeal over, the *Daily Student* editors as a group walked back to their offices in the Ernie Pyle School of Journalism to put out another edition of the paper. Many of the African American men followed Gerald Mitchell back to the Alpha Phi Alpha house, the IU chapter of a national black fraternity, for a separate meeting on affirmative action. Two worlds had met and had now gone their separate ways.

The administrators deemed the meeting a great success—what student life professionals call a teaching opportunity on the issue of diversity. Such moments are rare in a world in which like hangs with like, almost exclusively, at Indiana and all over North America. And in some important ways, the meeting was a success. People with very different perspectives and experiences had been forced to struggle when those differences clashed. The resulting discomfort was sure to remain fixed in their brains as they wrestled with the complexities and inconsistencies of college living.

* * *

Compared to most of the campuses I visited, Indiana had moved the least toward the numerical diversity so universally pursued and largely achieved by colleges and companies across North America. To be sure, IU is a public university in a state where only 8.4 percent of the total population is black, making it harder to create the kind of critical mass it takes for any minority group to feel it belongs. To be an African American on this campus of nearly thirty thousand students is to stand out. "Every day," Crystal Brown, secretary of the Black Student Union, told the newspaper editors, "I am reminded that I am a black on this campus."

Forty years ago—not only at Indiana but also on every mainstream North American college campus—to be black was to be flat-out lonely. Duke's first black undergraduate came in 1962. In my tiny graduating class of 196 at Hamilton in 1967, there were four black people, two of whom were African nationals. There was not a single surname of Hispanic origin and only one Asian on the Hamilton diploma list that June.

Nearly a third of all college students today are African Americans, Hispanics, Native Americans, Asians, or some mixture. That's double what their percentages were in 1980. In May 2004, out of a graduating class of some four hundred at Hamilton, there were fifty-six students of color, including eight cum laude honorees and a Phi Beta Kappa. In her salutatorian graduation address, native Sri Lankan Mary Beatrice Dias declared, "I am a third world, immigrant, bisexual, bilingual, working class woman of color in the sciences."

And Hamilton considers itself behind the curve in the recruitment and retention of students of color. Indeed, it is, when compared to Harvard and Duke and Dartmouth, where collectively more than a third of students now belong to one minority group or another. At Cal-Berkeley, where those of Asian descent alone make up 40 percent of the student body, Caucasians are a minority group.

Racial and ethnic diversity on college campuses has moved from being an aspiration to an expectation. Not only do administrators want their institutions to be broadly representative of the different racial and ethnic elements in society, so too does the majority of young people applying to college. In a 2000 national survey of incoming freshmen, two-thirds of the new arrivals thought they had a very good chance of socializing with people of a race other than their own while at college. Even a casual glance at the Web sites and glossy view books sent out by admissions offices reveals a purposeful effort to portray their campuses as energetically and happily multicultural.

Sometimes they overdo it. A few years ago at the University of Wisconsin–Madison, where students of color made up less than 10 percent of the undergraduate total, admissions staffers ran a photo in the UW view book that had been taken at a 1993 Badger football game. The exuberant crowd of happy, wholesome faces presented a great image of UW, except that they were all white. Utilizing computer technology, an art director superimposed a 1994 picture of UW senior Diallo Shabazz into the otherwise white crowd and instantly multiculturalized it. The clever bit of digital legerdemain might have gone undetected if Shabazz's dark smiling face had not been discernibly more sunlit than all the others—an anomaly detected by enterprising journalists at the *Daily Cardinal* student newspaper. A search of the photo archives produced the original, and the misrepresentation was exposed. Even more embarrassing was that Shabazz had never gone to a Badger football game during his four years in Madison.

Where two and three decades ago diversity was measured largely in terms of the enrollment of blacks, today it encompasses a far broader array of races, ethnicities, and even lifestyles. Add in Hispanics, Native Americans, and students of Asian descent, lesbians, gays, bisexuals, and transgender students, collectively referred to as the LGBT community, throw in half a million more students from other countries, and you have a sense of the scope of contemporary diversity. The watchword is *difference*.

There is a lot of difference in college today. How it got that way—including the ongoing debate over affirmative action admissions and retention policies, goals, and motives—has been the subject of countless studies, books, op-ed pieces, and talk-show debates. The questions that interest me are: What are colleges and universities doing with the expanded palette presented to them by their admissions offices? What is the objective in amassing all this diversity? And is the objective being achieved?

Only a few generations ago, the espoused purpose of having minorities in college was simply to provide them with access to the temples of knowledge, where they could obtain the wherewithal to succeed in life. As for the secondary aspects of collegiate life—the manners and mores, the social networking—the white establishment took it for granted that minorities, and for that matter women, would simply assimilate into its culture. The more minority students looked, dressed, and sounded like mainstream white collegians, the better their chances of success both on campus and in the larger society beyond. As for sexual orientation, "Don't ask; don't tell" was hardly a 1990s contrivance of the armed services.

Cultural assimilation, like parietal hours, dress codes, and standard curricula, came under attack during the student revolts of the sixties and early seventies. As the numbers of minority students rose through that decade, so too did the tensions, which in the spirit of the sixties were expressed through confrontation. In the winter of 1969, the Third World Liberation Front, consisting of various organizations representing African American, Mexican American, Asian American, and Native American students at Berkeley, launched a boycott of classes, demanding and winning the creation of a third world ethnic studies program. The following spring, militant African American students took over Cornell's student center on parents weekend, fought off a counterattack by white fraternity members, then armed themselves and held the building until the administration agreed to grant them amnesty. That same month, Cornell's board approved $240,000 to launch an African studies program.

Emboldened both by their larger numbers and by a growing ambivalence toward North America's traditional cultural values, minority groups became increasingly vocal about their wants and needs and more insistent about recognition of their own values. The proponents of black power, gay pride, and other expressions of group identity effectively silenced advocates of assimilation. Bolstered by a growing population of sixties-educated, progressive faculty members, student life administrators adopted policies that encouraged this cultural shift and in many instances codified them through speech codes that barred not only language deemed hurtful but even opinions about cultural values. By the early 1990s, nonjudgmental, politically correct speech was the dominant language of academia.

The initial forays in the PC wars were against traditional college curricula and the Eurocentric values they represented. Intimidated by protests, including a 1993 hunger strike by a relatively small number of Chicano students, UCLA agreed to create the Caesar Chavez Center for Interdisciplinary Instruction in Chicana and Chicano Studies. Beginning with its 1991 edition, Heath's widely used anthology of American literature had replaced samples of early New England Pilgrim writing with Native American oral narratives and the poems and diaries of Spanish voyagers.

The battle widened to include extracurricular matters. Many schools hastily abandoned sports team mascots—most especially Indians—that might be interpreted as racially or ethnically disparaging. Dartmouth was among those that dumped its venerable Indian, but as of this writing the college was still looking for a new mascot. From time to time, the campus suffers through bouts of acrimony, student assembly deliberations, symposia, and editorial comments in the *Dartmouth* newspaper over what the new mascot should be. In recent years, the mantle has rested uneasily on the shoulders of a White Mountain moose. To the

consternation of multiculturists, however, there remains strong
support for the brave of yore, especially among older male alums.
For a while, the student assembly tried to cleanse the old boy network of its Indian paraphernalia by offering to replace offending
jackets, shirts, and hats with more benign apparel—sort of a nee-
dle exchange program for Men of Dartmouth traditionalists.

To the frustration of the multiculturalists, campus speech
codes did not withstand the scrutiny of the courts. One by one,
beginning with Stanford's in 1995, they were deemed unconstitu-
tional. Without them as a tool of enforcement, student affairs
staffs have tried to use other policies to protect special interests.
In its effort to make sexual assault victims more comfortable with
the judicial process, Columbia University crafted procedures that
curtailed defendants' rights, including the right to cross-examine
witnesses, for example. Tufts brought sanctions against a student
Christian group that refused to promote a lesbian within its ranks.
At Cal Poly–San Luis Obispo, a white student was convicted of
disruption for trying to post a flyer promoting a conservative
black speaker in a public lounge on grounds that the subject matter was disturbing to a group of African American students meeting nearby.

In each of these cases, college administrators found themselves under legal fire from a group calling itself FIRE, the Foundation for Individual Rights in Education. Founded in 1999 by
Alan Charles Kors, an academic conservative, and his old college friend, Boston attorney Harvey Silverglate, a social liberal,
FIRE has emerged as a kind of American Civil Liberties Union
(ACLU) for college students and professors. On its Web site, the
foundation claims to have interceded in cases at over two hundred colleges.

On most campuses, where political liberalism continues to
dominate discourse, FIRE is viewed as an unwelcomed, right-
wing interloper. To be sure, most of the causes the organization
takes on are in defense of conservative issues. Among its signifi-

cant backers is the archconservative Sarah Scaife Foundation. But like the ACLU (which has sided with the foundation in court more than once), FIRE vexes its enemies by occasionally defending ideological opposites. It championed the cause of Nicholas DeGenova, the Columbia University anthropology professor who in the wake of 9/11 called for "a million Mogadishus" (a reference to the Blackhawk Down deaths of eighteen American soldiers in the streets of Mogadishu, Somalia, in 1993) against the U.S. government.

"In the academic world, we always should bend over backwards to accommodate the greatest possible freedom of expression," Kors wrote of the DeGenova case during an online colloquium hosted by the Chronicle of Higher Education. "But that applies both to speech deemed 'unpatriotic' and to speech deemed 'racist, sexist, or homophobic.' Freedom is a way of being human, not a tactic toward a partisan political end."

As I traveled around campuses, I heard very few racist, sexist, or homophobic remarks or even heard about them. What I found instead was a vast majority of students well schooled in the need to show ethnic and gender sensitivity and who seemed anxious to avoid any kind of confrontation. They seemed intent on not passing judgment on others' values. I sensed in many of them a low threshold of tolerance for anything that smacked of intolerance.

And when they're not sufficiently sensitive of diversity, they are reminded. At its November 2003 concert to introduce new inductees, the Aires, Dartmouth's oldest a capella singing group, performed a skit in which two black members tried to teach two white members a dance step. Their unsuccessful efforts clearly implied that the step was too complicated for rhythmically challenged Caucasians. Then the two whites attempted to teach their African American colleagues how to spell cat (C-A-T). The four freshmen wrote the skits themselves.

At the performance, many students laughed, apparently accepting it as the parody of racial stereotypes it was intended to be.

But some—whites as well as students of color—began grumbling about how the skit made them feel uncomfortable. Afterward, their grumbling spiraled into righteous outrage over Dartmouth's Blitzmail system. Though the group, including the two blacks and two whites who wrote the skit, continued to insist that it was intended to demonstrate in a humorous way that race is not an issue among the tightly knit Aires, others at Dartmouth chose to read insensitivity, if not racism, into it. The day after the concert, the Aires did ninety minutes' worth of penance before the Black Leadership Council under the watchful eyes of the college's Office of Pluralism and Leadership. That Friday's edition of the *Dartmouth* carried a formal apology signed by the group's musical director and business manager.

Overt institutional support for underrepresented groups is typical of our most selective colleges today. Every place I went had deans dedicated to minority students—in many cases one per ethnic group. Dartmouth has a separate dean for African American students, Asian Pacific students, Latino/Hispanic students, and LGBT students, as well as affinity housing for blacks, Asians, Latinos, and Native Americans. Stanford has theme housing for each of these groups as well, although there is a 50 percent limit on the space allotted to each racial/ethnic group. Pomona and Hamilton have no separate housing for minorities but do have cultural centers for African Americans, Latinos, and Asians as well as women's centers and meeting spaces for LGBT students. Wesleyan University in Middletown, Connecticut, began offering separate housing for transgender students in the fall of 2003. Apparently, enough students said they felt uncomfortable using public lavatories to warrant having a place of their own.

At Pomona, the Asian American Resource Center is a spacious office on the second floor of the Smith Campus Center. Director

Daren Mooko oversees ten to fifteen student interns who make it their business to go after each one of the sixty-some Asian students who arrive with each new Pomona class. They identify them during the summer before they register and send letters offering the center's services. Throughout the year, the center puts on events—a performance by the Spoken Word, an Asian Hip Hop group, a roundtable on queer issues among Asian Americans, or an Asian film series.

Most North Americans see Asians as the least needy of the minority groups. The stereotype credits them with being more diligent if not outright smarter than the norm and highly concentrated in the most rigorous academic disciplines. They are more likely than Latinos and blacks to assimilate in traditional ways by joining fraternities and sororities or the cheerleading squad. But some Asian cultural characteristics can work against them in a liberal arts setting. The same strong family ties that lead them to stick to their parents' detailed life game plan make it hard for many Asian American students to explore new possibilities—to switch from premed, for example, to studio art, thereby defying parental plans for them to become the family's principal breadwinner.

Asian families, said Mooko, might well expect their children to come home regularly to pay their respects even when such interruptions prevent them from participating in campus activities. Children of recent immigrants from certain Asian countries are frequently expected to handle their parents' finances—an obligation that may rule out a junior year abroad program. "It's often not important to Asian families what a student enjoys," explained Mooko, "but what will get them a lucrative job. For the eldest child, there's even less room."

Older Asian students can advise and share their own experiences. "Here's what I said to *my* parents," a mentor might offer a freshman who wants to drop biology to become an English major in defiance of her family.

More established support networks await incoming African Americans and Hispanics on these campuses. Indeed, some support systems kick in well before the targeted minority group registers for classes. One of the most aggressive is the POSSE Foundation, an independent foundation that bridges the gap between affirmative action admissions and programs designed to acclimate minority students once they are enrolled.

I was familiar with POSSE from Hamilton, which has had the program for nearly a decade. I came across POSSE at Middlebury and again at the University of Wisconsin. Launched in the early nineties, the POSSE Foundation identifies students from inner city environments, where more of their peers might go to jail than to college, and prepares them to cope with the pressures they will face at high-powered academic institutions. Not all participants are black or even of color. But because the face of most inner cities is more likely than not one of color, most POSSE students I've seen are either black or Hispanic.

POSSE gets its name from the old western movie notion of the sheriff riding into town with a platoon of allies by his side. It was inspired by a remark made by an inner city student who had dropped out of college and later explained that he would have stayed if only he'd been with his posse, meaning his inner city neighborhood buddies. POSSE forms teams of students who as individuals are capable of doing the work at these colleges but who might not survive the ordeal alone.

Athenia Fischer, from Trinidad-Tobago and Venezuela via East Flatbush, Brooklyn, was a member of Middlebury's class of 2004 POSSE. She had no idea where she wanted to go to college when she was told in February of her senior year in high school that she was accepted at Middlebury. It was the closest college with a POSSE contract to her home. She first visited the campus in April. Following a tour, the group waited in the basketball court until the bus went back to New York. It was not a good first impression. "As far as I could see, the school was near a cemetery and smelled like cow dung," recalled Athenia. As they waited to go home, she said, "the guys played basketball; the girls sat on the floor and cried."

It wasn't much better when the group returned in the fall. Finding it hard to operate without the stimulations of urban life, the students often left campus on weekends. It was not until April that the women collectively decided they were better off accepting Middlebury for what it was and making the most of it. "It was horrible here," said Athenia, "but not horrible enough that it was worth our lives. So we as a group decided to do more activities on campus to satisfy our city hunger."

Middlebury remained difficult for Athenia right up until her junior year, when instead of going abroad as so many of today's students do, she did a semester at Atlanta's Spelman College, one of the country's traditionally black colleges. "Being down there gave me an appreciation for Middlebury," recalled Athenia. "I got to appreciate being out in the woods camping. I appreciated the way the buildings are kept up, having a refrigerator and a microwave in your room." She also began to value Middlebury's academic rigor. Spelman, she said, was "an easy stroke for me. It wasn't as hard as here. Their 'hard' is different—more rote learning." And Spelman's strict rules (parietal hours for women) made it feel "like going backwards."

When I met her at the beginning of her senior year, Athenia was working as a POSSE student mentor herself, shepherding a new batch of students from the New York metropolitan area. She was at their exclusive orientation session, sitting in a circle that included college president John McCardell, dean of students Ann Hanson, and the new group's faculty mentor—all there to answer any questions these ten new minority students or their parents might have. Such high-level attention doesn't stop at the end of orientation week. Once enrolled, POSSE students meet at least once a week with their mentor. Twice a year, folks from the home office come to campus to see how they're faring. Though they are encouraged to see themselves as a unit, they are not allowed to live together. Instead, they mainstream into the full campus and are encouraged not only to get involved but also to go for leadership positions.

Athenia was earning $800 a semester as an RA at Palana Center, Middlebury's one example of racial affinity housing. She was a recognized leader on campus. Still, she was not entirely comfortable in a college that is a traditional bastion for white upper-middle-class New Englanders. When I asked her how as a senior she was getting on with whites, she allowed, "I'm still working on a lot of that."

"People kind of sort out diversity," she observed to me as we sat on a wall outside one of Middlebury's nearly brand-new, multimillion-dollar residential commons. "The common ground we have is hip hop and reggae—Bob Marley. When the Roots were here, a lot of white people came. We were very happy. And I've gotten to like some of the music they like."

POSSEs don't always take. Individual members, sometimes whole cohorts, fall short of expectations; either one or more prove unable to make the social adjustment or to keep up academically. Some question POSSE's value for the money. In addition to earmarking ten full-freight scholarships for each incoming group, participating colleges pay $30,000 just to belong, plus tens of thousands of additional dollars for staff training, retreats, and support services. Because the foundation staff insists on relatively hands-on oversight of its charges, some college officials occasionally carp about the program's inflexibility. "Yes, we increased the diversity on campus," wondered an administrator who oversaw minority programs on one POSSE client campus, "but how many more students could we have with increased efforts at $1.2 million [in total scholarship]?"

More than blacks these days, gays and lesbians say they feel threatened as they go about their daily lives on campuses. Most see the 1998 murder of University of Wyoming freshman Matthew Shepard as just the extreme end of a spectrum of hostile reactions to their sexuality and culture. Typically, they are not as supported as racial and ethnic minorities. Out of the nation's several thousand colleges and universities, noted Sue Rankin, an LGBT analyst at Penn State, only around a hundred have visible support systems for gays and lesbians.

As an openly gay student at Hamilton, Thomas Acampora experienced harassment in his first semester when he found anti-gay messages written on the whiteboard outside his room. That first fall he also got a late-night phone call from a group of obviously intoxicated males calling what he did unnatural, and threatening to drive him from campus. Sophomore year brought a respite. But a series of anonymous computer-typed notes broke the truce in the spring of his junior year. On a mid-April Saturday, he got up from bed to find one slipped under his door. "Fuck you, faggot," it read in oversized boldface type. "Stop bitching. I don't give a shit. It is unnatural and fucking disgusting. You should shut up and die."

As a coordinator for the Rainbow Alliance, Hamilton's LGBT organization, and visible in his gayness, Acampora was not a surprising target. The college was nominally supportive of the gay community, he said. Like other student organizations, the coalition was funded and had office space. Mark David, the associate dean for multicultural affairs, a heterosexual African American and the administration point man for gays, had dutifully held a couple of retreats that included LGBT issues during Thomas's time at the college. Res Life staffers tried to get a safe zones system started wherein members of the faculty and administration would sign on as official allies of gay people, so that any LGBT student with a problem would know who might help. But Acampora said it never really got organized. Far more effective in reassuring gay students was a full-page ad in the *Spectator,* the college newspaper, from Group Q, an assemblage of openly gay faculty members who offered to serve as mentors or counselors to any student needing support. Ironically, Hamilton is considered one of the more gay-friendly work environments.

The Rainbow Alliance has regularly called for a queer studies department at the college, but that did not seem to be forthcoming. The administration polled coalition members on whether they wanted to have a gay dorm on campus, but the consensus was that it would only provide homophobes with a target.

Historically over the past two decades, colleges have tended to bunch gay students in with ethnic and racial minority groups. While some campus political coalitions have grown out of their common sense of not belonging, it is not a natural alliance. "That LGBT falls under the multicultural umbrella is problematic," said Christopher Scoville, an openly gay Duke senior and columnist for the *Chronicle*. "Gays are incredibly diverse in terms of their individual backgrounds. But there is a lot of fragmentation among minorities. Blacks and gays, for instance, have nothing to do with one another."

That's true at Northwestern University as well, according to Tamar Carmel, a Rainbow leader there. "Politically, we are part of the Progressive Alliance, along with other liberal and ethnically based groups," she told me. "But we have virtually no contact with black students. I have a black lesbian friend who says, 'Either you're black or you're lesbian, not both.'"

Straight students seemed surprised to hear that gays on their campus felt hostility. One Hamilton student said that he knew of a gay couple who had been welcomed without incident at his fraternity's last party. Gays say the hostility is seldom expressed overtly but rather in sneers and snide remarks. A lesbian at Duke said, "There is an increased visibility around LGBT issues because of the center here, because of the okaying of same-sex marriages in the chapel, and because of marketing campaigns like the 'Gay's Fine By Me' T-shirts handed out around campus. But then there was a 'Gay Not Fine by Me' article in the *Chronicle* that did not draw much of a response. You can imagine the response to an article entitled 'Black Not Fine by Me.'"

Even at Harvard, where intolerance is held in check by a pervasive assumption that practically everyone there is smart enough to deserve respect, minorities and gays see subtle signals of opprobrium. Allana Jackson, class of 2003 and president of the Association of Black Harvard Women at the time of my visit, said that from what she has heard, race relations were a lot worse in the past. They're still not great, she said. "But I feel that if you ask that of a white person, they're more likely to say they're great because they often don't even see it."

The most egregious slight, she said, came at the end of the 2001–2002 year when editors of the yearbook inadvertently omitted mention of nearly a dozen black and Latino student organizations, including her own. Somehow they remembered to include Asian groups. African American students demanded a reprint or a supplement, but they were told it would be too expensive. A professor anonymously donated the money to produce a supplement.

More subtle and typical, said Johnson, was the response from some white students to her organization's general messages on Harvard's House Open computer message system promoting Black History Month. Each message contained a little factoid on black history. After a few days, someone protested online that these messages constituted spam and should be stopped. "It's not as if the House Opens don't have a lot of trivial stuff on them all the time," said Johnson. "But this time it's spam."

If the spam complaint had racial overtones, my guess is that it reflected a more generalized mainstream resentment of perceived special privileges granted to minorities. Few will say so directly, but my sense is that many white students feel the amount of space, money, and institutional attention administrations devote to racial minorities and LGBT students is disproportionate to their numbers. Duke's LGBT Center on the second floor of the Flowers building in the heart of the West Campus when I was there has since moved to a spacious suite of offices previously occupied by the Mary Lou Williams Center for Black Culture, which took over an even larger space that once housed the Oak Room, a private, white-tablecloth dining room near the center of campus. Virtually the entire third floor of Dartmouth's Collis

Student Center is devoted to the college's affinity deans and meeting space for students from underrepresented groups. Only the *Dartmouth Review* had the temerity to question newly installed dean of the college James Larimore's April 2000 decision to promote the college's African American, Hispanic, Asian, and LGBT affinity deans from half-time to full-time. "Apparently, the advice provided by class deans is inadequate, or culturally indecipherable, for students with minority backgrounds (or alternate sexual orientations)," wrote the *Review*. "As such, Dartmouth is providing special advisors just for them."

The cost and visibility issues exploded beyond the conservative *Review* in December 2002, however, when Dartmouth announced it was abolishing the college's varsity swimming program. More than six hundred students, many of them part of Dartmouth's entrenched jock culture, rallied in front of Parkhurst Hall in protest against the move. Openly echoing the *Review*'s complaint, many in the crowd demanded to know why the administration had chosen to balance the college's budget on the backs of its swimmers when it had just expanded the role of the affinity deans.

The Dartmouth swim team episode brought to the surface a vexing question about modern college diversity programs: For whose benefit do they exist? Mitchell Chang, professor of education at UCLA and a scholar of campus diversity, has conducted studies concluding that "racial diversity has a direct, positive impact on the individual white student: the more diverse the student body, the greater the likelihood that the white student will socialize with someone of a different racial group or discuss racial issues." That is an unassailably noble goal, not to mention logical. But more often than not, I found, it failed to materialize because rather than exploring beyond their own cultures, individual students prefer to remain inside the safe environs of their own crowd. Sociologists call it a silo effect.

"Yes, we have a multicultural community at Duke," said Heidi Schumacher, a white premed student. "We have this culture here, and this culture here, and this culture there," she said, moving her hand from one isolated spot on the table to another.

Silos are mostly invisible except for their effect. In one of the more popular food courts inside Indiana University's vast Memorial Union, all the tables in the far corner of the eating area were taken up exclusively by African American women who were talking and laughing at a notably higher decibel level than anyone else in the room and drawing furtive glances from the whites who passed by with trays on their way to other tables. In Pomona's Frary dining hall, every one of the twenty-some seats at the long table nearest the check-in desk was taken by a strapping white male who looked like he might have been a football player, each hunched conspiratorially over large plates of food. Women and students of color were scattered elsewhere.

When I mentioned my observations, minority students and their mentors tended to shrug it off, as if to say, "So what's new?" Such informal segregation is just the way it is for students of color all the time. Self-selection and informal segregation are okay, said Daisy Lundy, who is part African American, part Korean, and president of the University of Virginia's student council. "They [whites] don't acknowledge that they do it themselves." Besides, she said, "Total self-segregation is impossible." Even in Alderman, viewed by many on campus as U-VA's African American first-year residence hall of choice, she noted that blacks are still not in the majority.

One college administrator who openly bucked the multicultural trend was Rick Turner, the dean of African American Affairs at the University of Virginia. Turner couldn't care less what benefits whites might gain from diversity. He has one goal: black retention. "Everybody knows that Rick Turner is the dean of African American students, not Latinos, not whites," he told me in his second-floor office of U-VA's Luther P. Jackson House, the university's African American home away from home. "I have devoted my life to assisting these students in their efforts to graduate."

"I'm not the dean of students. What I promote is taking advantage of the University of Virginia." And if that means studying and living within a racial silo, so be it. "You can't force people on folks. I want students to take advantage of what's here."

A graduate of tiny Linfield College in Oregon, Turner was one of six black students out of a thousand—"a lonely experience," he acknowledged. "I don't want my African American students to feel the pain and anguish I felt." He completed his Ph.D. in education at Stanford on how blacks fare at traditionally white colleges.

His formula includes "showering love" on black students as soon as they arrive at the university or even sooner. "We jump on them as soon as they sign that letter." When they come to Charlottesville with their parents, he said, "I want [them] to see my black face and my Africancy." He also has a peer advisor program in which sixty second-, third-, and fourth-year African American students are trained annually to be big brothers and sisters to incoming first-years. Over the last ten of the fifteen years Turner had been at U-VA, African American RAs have gone from zero to 30 percent of the total.

At the end of the 2002–2003 academic year, the graduation rate for blacks at Virginia was 87 percent—the best of all the so-called public Ivies and not far behind Harvard's nation-leading rate of 93 percent. "African American students love it here," proclaimed Turner, "and they love their association with each other more than anything else."

But Turner is an exception even at U-VA. Most of the administrators I met were still struggling to resolve the inherent conflict between a desire to support and retain students of different races and sexual orientations and the hope of getting them to interact and learn from one another. Their efforts often backfire. Toward the end of a late-night discussion with a random group of Dartmouth students in Gile Hall, where my room was, a first-year girl approached me with the story of her arrival on campus the previous fall. She prefaced it by explaining that while she was of Korean descent, she had grown up in Los Angeles, attended a prestigious private school along with the children of a lot of prominent Caucasian families, and was a thoroughly assimilated, prototypical California girl by the time she arrived in Hanover. Then she got to Dartmouth, where, she said, "I was made to feel more Asian than Asian American. They force you into a box at Dartmouth, and if you don't fit comfortably into any one, they put you in one that is convenient." Others in the group nodded: the administration pushes the ethnic identity thing too hard, they agreed. One student said, "It makes it seem like it's a problem."

When irrefutably racist or homophobic incidents take place, they are almost always anonymous. The perpetrators are seldom caught and punished. Daisy Lundy was a candidate for student council president at Virginia when an unidentified white male attacked her as she opened her car door just off the Lawn at the center of campus. "No one wants a nigger to be president," her attacker allegedly said before running off. He was never identified. Nor did anyone ever figure out who rubbed black cigarette ashes in the crotches of the George Segal–sculpted gay liberation statues at Stanford. Most mainstream students simply walk around such incidents as they might a scruffy homeless person asking for money. Their lives go on inside a series of their own silos that provide the comfort of sameness to those within and protection from the difference that lurks outside. The common denominator of the few successful programs and events that integrated students was that the students were involved from the outset in the planning because someone had the courage to cross an invisible line.

Too often, college administrators try to engineer such things by organizing retreats and other events that more often than not end up attracting the same group of earnest students, most of whom are part of one underrepresented group or another. I found an exception at Duke. A contingent of thirty-five students accompanied by thirteen facilitators went off to a beach on the Carolina coast for a week of intense discussion and self-examination. Instead of just the usual suspects—ethnic minorities and gays—this gathering called Common Ground also included middle-class white frat boys and effortlessly perfect Duke coeds. With a little coaxing and safe surroundings, they were able to talk openly and honestly about their differences.

"I've been going to diversity retreats since high school and I thought it was going to be a bunch of hippies trying to change the world," said James, as I'm calling him, an African American sophomore. "But it wasn't the case at all." A devout Christian who had trouble dealing with the fact that his brother was gay, James found the retreat to be a way to appreciate common traits among people of different races, economic backgrounds, and sexual orientations. "It was a retreat where people actually shared how they really felt. People are usually afraid to share even with people they do know."

What made that year's Common Ground gathering significant was that the changes lasted more than a week back on campus. "Our social circles completely changed," said one participant. "The people who went began inviting people to their parties they'd never associated with before." White frat guys started arranging mixers with black fraternities and sororities. For James, who told me that he's always mixed pretty well with whites, the dramatic change came in his attitudes toward gays. A year after the retreat, not only was he better able to understand his brother, he also made lasting friends among white gay men at Duke.

Where I found housing integration efforts to be most natural was at schools that intentionally integrated everyone. Most notable was Harvard, whose twelve residential houses weren't always broadly representative of the student body. Prior to 1995, students applied to the houses in which they saw a reflection of themselves.

As a result, Adams House acquired a reputation as artistic and gay-friendly; Mather was where the jocks lived; Lowell attracted intellectuals; rich preppies were at home in Eliot, as were blacks in the old Radcliffe Quad houses—Cabot, Currier, and Pforzheimer. In 1995, however, then newly appointed dean of the college Harry Lewis randomized the houses, assigning membership by lottery and counting on probability to break down the silos.

A lot of people were unhappy with randomization. The old guard mourned the loss of a level of belonging just below that of the private fraternity-like final clubs; minority students and their mentors protested the breakup of their clustered comfort zones. Harvard's houses did indeed lose their distinctive personalities, but they appeared to gain from a broader, more egalitarian distribution of types, talents, and skin colors.

Where racial interaction works best, say most administrators, students, and professors, is in the classroom. Discussions in social science and humanities courses in particular, they say, often draw out perspectives from minorities or gays that are different from those offered by middle-class heterosexual whites. Assigning students of differing backgrounds to study groups or team projects where they share a common goal produces the kind of interaction that students rarely produce in the residence halls and dining rooms when left to their own devices.

Exploiting the classroom as the sole venue for cultural interplay has its risks, however. When Pomona conducted extensive surveys of student attitudes during the 2002–2003 year, one of the complaints that emerged from minorities was that they often felt professors were singling them out to be spokespersons for their race, rather than simply allowing them to volunteer different perspectives on their own. Ava Robinson, class of 2006, originally from Jamaica, told me how predictable it was that sometime after the first month or two on campus, an exasperated first-year African American would come up to her and say, "I'm so tired of speaking for every single black person on earth."

At Virginia, Daisy Lundy observed, "Black students are seen as monolithic. Talk to one, you assume you've talked to us all. That's outrageous."

For many whites, who enter discussions about race these days with more trepidation than conversations about their personal sex lives, such complaints seem only to intimidate them and sometimes their professors as well. Larry Sabato, Virginia's renowned political scientist and pundit, alluded to a chill that has been cast over classroom discourse at U-VA not only about racial matters but about anything that's ideologically controversial. "The effect on discourse has been enormous," he said. "It's made us very timid. I end up avoiding controversial subjects because I'm afraid I might be misunderstood or misinterpreted."

I observed to him that many students I'd met seemed generally tentative in making judgments, particularly about each other. Speaking as a faculty member, Sabato replied, "We are too."

It is only human nature that like seeks like. In college that happens within a few weeks of arrival, as even the most self-assured students seek the comfort of being around others who look and dress and think as they do. Encouraged by their own affinity groups and by increasingly electronic media that offer to isolate them even further according to their views, they will only nestle deeper into their silos. "We are increasing our happiness by segmenting off so rigorously," commentator David Brooks once observed. "We are finding places where we are comfortable and where we feel we can flourish. But the choices we make toward that end lead to the very opposite of diversity."

I get what the campus champions of diversity are saying about assimilation: For too long it has presumed that the outsiders would adopt all the characteristics and values of the native-born Caucasian majority. Those who didn't risked ostracism. I also understand the value of critical mass: that only when there are enough people around them who look and think as they do will minority students feel truly at home on a campus.

But as the best of our colleges so laudably achieve the critical mass of minority students they have been seeking for forty years, they need to do more to create the natural environments in which truly multicultural assimilation and good old-fashioned integration can take place. If they don't and if they continue to capitulate to the forces that demand ethnocentric comfort zones, they will risk losing the benefits promised by the multicultural campus society they have worked so hard to create. That would be a tragic waste.

8

Fraternities and Sororities under Siege

O nce the backbone of campus social life in the heyday of
the American collegiate era from the 1920s through the
mid-1960s, Greek fraternities and sororities, along with
their purer cousins, the secret societies like Yale's Skull and Bones,
have in recent years become touchstones of controversy. Derided
by egalitarians as antipluralistic, antediluvian, and outright dangerous havens for underage drinking and misogynistic behavior,
they are equally championed almost exclusively by their members as builders of character, guardians of tradition, and breeding
grounds for leaders.

The subject of fraternities is deeply personal to me. I was a
member of Delta Kappa Epsilon, or DKE. My Deke label is a
part of my identity as a Hamilton graduate. But the thin wedge
that separated those two mutually dependent identities came into
stark relief when I was asked as a trustee of the college in 1993 to
serve on the Residential Life Committee charged with evaluating
the relationship between students' residential and academic lives.

When I was a student in the mid-1960s, Hamilton was still all
male. Almost 90 percent of students belonged to one of eleven
fraternities. A third of upperclassmen lived in fraternity houses,
where they were responsible for upkeep and for working with
local alumni to maintain financial records. Like Greek organizations on most campuses, Hamilton's fraternities rushed students

they liked and offered them bids to join. For a few frantic weeks in the late fall, anxieties ran high as factions of friends formed, fractured, and reformed, and a new wave of freshmen was absorbed into a social system whose roots were in the middle of the nineteenth century.

In the late nineteenth and early twentieth centuries, college deans welcomed the proliferating Greek organizations as "ready-made administrative units," according to Berkeley historian Paula Fass. They provided much-needed housing for an exploding population of college students. More importantly at a time when college students came mostly from Sinclair Lewis's conformist middle-class America, Greek organizations enforced social standards of conduct and dress and fed the ranks of student leaders with whom deans could do business.

Originally admirers of Greek societies, whose charters typically held scholarship among their highest ideals, professors lost their enthusiasm as fraternities became more social. In recent decades, faculties have become increasingly vociferous in denouncing them as elitist and "inconsistent with the academic mission of the institution." But at Hamilton, as elsewhere in the 1960s, faculty grudgingly acknowledged them as an intrinsic part of the landscape. For the most part, anti-Greek professors channeled their animosity toward those houses that harbored the least scholarly among us. When I joined DKE, a professor whom I knew sourly predicted that it would be the ruin of me.

The Tau chapter of Delta Kappa Epsilon, like DKE chapters on many other campuses at the time, was something of a jock house. At one time or another during my four years, we counted among us the captains of football, basketball, ice hockey, swimming, and lacrosse, as well as a plurality of starters on many of those teams. We had a handful of scholars and other campus leaders to be sure. But the collective testosterone count among so many helmeted sport athletes was high, as was our aggregate consumption of beer during house party weekends. Our Sunday morning gin-and-juice parties, with huge garbage pails filled with various liquors and fruit juices generously meted out to the ear-splitting sound of the raunchiest band our social chairman could book in central New York, were signature DKE house events that made us legends, in our own minds at least. Stories of brothers passing out and getting rolled up in rugs only to be found days later during the postparty cleanup, of the destruction of pianos and couches, have grown more lurid with age. But the friendships formed and sustained for decades beyond college were the real currency of fraternity life. So it is with every house on every campus, which is why fraternity loyalties run so deep.

Coeducation and changes in the law conspired to challenge the fraternity system, however. When Kirkland College merged with Hamilton, fraternity members inherited control over social life. Women tended to view the relationship as inequitable but went along with it because it was the only game in town. By the end of the 1980s, however, there were emerging signs that a growing number of the better-qualified female applicants were turned off by fraternities and choosing to go elsewhere. There were other forces at work as well: the national twenty-one-year-old drinking age, by then in effect only a few years, was providing an unhealthy boost to Greek membership nationwide. It became legally convenient for colleges to view the fraternity houses as off-campus housing and therefore not subject to the regulations governing their residence halls. That distinction virtually ensured that the fraternities would become havens for underage drinking.

Hamilton's trustees decided in the early 1990s to revisit the issue of fraternities and sororities, which we called private societies—this time with a specific focus on gender imbalance as well as the deepening problem of underage drinking. Nine out of seventeen members of the Residential Life Committee were former fraternity graduates from the old, all-male Hamilton. If there was a bias on the committee, it was on the side of the houses: each of us had similarly fond memories and strong ties to a fraternity and wanted to preserve the system if we could.

Over the course of almost two years during which we studied the issues, visited other campuses, and talked to current and former students, however, we old boys were drawn inexorably to a recognition that fraternities in the 1990s were dramatically different from the ones we remembered. So was the world in which they existed. Where nine in ten Hamilton undergraduates belonged to a fraternity in the 1960s, one in three men—less than 20 percent of the student body—belonged by the mid-1990s, and only eight of the original eleven houses were still active. Some sororities had formed since coeducation, and one former fraternity had opened its membership to women. But the means to host parties remained in the hands of what the committee's final report characterized as a relatively small cadre of male society members. The women were just guests at their parties.

As troubling as the gender inequity was the obvious erosion of upkeep in many of the fraternities. We toured one house, which had been suspended because of an alleged sexual assault that took place on its premises, and found not a single functioning doorknob in the building. Most houses had very little furniture below the sleeping floors; they had devolved into lean, mean party machines in which other aspects of residential life had atrophied. When leaders of the Interfraternity Council promised the committee that they would ban parties on Monday, Tuesday, and Wednesday nights as a show of good faith, even the staunchest Greek defenders among us were dismayed.

We considered a wide spectrum of solutions: the status quo but with stricter administrative control of the houses; mandatory coeducation, as Princeton had done with its eating clubs in the 1980s and Middlebury with its fraternities earlier in the 1990s; and complete abolition. What emerged as the middle-ground solution was a proposal to decouple the memberships from their houses. The college would continue to recognize students' rights to associate, while removing them from their inherited mansions.

The plan gained support because it seemed to address both the gender inequity and the off-campus drinking issues while avoiding complete abolition.

Beyond a philosophical resistance to abolition, many of us were influenced by testimony from other colleges that had done away with fraternities altogether: in almost every instance, the brotherhoods resurrected themselves underground even at the risk of expulsion. More than forty years after Williams abolished its fraternities, a number of the old chapters were still pledging classes and holding secret ceremonies. Recognized by the college, fraternities were amenable to supervision. Illegal and underground, they had nothing to lose.

The rationale for decoupling was an assertion that as a residential college Hamilton should require its students to live in college-owned housing. In order to prevent the societies from giving up just their bedrooms while keeping their social spaces, we further recommended that all students be required to participate in a college meal plan and to host social events in college spaces under college rules. That left the fraternities with little choice but to sell their houses to the college. We would negotiate a fair market price and reconfigure them into dorms or office spaces.

The truth was that without the space provided by the fraternity houses, there was no way we could provide residential space for all students, as our report promised. In a sense, we had leapt into a void without complete answers to a number of critical questions: Would the fraternities, controlled by their alumni and in most instances beholden to national organizations, cooperate and sell us their houses? Or would they withhold these grand old buildings, some critical to the architectural integrity of the campus, and convert them to private homes, bed-and-breakfast inns, or even fast-food franchises? How long would it be before this residential college could house all its students? And most importantly, what kind of social infrastructure should replace the system, however flawed, we were about to destroy?

I use the word *destroy* with some trepidation. Like many of my alumni colleagues on the Residential Life Committee and the board, I was persuaded that by preserving the right of students to organize private societies, including the old Greek chapters such as DKE, we were not destroying the fraternity system. Hamilton fraternities would still be allowed to rush and pledge classes, to hold meetings and host parties, to live together in dorms in self-selected groups up to twelve, and to pass the baton of brotherly (and sisterly) friendship from one generation to the next, as we had done decades earlier. The bonds of brotherhood, I argued in a letter I wrote to all Hamilton DKE alumni in the wake of the Residential Life decision, were surely made of more than bricks and mortar. It remained to be seen whether that was true.

Support for the decision came from predictable quarters. Many faculty members were ecstatic. By and large, women alums approved. And some of my contemporaries would later quietly acknowledge that daughters who had followed them to Hamilton had confessed that they had felt like second-class citizens in a male culture, detracting from an otherwise satisfying academic experience.

Those who had benefited from the old system, however, felt angry and abandoned. Even for some current women students, though they might have felt like second-class citizens, fraternities were the only social life they knew. At the end of the year, the departing brothers of Delta Upsilon set fire to their house, though it did not burn down. The Chi Psi house was vandalized, almost certainly by its own members. Everywhere President Eugene Tobin went to speak to alumni groups about the decision, he was met with sharp, often vitriolic questions, usually from younger former fraternity members. As a member of the committee, I too felt the brunt of disapproval from a number of my contemporaries and fellow Dekes who saw me as a traitor to the brotherhood. I had some uncomfortable conversations with old friends, one of whom stated he did not understand why we felt compelled to throw the baby out with the bathwater. Many suspected that by taking the houses and leaving the organizations, the board had chosen a devious route to eventual abolition. Without the houses, they predicted, the fraternities would wither and dry up.

One by one, the property-owning private societies agreed to cooperate with the decision and negotiated the sale of their houses to the college. But four of the most prominent fraternities on campus joined forces to sue the college. They ultimately lost the case, but the protracted legal process delayed plans to reconfigure the houses into dorms, which only further prolonged the sense of disarray among students. The pending suit also kept current society members from participating in efforts to restructure social life because their alumni were encouraging them to hope for a return to fraternity house living. It took almost eight years after the decision before the last holdout, whose chapter was bankrupt and on the verge of losing the house to repossession, capitulated.

As of this writing, almost a decade after the Res Life decision, Hamilton is a different place. Several of the repurchased fraternity houses, expanded and converted into residence halls, have become popular draws in the annual housing lottery. Responding to a request by students, the college built a new 11,700-square-foot social annex behind the student center big enough for a party of six hundred with a band but with built-in wall dividers that allow it to be converted into smaller rooms where, for example, private societies can dine together or host parties.

The best outcome has been that the academic qualifications of applicants—women in particular—have increased dramatically. In a class entering at the time of the Res Life deliberations, just under half were in the top 10 percent of their high school class; this figure increased to 71 percent for the group that entered in the fall of 2003. From the standpoint of overall selectivity, Hamilton has become almost twice as hard to get into as it had been in the early nineties. Faculty members have testified with delight that there has been a palpable rise in the intellectual quality of class discussions. Not only are smarter women coming to Hamilton, smarter men are too.

The results have not all been positive. Even setting aside the drag of the lawsuit, it was clear that Hamilton students were still floundering in their efforts to build a new social structure. Before the annex was completed and without the fraternities, they were hard-pressed to find a decent place on campus to have parties. And when they did, the college rules, which limited the amount of alcohol and required trained bartenders, ID-checkers, and insurance coverage, made the process of throwing a party so onerous that only the societies had the wherewithal to do so. Res Life was supposed to broaden party sponsorship to all students. Ironically, the liability requirements mandated by the twenty-one-year-old drinking age were conspiring to keep social life under Greek control even without their houses.

An even greater irony has been that the binge drinking, which we had broadly blamed on fraternities, remains as much a problem as it was before the change. In one respect, it is arguably worse: with the close of the houses, drinking has shifted from the frat house basements to students' rooms and to local taverns. Instead of swilling beer from a tap in the cellar of a fraternity house, students are drinking vodka or bourbon in their rooms, getting drunker and sicker—faster. Or they are climbing into their cars and driving a few miles on a winding two-lane road to the bars on Route 5. The traditional DKE gin-and-juice party has moved from the house living room five minutes from the college chapel to a rented fire station several miles out of town.

Contrary to predictions that homelessness would kill them off, Greeks actually rose in number: by 2004, one in three Hamilton students belonged to one of nine national fraternities and six—twice the number in 1995—sororities. Yet despite the resurgence, there is at Hamilton, as on every campus I visited, an abiding feeling among Greeks that their days are numbered. Sitting in his dorm room a few weeks before his graduation in 2004, senior Jeff Corey and two of his Psi U brothers recited to me the litany of moves they interpreted as calculated efforts by the college to tighten the noose around the necks of societies: reducing the size of housing blocks from twelve to six, raising the requirements for hosting a party, and the latest, a recommendation by yet another committee examining college alcohol policies that has proposed an annual review of societies, including an account of social violations accumulated by their members. "In the next three, four years," Corey predicted flatly, "societies at Hamilton will be eliminated altogether."

The trend would seem to favor Corey's prediction. The Res Life decision at Hamilton was only one of a series of dominoes that fell on Greeks nationally in recent decades. Administrations at other eastern small colleges—Amherst, Colby, Bowdoin, Middlebury, Trinity, and Colgate—eliminated private societies altogether, forced them to go coed, or denied them the right to occupy houses. Among the Ivies, Yale's last chapter house closed in 1973, four years after coeducation. A sex discrimination lawsuit against three of Prospect Street's most prestigious eating clubs forced Princeton's analogous societies to go coed during the 1980s. A mid-1990s report by the dean at Harvard noted a "disturbing increase in the reports of inappropriate behavior occurring at various final clubs" (Harvard's private societies), including extreme drunkenness, underage drinking, reports of drug dealing, lewd sexual acts performed by hired women, and more than one case of sexual harassment of women.

On almost every campus I visited, Greeks felt similarly under siege. At Duke, they saw the beginning of the end in each of a series of administration moves: a 1995 delay of rush from the fall to the spring of freshman year; a reconfiguration of housing in 2002, wherein fraternities were evicted from their prime positions fronting the Main Quad; and the institution of a seven-point annual review procedure requiring each organization to submit a detailed report on what its membership has done to deserve rerecognition. At Stanford, where fraternities have been going on and off suspension like a badly wired Christmas tree, many students complained about draconian rules and blanket police surveillance of their parties. Even the renovation of a building previously occupied by a suspended fraternity, in which the urinals were replaced with sit-down toilets, was interpreted as evidence that the end was nigh. When he arrived as a freshman, New Zealander Mike Wilson was awestruck by Stanford's frat blowouts, like the Theta Delta cave party or Sigma Chi's luau, stocked with alcohol and breathtaking girls in grass skirts and leis. "You feel like you're on a movie set with disco lights," he said with wonderment. By his senior year, all that was disappearing. "Fraternities used to be the nexus of social life here," he told me. "Now they're afraid to be."

Given the scope of this anti-Greek movement, Dartmouth's decision to stand by its Greek system, at least for the moment, was all the more intriguing. In 2000, the college unveiled an ambitious student life initiative (SLI) that committed nearly $200 million for the creation of a new residential infrastructure not unlike a Harvard house or Yale college. It included plans to transform the central dining facility into a new social space for all students and add other entertainment features, such as a nightclub and a coffeehouse. In effect, its goal was to provide an alternative to the Webster Avenue basement keg parties as Dartmouth's principal source of entertainment.

As for Greeks, the SLI Committee proposed a plan to hold them to new and higher standards of conduct. The dean's office posited six guiding principles: "scholarship, leadership, philanthropy/community service, brotherhood/sisterhood, inclusivity, and accountability." Every organization had to maintain a composite 2.3 GPA. Each was required to add a philanthropy chair to its slate of officers. At the beginning of the academic year, each had to submit an action plan that laid out its objectives for the year and outlined how the membership was going to meet them. "We are using a management by objective method," said Marty Redman, Dartmouth's Res Life dean. "We ask every house: 'What are your goals? What are you going to do to meet them? How have you done?'" Like the business model it mimicked, the guiding principles system was designed to make the Greeks take ownership of their own behavior—hence their destiny. The college even threw in a $5,000 prize for the best-performing house.

Some saw the guiding principles as onerous. But they at least left Dartmouth's fraternities and sororities intact, which was not the outcome many expected from the SLI. Formed by James Wright shortly after he was named Dartmouth's president in 1998, the Committee on the Student Life Initiative was widely viewed as the Greeks' high executioner. Wright did little to assuage Greek fears when he predicted in a speech to the Alumni Council in May 1999, "a full discussion about how we might introduce some fundamental changes to the current fraternity/sorority system." These private organizations, he said, "need to be more inclusive, more representative of the student body, and should be fully integrated into the residential and social life of the college."

Cochairing the SLI Committee were Dartmouth trustee chair Susan Dentzer, class of 1977, senior correspondent for the Public Broadcasting System's *News Hour* and a survivor of the pioneer years of Dartmouth coeducation; and board member Peter Fahey, class of 1968, an investment banker and a product of the old, all-male Dartmouth. Fahey had been a member of Phi Delta Alpha, a Dartmouth jock house; Dentzer, as a member of Dartmouth's first female class, was initiated into campus social life when someone poured a beer over her head in a fraternity house basement. Other committee members, like Dentzer and Fahey, tended to pair off according to their views of the Greek system.

According to Lucy Buford, class of 2000, who wrote her senior thesis on the history of women and feminism at Dartmouth, if the SLI was to decide the fate of fraternities, the case against them had been building since the college first admitted women in 1972. Their numbers purposely held to no more than a third of the student body in those early years, Dartmouth women had little choice but to operate by the rules of the male culture. Buford wrote that they "experienced extraordinary expressions of violent misogyny—acts that went virtually unacknowledged and certainly unpunished by the college administration. Men broke into women's dorm rooms, urinated and/or vomited on their doors, and smashed their windows." Openly referred to by male counterparts as cohogs, they were allowed into the fraternal sanctuaries essentially as sex objects and were subjected to abuse as a rite of passage. They had to be tough to survive. As a result, Dartmouth tended to attract female versions of the prototypical Dartmouth Outing Club male. When sororities began to form, they often emulated the fraternity culture, taking up Pong and other beer-centered rituals common to the Webster Avenue culture.

While those who felt comfortable with the traditional male culture opted to join the Greek system, a new wave of active feminists in the 1980s chose confrontation over assimilation. And as Dartmouth's admissions office succeeded in recruiting more minorities as well as gays and lesbians, the fraternities found themselves living in a fishbowl surrounded by cultural change. When word spread that there was a strategically cut hole in a wall of one frat house that allowed members to view one of the brothers having sex, the entire memberships of two sororities put their signatures on an ad in the *Dartmouth*, the campus paper, denouncing the fraternity.

Sentiment to dissolve the system grew during the eighties and early nineties, but backed by strong alumni opinion, the board of trustees resisted change. On campus, however, a schism had solidified, creating what Buford called "two basically distinct Dartmouths": the traditional Men of Dartmouth culture centered around the Greek system on one side and everybody else on the other.

The divide was not strictly along gender lines. The sorority women whom I met at Dartmouth appeared to have their feet planted firmly in both camps. Sigma Delta, with a hundred members during 2003–2004, was one of the strongest of Dartmouth's six sororities, with its own house where sixteen members lived. The sorority attracted many of the players on the women's rugby team. They too had Pong tables, albeit much nicer ones than the battered pressboards in most frat houses. Their center court table in the basement was elaborately decorated with a portrait of the Goddess Shiva, Princess of Power.

With no national Pan-Hellenic ties, the Sigma Delts allowed alcohol in the house. Other sororities with national headquarters that mandated strict abstinence at least pretended to stay dry. Many had informal affiliations with one or another of the fraternities, with whom bonds were likely to be as close as with their own sorority sisters. The day I arrived at Dartmouth, Amy Catlin, a member of the women's hockey team, took me on a quick tour of the Chi Heurot house, home to many members of the men's hockey team. She walked me through, upstairs and down, as if she were one of the bros, which as a women's team member she almost was.

By the time I arrived on campus, the SLI rules governing Greek conduct were in full effect. Proponents claimed that the Greeks rose to the occasion. Despite the new constraints, one hundred more students rushed in 2003 than had the year before. "It's grass roots," said Deb Carney, an associate dean for Greek affairs. "It's not us doing it."

The brothers saw it through less rosy lenses, however. In the system's maiden voyage during the 2002–2003 year, members complained about the red tape involved in producing what amounted to a forty-page action plan devoted to detailed agendas for things that hadn't happened yet. And it was still too easy to fulfill commitments with hollow gestures. The Chi Gams knocked off their brotherhood requirement by getting the whole house up at dawn to watch the World Cup on television. "Too often," said another associate dean, Cassie Barnhardt, one of two administrative overseers of the plan, "the Greek idea of diversity is, 'We've got a Latino in the house,' or 'We have some Asian girls,' or 'We have some people who are not on the lacrosse team.'"

The exercise was not totally pointless, several students admitted. The ADs (formally Alpha Delta Phi), fraternal heirs of *Animal House*, made a date with the sisters of the African American Alpha Kappa Alpha sorority as a demonstration of their commitment to inclusiveness. "It was one of the most fun nights we've ever had," testified Mike Curley, class of 2004, a house officer, and, like many of his fraternity brothers, a white Dartmouth rugby player.

Planning for a traditional drinking party is not so fun. "Every year it's something new," complained an officer of one house. To host a party in 2004, a Dartmouth fraternity had to declare at least three days in advance how many people would be in attendance, which would help determine which of the three tiers of regulations the house would have to follow. Any gathering of more than forty qualified as a party requiring prior registration, two walk-throughs by a campus Safety & Security officer, and a minimum amount of "unsalted" food service. By those standards, the regular weekly house meeting at most Dartmouth chapters should be a registered event. How do Dartmouth's houses handle that? "We just lie," said a fraternity officer flatly.

Under the pre-SLI rules, kegs were permitted, although they had to be tagged and limited in number according to the size of the party. Since SLI, kegs are banned at Dartmouth parties; houses are required to dismantle their tapping systems. Keystone in thirty-packs has become the operative beer delivery system.

The tighter and more explicit Dartmouth's rules get, the more fraternities seem to get in trouble. Right in the middle of the SLI deliberations, four members of Phi Delta (trustee Fahey's old fraternity) set fire to a neighboring house. A year later, Zeta Psi, one of the more popular houses on Webster Avenue, was caught printing a series of internal newsletters describing and rating the sexual talents of Dartmouth women, color photos included. The copy of the "Zetemouth" dug out of the garbage behind the house following a Wednesday night meeting in April 2001 was not the first that Dartmouth women had heard of the fraternity's in-house newsletter. But when four of them finished cleaning the vomit off the torn copy and confirmed its lascivious contents, they turned the document over to Marty Redman, the Residential Life dean. A lengthy description of the publication, along with a history of Zeta Psi's previous newsletters, appeared in that week's edition of the *Dartmouth*. All hell broke loose. The story made national news, and President Wright issued a statement that "Zeta Psi undermined fundamental values we hold dear." Within a few months, the Zetes were permanently derecognized.

You would think that would be the end of Zeta Psi at Dartmouth. Yet when I wandered by the officially defunct house on a Wednesday evening, when Dartmouth fraternities hold their meeting-cum-midweek-drink-ups, I heard the distinct sound of Ping-Pong balls and the singing of songs emanating from the Zete basement. Though I had been told that the building, which was still owned by the Zeta Psi alumni corporation, was being used to house graduate students upstairs and as temporary editorial offices for the *Dartmouth Review*, what I found instead were a dozen or so college men wearing identical blue T-shirts and baseball caps playing Pong. When I later mentioned the episode around campus, the response was usually a wry smile. They weren't supposed to be there, I was assured, and they wouldn't be foolish enough to have an outright party with women. But the building on Webster Avenue was off-campus private property under the jurisdiction of the Hanover Police, not Dartmouth College. As long as they kept under the radar, the Zetes would keep the flame alive.

They may have been mere harbingers of things to come. By the time of the 2003 winter carnival at Dartmouth, twelve out of nineteen Greek organizations were facing social probation, prompting student leaders to charge the administration with targeting their organizations. All over campus there remained a resignation among fraternity members about their ultimate fate. Yes, they dodged the bullet with the SLI. "We're okay for now," said AD brother Curley, class of 2004. "But in another four, five years, there will be another round like the student life initiative." Under different circumstances, Curley had come to the same conclusion that Jeff Corey had at Hamilton.

Staunch fraternity boosters in other regions of the United States argue that the eastern chapters have brought about their own misfortune by allowing drinking and by the failure of alumni to keep a tight rein on undergraduate behavior. To be sure, there are colleges in the South and Midwest where Greeks toe the line and thrive under the benevolent eye of the administration. But as I moved south and west, I found that while Greeks are more entrenched than in the Northeast, they too find themselves inside an ever-tightening noose.

Greek organizations have played an integral role in almost all the big midwestern state universities. At the University of Wisconsin, Paul Hohag, class of 2004, presided over a Sig Ep house that had grown from 40 to 130 members in eight years. The chapter house on Langdon Avenue, Wisconsin's fraternity row, while not a candidate for a spread in *Architectural Digest*, was at least in presentable shape when I met him there. Curiously categorized by the administration as learning communities, each Wisconsin fraternity had a faculty advisor. The Sig Eps even had a scholar in residence, though the grad student who fulfilled that role lived half a mile away and dropped by only occasionally. Members were required to do a minimum of community service each semester. The house was known for its annual Tour to Touchdown bicycle rally each fall, wherein 58 members carrying the banner of the mighty Badger football team rode across the state to raise money for local charities.

They still do lots of old-fashioned things in the Wisconsin Greek community. The week before, Hohag informed me, Sig Ep held its formal tie-and-jacket initiation dinner at Gino's, a restaurant in town. After dinner, they came back to the house, where the new members were taught the old fraternity songs. Then they marched over to the Kappa Kappa Gamma sorority, where each new member handed a rose to a counterpart sorority initiate.

Even so, Greeks in this big midwestern university still suffer from the same image problems as their brothers in the eastern schools. Ed Mirecki, the Greek liaison officer from the student life division, told me that the stereotype of the Republican-leaning suburbanite with an SUV parked out in front of the house holds up pretty well in Madison. "A disproportionate number are out-of-state, mostly East Coast types," he said. While they number some two thousand in twenty-six fraternities and eleven sororities, Greeks represent less than 10 percent of Wisconsin undergrads. And they are not the only students who drink in town. Said Mirecki with a sardonic smile: "Greeks enjoy a situation here where alcohol problems are so prevalent and campus-wide that there isn't a spotlight focused on fraternities."

Greeks at Indiana University wished they had such a low profile. With an aggregate membership that includes less than 20 percent of undergrads and plenty of other party opportunities available in off-campus apartments and bars, IU fraternities and sororities don't have the command of social life that Greeks do in smaller colleges. But they are highly visible in their grand mansions surrounding the Bloomington campus, some of them valued at well over $1 million. And in the relatively small town, they are a naturally more visible entertainment venue. In many ways, they have been victims of changing attitudes toward alcohol and the legal crackdown that has accompanied that change. "We've set standards," said Richard McKaig, the dean of students. "And we've simply said that if you don't meet those standards, we will act."

Both the university and the national headquarters of houses that have broken the rules have indeed acted. During the four-year tenure of the class of 2003 alone, IU lost nine chapters—one an African American sorority for a hazing incident, the rest fraternities for alcohol violations, two of which involved student deaths. A secondary by-product of the crackdown has been a change in the leadership of the fraternities: upperclassmen have been leaving the houses and moving into off-campus apartments, where they can have a few beers without being harassed by campus police, leaving sophomores to run the houses and often to serve as senior officers.

At Indiana, as elsewhere, there have also been signs that general standards of self-reliance and decorum are eroding. Fraternities used to have better food than the university dining halls. But with food courts replacing institutional cafeterias and the cost of keeping a decent chef on the payroll, that trend has reversed. Where brothers once learned management techniques by keeping their own books and managing their houses, increasingly they have been hiring professional accountants and managers to do the work for them.

The decline in decorum could be seen in the deterioration of an old IU tradition known as Serenade. Generations back, fraternity men would go to front lawns of the sorority houses and sing for girls crowding the windows above. Sometime during the seventies, the pattern reversed: the women started going to the fraternity houses and putting on dancing exhibitions. By the mid-nineties, Serenade had become a massive lap dance, with the brothers hooting and hollering on the sidelines as women gyrated and sometimes stripped down to nothing. In recent years, there has been a concerted effort led by the Division of Student Affairs to take Serenade back to its innocent roots.

Further west, at Berkeley, I sensed that Greeks were just another piece of a vast collegiate mosaic. Clustered uphill along Piedmont Avenue and Warring Street, their houses were no more central than the cooperative houses along the northern edge of campus. After freshman year, most Berkeley students move to off-campus apartments. Together the Greeks and the co-ops fell somewhere in between university housing on the one hand and independent apartment living on the other. But they were socio-economically worlds apart from one another: The co-ops offered low-cost room and board to students in exchange for pitching in with the cooking, cleaning, and maintenance. The fraternities were social clubs that attracted the well-to-do suburbanites from southern California. Not surprisingly, there was no love lost between the two factions—there never had been. One cooperative resident claimed he knew for a fact that one of the frats required pledges to hand over their parents' income tax returns as proof of their eligibility. "Only losers join fraternities here," he assured me. When one of the Warring Street fraternities closed down in the late nineties, the collective board that maintains the cooperatives bought the building and reopened it as a co-op for gays and lesbians, naming it Wilde (as in Oscar) House.

Most of the recent controversy about Greeks has been centered on fraternities. Their houses have been where alcohol-related deaths, including those of women such as Colorado State's Samantha Spady, are most likely to occur. Sorority life is generally more restricted, either by local or national Pan-Hellenic rules or by the nature of the individual chapter. The rap against sororities is typically that they are elitist, materialistic, catty, obsessed with appearance, and prone to foster such problems as eating disorders.

It's unusual for a sorority to get caught for doing anything that results in physical harm, as occurred in the fall of 2004 at Berkeley, when a nineteen-year-old Cal student was found unconscious on a sidewalk. She was hospitalized and treated for alcohol poisoning; she later told police that she had been drinking as part of a sorority initiation. Sororities are more likely to get in trouble for minor hazing incidents such as forcing new pledges to walk around campus in bizarre outfits or keeping them awake all night doing demeaning chores for their older sisters.

There appears to be much more hands-on adult supervision of sororities than of fraternities on most of the campuses I visited. Many of the Dartmouth, Duke, and Stanford sororities are dry by charter. Duke does not even allow sororities to live under the same roof, following an arcane North Carolina law that construes such concentrations of females as potential brothels. National headquarters seem to check up on sororities more often than fraternities. Many have officers who police drinking in the house. Unlike fraternities, where women shack up with their boyfriends regularly, most sororities take a dim view of cohabitation on the premises, at least officially. "Boys were banned—in word, yes, in deed no," said Holly Johnson, a Delta Gamma at Indiana. "I know a sorority where a guy slept there every night."

Holly had what they call a perfect rush in that no sorority cut her from their invitation list and she had the pick of the best houses on campus. "Those girls were my foundation, especially through my sophomore year," she recalled a few months after graduating in the spring of 2004. But after she returned from a year studying in England, the sorority scene seemed smaller, tighter, "more rigid and stratified." She thought of quitting but decided to stay, living in the house with over a hundred other sisters her senior year.

House living had its burdens, she admitted. Sunday meetings were mandatory and could last for more than two hours; no-shows were fined $50. "Some girls just paid the fine and didn't go," said Johnson. Most of the business centered on social life, with some left over for charity work. Delta Gamma had social events two or three times a week: informals, formals, and, in the spring, pairings with fraternities during Little Five Week, the prelude to Indiana's renowned Little 500 bicycle race. "Basically, we spent the whole week getting drunk, to put it bluntly," said Johnson. Rush week was another matter. Sisters were technically not allowed to drink or leave the house at night for the entire week in which prospective pledges were courted. The intense jockeying and the emotional roller coaster, said Johnson, made it "a week you'll never forget."

Pledging and initiation were big deals, as they are for most sororities around North America. "We had certain rituals—long, half-day ordeals," said Johnson. "But it wasn't anything weird." Older sponsoring sisters would lead their younger aspirants from room to room in the house, each stop a venue for a reading from the Delta Gamma book. "There was not anything like hazing," said Johnson. "A senior might take us out and give us fake beer to see if anyone pretended to be drunk. But we didn't have anything like some houses, where older members come and circle areas of fat on pledges' bodies where they need to lose weight."

Appearance was important, however, Johnson said. "We had a huge eating disorder problem. A lot of women were very put to-gether, very thin, or fit." Sorority women on many campuses echoed this observation. "I came to recognize later," said Carla, who pledged and then depledged one of Duke's more popular sororities, "that it was not a coincidence that a lot of sorority girls were really attractive."

And talented, as she discovered. "The sorority was made up of remarkable, amazing women," said Carla. "I was so blown away by how accomplished everyone was, by what they did and how together they were, even by Duke standards. At meetings they'd talk about the summer internship they'd had at Goldman Sachs or working as a senator's aide in Washington."

As at Dartmouth, while fewer in number than fraternities, sororities at Duke often had more members. A Dartmouth senior confessed to me that there were sophomores in her sorority she didn't even recognize. At Duke, said Carla, "sororities tend to be larger in number and as such not as tight as fraternities. And because there is no residential system, there isn't a stomping ground the way there is for the fraternities."

Meetings were also mandatory at Duke and members were fined if they didn't show. Most of the time was spent on administrative matters—planning parties or fund-raisers for community service. "Planning the social calendar was big," said Carla. "They had that down pretty pat. We had parties once a week—mixers at local bars. There was alcohol if you were twenty-one, and we had sisters who were designated as monitors to keep tabs on people's drinking."

What kept popping up in my conversations with sorority members as a reason for joining was the need to have a known circle of friends and the mutual support that comes with it. At Carla's sorority meetings, they'd have shout-outs—that whooping cry today's young women give in groups to show support for each other—for a sister who did well on her MCATs (medical college admission tests), for example, or who got elected to some office. At Harvard, which officially doesn't acknowledge its growing Greek presence, a junior who belonged to one of the three nationally affiliated sororities said her sisterhood showed mutual support with "Snaps—just like in *Totally Blonde*, where you applaud something that somebody has done, like 'Snaps to Lindsay for having lunch with me last week when I was totally down.'"

Once safely ensconced among friends, sorority women often stay within the confines of that circle. "A lot of people get sucked in and they totally forget about the life they had before," complained a University of Buffalo student who depledged her sorority. A schoolmate who stuck with another Buffalo house agreed: "Sorority life can be pretty limiting in terms of friends."

The opposite was true at Harvard, where a junior (who asked for anonymity because her sorority forbade discussion of house activities with outsiders) said most women she knew joined to broaden their social circles. "At Harvard, you tend to meet people whether in your house or through extracurricular activities. There is much more transcending of social boundaries than anything else at Harvard I can think of. You get to meet different girls from different social circles."

Almost every sorority woman I talked to admitted that one of the principal benefits of membership was having a formal structure for meeting guys that avoided the perils of hooking up. Formals and mixers provided an excuse for asking guys or whole fraternities to mingle socially. Events like My Ties, where Harvard men's neckties are given to sisters, designating them as their date for the night, or Grab-a-date, in which members are given only three hours to ask a guy to attend a sorority function, take the pressure off women seeking relationships that last more than a night. "For whatever reason," said the Harvard sorority member, "having a formal structure lowers the threshold of importance of asking someone out on a date."

I have very mixed feelings about the beleaguered state of Greek organizations these days. I understand the forces working against them, and I recognize the poor fit they have in a microsociety hell-bent on inclusion. Yet I had the opportunity in my travels to spend time with some fraternity brothers in their houses, listening in on meetings, sharing meals with them in their own dining rooms. I liked that they kept the traditions alive but for the most part didn't take themselves too seriously. Was their almost romantic adherence to these old rituals so misplaced? What was wrong with having a good time with friends and helping each other through one of life's more challenging sequences? Was all this so antithetical to the values of higher education?

The questions got thornier when I tested my natural empathy for fraternity brothers against some of my other conclusions about modern campus life. Was it consistent, for example, to oppose racial affinity houses on grounds that they undermined diversity, then turn around and say it was okay for middle-class white guys to live together? I concluded that as long as it was not intentionally exclusive, then yes. Blacks and Hispanics as well as whites were choosing to join with one another in fraternities and sororities on many of the campuses I visited. (Black students at Dartmouth refer to other blacks who join predominantly white fraternities as Incognegroes.) A white female student at Duke told me that black fraternity guys, with their rigorous pledging standards and step dance routines, "are considered definitely cool." Somehow an independent association formed on the basis of friendship, whether black, white, or Hispanic, feels different from an administration-sponsored residence specifically designated as a haven for a single race.

Diversity is breaking the traditional template from which fraternities like DKE were molded. The Dartmouth fraternities along Webster Avenue now have neighbors who belong to Latina sororities and nontraditional coed societies that reject the frat house kegger ethos and party with milk and cookies. Out gays and lesbians are showing up at parties and sometimes even joining houses. All this is happening with or without college Res Life staffs institutionally mandating who associates with whom.

Though the forces of social change appear to be aligned against classic single-sex residential private societies, I predict that they will survive in various guises: the highly disciplined residences operating under the close supervision of alumni and national bodies; the hybrid social clubs that open their doors to all comers and reach out beyond alcohol as an organizing principle; the homeless chapters with members who meet in dorm rooms and party in firehouses just because they're friends; and even the underground cults determined to keep the forbidden flame alive at the risk of expulsion. Wise deans, presidents, and trustees will accept the inevitability of like seeking like and concentrate their efforts on educating all students against the corrosive effects of exclusion. If they teach them well, the Greeks as well as the affinity house dwellers will abandon their silos of their own accord. But they won't abandon their friends.

Fraternities may have become the nexus of the social disequilibria so evident on many college campuses, but they are not the source. The fault lies at the confluence of all the forces that have conspired to isolate fraternities. I look back on our decision to close the houses at Hamilton with a mixture of satisfaction that we corrected a corrosive imbalance of social options along with a melancholy recognition that in doing so we at least preserved the right of students to associate, if only to fulfill a common desire to laugh over a few beers and to seek common values.

I also took solace in hearing Ben Townson, a Hamilton Deke years after there was no longer a DKE house, sum up his four-year experience as a member of the fraternity: "What I will remember most fondly about Hamilton was the group of guys I spent time with," he told me. "These are my closest friends in the world. That matters." Indeed it does.

9

The Morphing Drug Scene

C olleges and the government lump all chemical mood-altering substances, whether legal or not, into one basket they call AOD, which stands for alcohol and other drugs. For most parents, drinking is one thing, drugs quite another. The mere mention of drugs in the context of their children's college experience strikes fear in their hearts, even though many of them blithely experimented with whatever was available in their own heady days of freedom. Many view drug use as one of the highest risks of campus life. When I started out on my journey inside these various social microclimates, I expected to hear a lot about drugs.

I didn't.

Not that they aren't there. Marijuana has become so common-place that it has nestled into the landscape and hardly registers with anyone. According to various surveys, its use increased slightly over the decade of the nineties, but it seemed like incidental back-ground noise on the campuses I visited. Other than during my evenings at Berkeley, I didn't come across it. Students tended to be cautious in discussing its use. "It's a matter of trust, really," said one Dartmouth student. Those who do it tend to do it in intimate settings, sitting in a circle in a room and passing a joint (almost invariably to the left, noted one user) and otherwise engaging in conversation without much reference to the joint or the bong that is in fact the focal point of their being there.

When I asked Richard McKaig, Indiana University's dean of students, about drug use on campus, he hauled out the previous year's survey data from his files. "It says here that 56 percent of students did not use marijuana in the past month, which means that 44 percent did." Some quick mental math told me that about thirteen thousand IU students had used the drug within the last thirty days. "But for alcohol," continued McKaig, "that number was 80 percent. So that should put it in perspective." What struck me was the similarity with which campus police and judicial systems dealt with patently illegal drugs like marijuana and age-proscribed alcohol. College administrators generally treat marijuana use much as they do underage drinking: with a fine, maybe a letter home, or probation for first offenses. "The campus doesn't get too excited about it, unless they're selling," said a Wisconsin student health administrator.

Just past midnight on a football weekend at the University of Virginia, I was traveling in a patrol car with a U-VA police officer when she received word of an anonymous tip that two young men in Holmes Hall were smoking pot. I asked the officer if it was common for students to turn in other students for drugs. She shrugged her shoulders and looked at me with a half smile/half wince I interpreted to mean "Not really."

We arrived in the parking lot behind Holmes, where another female officer was waiting. Together we walked through the corridor to the room indicated by the informant. The officers knocked. There was no response. They knocked again. Beginning to wonder if they had the right room, the two officers sniffed around the frame of the door but detected no odor. So the officer who had received the initial tip went outside to call the informant to confirm the room number. Within a couple of minutes, a young woman's head peeked through the doorway at the top of the stairs and nodded in the direction of the room they had been trying. I guessed she was the snitch.

After a third set of whacks on the door, this time with the butt end of a billy club, they got a response: the door opened and a fellow clad in cords and a T-shirt peered out through an opening. Behind him was another guy. It took some time for the full implications of what was happening to sink in. When it did, it was clear the students did not like what they saw.

The senior officer present, a woman not more than five or so years older than the students, said that they had received a disturbance report and asked if they could search the room, making it clear that if they were not given permission, they would go to a judge and get a warrant. The occupant of the room calmly asked a question or two about procedure but ultimately acceded to their request. It didn't take long before the officers came up with a small bag.

That triggered another call, and within ten minutes a sergeant appeared with a test kit with which he quickly confirmed the presence of THC, the active ingredient in marijuana. Out came the citation pads. I took one of the officers aside and asked about the penalty for being caught at U-VA with marijuana. "A fine of a few hundred dollars and one year's suspension of their driver's licenses," she replied. That was a State of Virginia penalty. The university would most likely sentence the two to some community service hours and a few class sessions on the dangers of drug use.

"Can I say something for the record?" asked the second man, who apparently did not live in the room.

"Of course," said the sergeant.

"Everything in that bag belongs to me," he said.

A touch of old Virginia honor, I thought: he was trying to get his pal off the hook. That made as much ethical sense to me as anything else I'd seen since this episode commenced. Here were two people, both of whom were twenty-one, sitting in a room consuming something that was by all the evidence I had ever read decidedly less harmful to them than the bourbon the guys down the hall were drinking. Recalling the scene as I write brings to mind something a Berkeley junior named Carlos said to me: "For the life of me, I can't understand why marijuana is illegal and alcohol is legal. People do so much worse shit when they're drunk."

The establishment line on marijuana remains that it is bad for people: regular use can lead to loss of cognitive skills, heart disease, and lung cancer, and from a sociological perspective, it is still seen as a gateway drug to harder stuff such as cocaine and heroin that is indisputably harmful. Fewer scientists accept that conclusion these days and more are likely to raise the possibility of its medicinal benefits. When Dr. Pierre Tellier, the director of McGill's student health clinic, spoke about drugs to the resident fellows in their training session, he told them that the physical danger of marijuana is limited to its effects as a smoke inhalant: one joint a day, he said, affects the lungs the way smoking somewhere between a half and a whole pack of cigarettes would.

What is striking about today's pot—or weed, as most students call it—is how much stronger it is than the grass typically consumed in the mellow seventies. Marijuana seized in DEA (Drug Enforcement Administration) raids in the late nineties tested out to be twice as powerful as that seized in the late 1980s. There have been reports of some stuff up to ten times more potent. Duke officer Sara-Jane Raines told me about the discovery of "one of the finest marijuana plants you've ever seen—it had six-inch buds"—growing in a window planter outside the room of a biology major.

Marijuana is easy to get on almost any campus and in some places easier than alcohol. In the midst of Indiana University's crackdown on underage drinking, Christina Scolli, a recruited tennis player from Norway, told me that freshmen at IU had a tougher time getting beer than marijuana. A story in the Vanderbilt student newspaper in the spring of 2004 cited a survey indicating that four in ten Vandy students had tried weed. "My freshman year, there were three guys dealing it on the same floor," said one. "It's not hard to find, even if you're not looking." A student at Auburn University in Alabama confirmed to his school paper, "It's easier than getting pizza."

Cocaine use shows up far less often than weed but more often at schools that attract wealthier students. "There's some coke here," said a Stanford senior from New York. "But I'm surprised by how small the contingent is that does it." Sara-Jane Raines, the campus police officer at Duke, called coke a moderate problem at her school. At the University of Wisconsin, health officials associated its use with "some of the younger, out-of-state students from pretty much the same zip codes," explained Kathy Poi, director of health services in Madison. Those zip codes, she said, would be the New York and New Jersey suburbs of Manhattan.

They are the same zip codes attached to communities that feed many of the better private colleges and universities, which support the widely held assumption that a lot of the college drug use started someplace else—like home. In the fall of 2003, two freshmen at Hamilton, both graduates of one of New York City's most prestigious private schools, were caught buying cocaine from a supplier one of them had done business with while still in high school. In exchange for setting up a sting in which the supplier— a high school dropout from New York's Lower East Side—was busted as he delivered a payload of 70 grams for $2,000, the college boys were given reduced sentences and had their records sealed. But they will never return to Hamilton.

During the same week in which the Hamilton bust went down, the University of Virginia saw a much more spectacular sting pulled off by a task force with the help of university students and employees. The bust was dubbed Operation Spring Break Down, and it involved agents from seven different state and federal agencies. Following a fifteen-month investigation into the sale of marijuana, cocaine, opium, Ecstasy, and psilocybin mushrooms, task force members lured suspects by inviting them to join a secret society, Zeta Tau, and to indicate their interest by showing up at a van parked near the rotunda. Five students did and were informed they were under arrest. Others were nabbed in bars along the Corner, the cluster of taverns just off campus. Thirty-three people were arrested in all. The inside joke among the law enforcement agents was that Zeta Tau stood for zero tolerance.

In the fall of 2004, Berkeley's campus was rocked with news of the death of a senior and the discovery in his off-campus apartment of fourteen pounds of marijuana as well as methadone and weapons. Three of the dead student's roommates were subsequently arrested in what police said was the breakup of a major campus drug ring.

The drug that scared campus officials in the late nineties was Ecstasy, often referred to as E. Scientifically it is known as the compound MDMA. E has been around for more than a century and was actually patented by Merck in 1914. It made its debut as a club drug in the early 1980s in the Dallas area, and the DEA promptly listed it as a schedule I substance, which ended its legal availability.

By playing with the brain's neurotransmitters, including serotonin, a major influence on mood, Ecstasy induces a combination of cocaine-like bravado, amphetamine-like stimulation, and pot-like sensuality without any of the perceptual distortions created by hallucinogens. One Berkeley undergraduate told me that she tried it once and felt extremely nauseous for the first half hour, but then she was overwhelmed by a nerve-tingling sensuality and a self-confidence that wiped away all inhibitions. A University of Michigan student recalled his first experience with the drug: "The second the powder entered my nasal cavity, it burned intensely. I reeled back from the dresser, eyes watering. Seconds later, a tingling started up and down my limbs, followed by a warm rush of chemicals surging through me. I remember walking out of the bedroom, floating down the narrow hall with a gigantic smile on my face, feeling so overwhelmingly wonderful, a thousand times better than I had ever felt in my life."

In the 1990s, E hit the all-night dance club scene like a tsunami and was treated with relative kindness by the mainstream press, including a *Time* magazine cover story in June 2000. For $20 a pop, users could dance or make love all night, and they did. In 2001, roughly 15 percent of college students reported using Ecstasy—more than a sevenfold increase from a decade earlier.

The bad news, which didn't get much attention early on, was that Ecstasy occasionally set off psychotic episodes and appeared to have some long-term—perhaps permanent—effect on the body's serotonin levels, meaning it might lead to chronic depression and permanent personality change. As this word spread, along with a few hairy stories about kids who fried their brains on the stuff, the college Ecstasy scene faded.

But it did not disappear completely. Shortly after I visited Indiana University in 2003, a joint federal/state task force busted a ring of current and former IU students who had been importing large quantities of Ecstasy from Amsterdam by taping strings of tablets to their legs and getting through customs at the Detroit Metro airport. They had been selling the tabs on campus for $15 to $20 apiece. A health official at the Claremont Colleges, which includes Pomona, told me that students would occasionally show up at the clinic with mouth blisters induced by sucking Ecstasy-laced Popsicles. But as one Dartmouth senior told me, "People are beginning to read that it can have serious, lasting impact, which is moving it into the second category of drugs like cocaine and heroin."

When the rave scene died, the same Michigan student, whom I'll call Steve, moved from Ecstasy to cocaine, which he said was "a lot more subtle" than E but easier to get in his fraternity. Quick to deny that the Greek system was a haven for Michigan's cocaine users, he said that the fraternity just happened to be where his friends were. "Drug use, at least, is about the same with fraternity members and nonfraternity members. It's just a social situation, and we happen to have a big Greek system here."

"I was addicted to cocaine by the time I realized it," he recalled. "I suppose it was obvious to everyone outside of my similarly dependent friends, but that is also one of the realities of the drug: the habit hides itself from you until it's too late." Steve would spend about $100 a week buying coke but ran in a crowd that was generous with their own supplies. Most of them, he acknowledged, were from well-to-do families. Someone would just throw a batch on a table in the house while a party was going on; they'd divide it up into lines with a razor blade and snort it with a straw or a rolled-up dollar bill. High on coke, and also smoking weed and drinking, the partiers would go through the night, sometimes into midmorning. "I was already seeing the sunrise five days a week—the only daylight I really saw anyway—and I began to hate it. By late morning, all I wanted to do was sleep, but insides twisting, mind racing, nose bleeding, face sweating, my bed offered no comfort, and even a blanket nailed over the window did not keep out the sun."

When he crossed the line from recreational use to addiction isn't clear, but by the spring of that year, he had shed 30 pounds from his six-foot frame, dropping to an emaciated 130 pounds. His relationship with a girlfriend deteriorated and finally collapsed. He stopped answering or returning phone calls from his parents. When he finally returned home to face them, it was after a coke binge that kept him up all night and all day. At some point he collapsed, and his mom and dad were standing over him when he awoke, shaking him and yelling in his ear. It had taken them twenty minutes to revive him. It was only after his subsequent confession to them that Steve tried to break the habit.

He stayed clean for a month, but he fell back into it when school started up again in the fall. Finally recognizing that he had a problem he couldn't deal with alone, Steve dropped out of Michigan and went into rehab. With help, he kicked the coke habit. But back in college, he continued to drink and smoke weed—in moderation, he maintained. "I know people who can do coke and not get addicted," Steve told me as he approached midyear graduation from Michigan. "But I also know a certain type of person with an addictive personality who can't do it. I feel like I have managed my drinking very well."

Such horror stories notwithstanding, hard drug use has stayed at relatively manageable levels in recent years. What's new about the college drug scene is the propensity to mix substances like GHB, roofies, crystal meth, and ketamine (known as Special K) with alcohol. Some students have been known to mix in anti-depressants, which typically come to college along with a psychiatrist's prescription. For guidance on what works and what kills, they go to Web sites such as Columbia's Go Ask Alice (www. goaskalice.columbia.edu) and check out the startling permutations other site users have questions about—Ecstasy and alcohol, crystal meth and Paxil, nitrous oxide (laughing gas) and marijuana. They are seeking to avoid the fate of people like Josh Duroff, a senior at Connecticut's Trinity College who died from sniffing a concoction of ground-down Valium and Xanax, a double dose of downers, having already had alcohol and heroin. A woman at Rollins College apparently thought it would be interesting to mix Inderall, a prescription heart drug often used to treat migraines, with an extra dose of her antidepressants before going to a fraternity party. She went to the morgue instead.

An ER doc in Madison regaled me one afternoon with stories from a hospital near the UW campus. "We get a lot of poly-drug stuff," he said. "Paxil and Welbutrin [antidepressants] mixed with alcohol—mostly college kids but not necessarily UW—marijuana, heroin . . . that's how people die. Five or six years ago, we had a nineteen-year-old fall off a window ledge at a party. When she got here, she was a quadriplegic—and pregnant. Three years ago, we had a kid on PCP who was out swimming in Lake Menona in November. Another kid on coke went psychotic and ran around the ER naked and screaming. When Ozzie Osborne played at the Dane County Coliseum a few years ago, every bed in the ER was filled."

In one of the several lawsuits filed against MIT, the family of Richard Guy Jr., a student who in 1999 suffocated inside a plastic bag while inhaling laughing gas, claimed that the nitrous oxide canister their son used was kept in a fifth-floor room painted black with pink and purple lightbulbs. Residents referred to it as the "dorm bottle." Subsequent to his death, two students, including the woman in whose room Guy had died, were charged with possession and intent to distribute not only nitrous oxide but also hallucinogenic mushrooms, amphetamines, and marijuana.

One psychiatric services administrator told me about a student who had combined Ecstasy with Viagra—he called it Sextasy—and had to be treated in the health center for priapism, a persistent erection that could have serious health consequences. But at least he lived to tell about it.

I should not have been surprised, but I was, by the frequency with which a rather banal new addition to the American pharmaceutical palette came up in campus conversations about drugs. That is the growing popularity of Ritalin (methylphenidate) and its pharmaceutical cousin, Adderall, a mixture of amphetamine salts—both of which are used mainly in adolescents for the treatment of attention deficit disorder. Literally millions of kids are prescribed one or the other of these drugs, and many of them eventually end up in college. Odds are good that by the time they reach age eighteen, they no longer need these drugs (if in fact they ever did). But many manage to extend their prescriptions to avail themselves of the drugs' ancillary uses.

The widest use on campuses is as a study aid. In the old days, we used to get a mild over-the-counter stimulant like No-Doz, or in some cases a mysterious black capsule some guy down the hallway had for the serious all-night cram sessions. But Ritalin and

Adderall (the preferred choice, I was assured) can really focus the mind. "It's helped me a lot," a Harvard junior told the *Crimson.* "I can sit down for three hours and it feels like ten minutes." A U-VA student claimed that it "kicked the ass out of coffee," which has the negative side effect of causing jitters. A pill typically sells for $5, I was told, though one senior at Indiana said there was a guy there who sold his prescribed 100-milligram Adderall pills for $10 a pop.

Some who have studied with the help of these drugs have also discovered that it's not a bad party aid either. By grinding a tablet back into powder form and snorting it through a rolled dollar bill the way one would cocaine, a user can take a hit that will make him either the life of the party or an A student—maybe both. Ideal though they might sound, these drugs have long-term ill effects, including anxiety, insomnia, high blood pressure, and impotence.

As disturbing as these tales might be, they live in a context that is, relatively speaking, heartening: illicit drug use in the United States has been declining, albeit gradually, over the past two decades. College students in particular seem open to being educated by the facts about drugs. Their attitude toward alcohol, by contrast, remains fixed at a level that borders on the obsessive.

10

College Sports and Res Life

D eep inside the McLean Athletic Center, under the shadow of the University of Wisconsin's Camp Randall football stadium, is the Fetzer Center, named for Wade and Beverly Fetzer, who donated $2 million to help ensure that Badger athletes get all the academic help they need. Built in the late 1990s, the Fetzer, as Badger athletes call it, has nine separate study rooms, an auditorium, a separate study hall just for freshmen, and a computer lab spread over 10,000 square feet. It has the capacity of a small high school and more: the Fetzer has a full-time professional staff of fourteen, five special advisors who help athletes select courses, three learning specialists who deal with those who are underprepared for college, and a call list of over a hundred tutors.

Since it is under the same roof as the training rooms and indoor practice field, Fetzer is very convenient, especially for football players. In season, the average Badger lineman spends at least ninety minutes a day working out in a weight room just down the hall, another ninety minutes in team meetings watching game films, and two and a half hours of actual practice every weekday. With another twenty minutes to shower and dress and two more hours of mandatory study hall at night for freshmen, most of Wisconsin's eight hundred or so varsity athletes spend a majority of their time in and around the Fetzer.

Fetzer is a vital safety net without which the more academically challenged athletes likely wouldn't survive. Those who maintain a 3.0 GPA or better can ignore Fetzer. But anyone under that
is monitored, with particular attention paid to freshmen and
transfer students. The staff keeps its own database of grades and
attendance records. Twice a semester, beginning at the five-week
point, the staff e-mails professors asking about athletes. "We may
require extra tutor meetings for problem areas," said David Har-
ris, the center's director. Sometimes it takes a direct order from
the coach to get results (for example, "If you don't sign up for
tutoring, you're not playing Saturday"). On average, about five
athletes a semester flunk out.

Andy Wheeler was one athlete who didn't need Fetzer, though
he had many hockey teammates who did. "School was never hard
for me," admitted the Duluth-born history major who managed a
3.2 GPA as well as the captaincy of the Badger team, one of college hockey's perennial powers. But freshman year, he was required
to spend three evenings a week from seven o'clock until nine
o'clock in what was effectively a proctored study hall. Mostly, athletes learn good study habits and time management skills in Fetzer.
But there were tutors available who "catered to our every need,"
recalled Andy. "They gave you everything you could think of specifically tailored to your classes. It was thoroughly customized."

That's the way it's done at big-time athletic colleges these
days. Gone are the athletic dorms where few people knew what a
textbook looked like. Now every NCAA Division I college has its
own version of the Fetzer. Indiana University's tutoring center is
beneath the stands in Assembly Hall, where the famed Hoosier
basketball team plays. Varsity athletes at Berkeley do study hall at
the Cesar Chavez Student Center on Lower Sproul Plaza. Football players must spend fifteen hours a week; soccer players, who
generally do better academically, spend only six. At archrival
Stanford, a couple of dozen tutors on the payroll provide help for
struggling jocks. "If someone is not doing well in class, I will get
a phone call or an e-mail," said Verity Powell, who lines up tutors

from a large room in the basement of the Arrillaga Family Sports Center. "We try to pair athletes with grad students who were former athletes themselves."

Combined with training, travel, and practice time as well as the natural penchant for athletes to hang out with their own kind, college life for a typical Badger athlete is nothing like it is for other Wisconsin students. For athletes who go on to play for the pros, that's not an issue; college for them is little more than a farm team with books; Andy Wheeler skated with several Badger players who went on to the National Hockey League. Though he kept one foot in conventional campus life and loved his Wisconsin experience, Wheeler's life was so involved with hockey that he really didn't know what was going on in the larger world outside of what he read in the student newspaper. That was common. "When I was rowing, I had no clue about anything else," said Jen, a member of the Wisconsin women's varsity crew before the grueling schedule burned her out. "I didn't know that I had a regular advisor other than my athletic advisor. I didn't even know that Al Gore had come to campus to speak. And there's not much partying when you're getting up at five A.M. and rowing a boat at six."

Like Greeks, athletes feel under siege these days. It is widely assumed that they are uninterested in and most likely incapable of intellectual pursuit, that they're on campus as part of a business proposition and live by different rules. Unfortunately, those assumptions are often well founded. The two dominant college sports stories at the time I was touring campuses involved the University of Colorado football program, sullied by the accusations of nine different women who said they'd been raped by Colorado athletes during the previous five years, and Maurice Clarett, the star Ohio State running back who was allowed to take a special oral exam in an African American history course after he walked out of the regular midterm.

The Colorado scandal revealed an elaborate recruitment scheme in which female students were brought in to "entertain" top high school prospects. Clarett's tale uncovered a laundry list of dubious practices that led to his suspension from OSU, after which he had the audacity to sue the National Football League to be allowed to sign up early as a pro.

The two big universities were not alone in this morass. According to the *Sacramento Bee*, the basketball statistician at California State University at Fresno admitted that he was paid to write papers for members of the men's team. In 2003, Penn State's Nittany Lions had ten players arrested on a variety of charges, including rape. During roughly the same period, archrival Ohio State's Buckeyes ran up fourteen arrests of their own on charges, ranging from theft to felony drug possession. Other sports headlines included stories of shootings, sexual assault charges, cheating, drugs, child pornography, and a beheading.

Of course, the vast majority of college athletes are not crooks, thugs, rapists, or morons. But even the smart, honest ones, whether they want to be or not, just aren't like regular students. Their world is a combination of relentless training and royal treatment by fans and the media. At Duke, I learned that the phone numbers and addresses of varsity basketball players were not listed like those of every other Duke student. At Berkeley or Stanford, students still pointed and whispered when the quarterback or the point guard actually walked among them in the dining hall. Indiana University professor Murray Sperber blames an unholy alliance of ambitious coaches, zealous alums, the alcoholic beverage industry, and network television for forging "a powerful synergy between big-time college sports and contemporary student life." A culture has built up around a quasiprofession that has placed the quest for knowledge well behind the drive for an NCAA bid in the hierarchy of reasons athletes go to college.

What is in many ways more disturbing is that these practices have infiltrated the academic elite, including the Ivy League and the small Division III schools. It is all part of the ratcheting-up process that has distorted the college experience no less than Budweiser or ABC's *Game of the Week*.

That's not just my observation. It is a conclusion supported through research directed by William G. Bowen, the former president of Princeton, who now heads the Andrew W. Mellon Foundation, one of the nation's premier academic think tanks. *The Game of Life* and *Reclaiming the Game* provide disheartening evidence that the gap between athletes and nonathletes in the Ivy League and comparably distinguished schools such as Duke and Stanford as well as among the small, highly selective eastern liberal arts colleges that compete under the banner of NESCAC (New England Small College Athletic Conference, the league in which both Hamilton and Middlebury compete) has grown wider than it has for colleges in general. And because these elite schools are smaller, field more teams, and have a greater percentage of their students participating in varsity sports, the impact of what Bowen and his coauthors call the "academic-athletic divide" is far greater and growing. At NESCAC colleges, nearly 40 percent of men play on varsity teams. By contrast, at a large Division I school such as Michigan, varsity athletes might make up 5 percent of the student body.

Despite lofty assurances by the Ivy League and the elite liberal arts colleges that their athletes are truly representative of the student body, according to the Mellon research, "the average SAT scores of recruited athletes in these two leagues are about 150 points lower than those of students in general." A recruited athlete "has more than four times as good a chance of getting into an Ivy League school as a comparable male applicant not on a coach's list." His (or her) chances of admission are almost twice those of a legacy (an applicant with a family connection) or a member of a minority group. And once admitted, these athletes do even worse than their SAT scores and grades would predict; 70 to 80 percent of high-profile (football, basketball, ice hockey) sport athletes in the Ivy League end up in the bottom third of their class even though they typically take less challenging courses. This academic underperformance occurs even after they stop competing.

*   *   *

The allure of competing at a world-class level at a world-class university is enormous. One afternoon at Stanford, I strolled across Campus Road into the land called Arrillaga, the university's sports complex and one of the great meccas of college athletics. At the 2,393-seat Taube Family Tennis Stadium, a plaque testifies that the men's team had captured seventeen out of the past thirty NCAA championships; the women had been champs in twelve of the past twenty-one years. Altogether, Stanford teams have won seventy NCAA titles since 1980; collectively, Stanford athletes won forty-seven Olympic medals in the 1990s alone. In a quick scan down a list of individual champions, I caught the names John McEnroe, Alex Mayer, and Kathy Jordan. And they have the facilities to match. There is a four-pool aquatic center where swimmers, divers, and water polo players have dominated their sports for decades. The 85,000-seat Stanford Stadium is where John Elway played quarterback. The course on the edge of campus is where Tiger Woods played his collegiate golf.

Stanford officials like to say that they do it without sacrificing their high academic standards. *The Game of Life* suggests that while Stanford and other academically strong Division I-A schools, including Duke, Northwestern, Notre Dame, Rice, and Vanderbilt, are impressive in their ability to recruit great athletes who are also strong students, the gap between recruited athletes and other students is greater among these schools than in any other category of college: more than 80 percent of the high-profile athletes at these institutions rank in the bottom third of their class.

The anecdotal evidence I saw supports those numbers. More with a sense of sadness than indignation, professors have described how athletes—especially men who play contact sports—tend to congregate at the back of the classroom and sit through a lecture as if it were something to be endured rather than absorbed. I'm convinced that the anti-intellectual jock image has brought about a cultural estrangement between faculty and athletes that continues to grow more than the actual problem and in doing so creates a self-fulfilling cycle.

Kelley, a varsity women's soccer player at Cal, first started playing at age four. "It was my whole life," she told me. "I stayed on the honor roll in high school because I knew that's what it would take to get into the colleges I wanted to play at." Soccer was so central to her and other players at her level that when the fledgling women's professional soccer league folded, "they were all crushed," according to Kelley's boyfriend. "For many of them, that was the next goal in life."

Dave Racine, a hockey defenseman at Division III Hamilton, started playing the game when he was four and never missed a season the whole time he was in school. Summers included a week or so at a hockey camp, working on power skating techniques and basic skills. He coached in the summer during high school. Hockey was his life.

As a member of the Culver Military Academy team in Indiana, Racine went east to play in a tournament at Phillips Exeter Academy, where Hamilton coach Phil Grady spotted him. Though he was also being recruited by some Division I programs, Dave chose Hamilton largely because he was assured he would play a lot. To his shock, he didn't make the team his freshman year. "I was real bitter for a while," he admitted. Even his parents felt betrayed. Luckily, he stuck with it, made the team his sophomore year, and regained his equilibrium and his identity as an athlete.

Even at the Division III level, where there are no athletic scholarships, aspiring athletes who don't make it often feel betrayed. The resilient ones readjust and take advantage of being at a top-notch academic school they probably wouldn't have gotten into without their athletic talent. Less flexible ones can get lost for life.

Those who make the team find themselves looking at college life through an entirely different lens. Coaches are the adults they most often see. Kelley remembered how her Berkeley coach, affable as a recruiter, was a relentless taskmaster on the field. "I expected it to be like a business," she admitted, "but I didn't expect it to be such an intense environment." The arm of his law extended into her first-year dorm, where after nearly an entire fall semester she had never even met her RA. "The only authority we answer to," she said, "is the coach."

Coaches who invest so much time in recruiting a strong prospect understandably follow up with rigorous oversight aimed at keeping that prospect playing. Hamilton's Phil Grady orders his players to alert each and every professor at least two weeks before they're going to miss a class because of a game. When he once learned that his team captain had cut a class because of a hockey conflict without informing the professor, Grady benched him for a game. A sophomore who tried the same stunt was called into Grady's office and asked, "Why are you ruining your life?" When Dave Racine confided to Grady during his sophomore year that he was getting a C in a course, the coach picked up the phone right in front of him and set up an appointment with a tutor.

Student athletes who run afoul of tough coaches like Grady can end up in prolonged anguish. But many lean on their coach for advice well beyond the scope of their sports and into their personal and academic lives. When Roger Brown was brought up on a cheating charge at Dartmouth, the first person he told was his ski coach. Christina Scolli, the recruited tennis player at Indiana, said, "If I had a serious emotional problem, I'd probably first turn to my coach." Duke chaplain Will Willimon praised basketball coach Mike Krzyzewski as "the last Aristotelian mentor we have here."

The mentor/mentee relationship is solidified by the demands of a varsity sport daily regimen. At almost any level, time management is almost as important as physical talent. With athletes spending at least four to five hours a day in season at their sport, they must learn to fit in everything else around that time. Andy

Laskowski, a rare two-sport athlete at Hamilton, where he was co-captain of the hockey team and captain of the lacrosse team, spent all but a few weeks each year working under the demands of his teams' schedules. With films to watch and no less than two hours of field practice in season, Andy was focused on lacrosse from four-thirty P.M. until ten P.M. every weekday of the spring term. But he saw a good side to it: "What athletes teach other students at Hamilton is how to be efficient with their time," he said.

The hockey team started skating informally in mid-October and went at a furious pace through early March, by which time the lacrosse team was already practicing. Off-season wasn't much lighter. Coach Grady had his athletes on a weight program consisting of a full upper body workout one day and a full lower body regimen the next, followed by a day off before the cycle repeated itself. They were expected to run five miles on their days off and were asked to send periodic training reports back to Grady until September, when they were tested back on campus. As did many of his teammates, Andy also worked as a coach in summer hockey camps. All this was for a Division III team. At Indiana University, 70 percent of varsity athletes, almost all of them on scholarship, routinely stay in Bloomington over summers to train.

This constant protecting and nurturing seems to thrust the wedge between athlete and professor that much deeper. A number of student-athletes with whom I spoke evinced a firm personal belief that many of their professors held their team memberships against them. "There are some who just hear the words *athletic* or *game* and just turn off," said Andy Laskowski at Hamilton. "Their view is that anything that gets in the way of academics is bad. I asked one professor if I could leave class thirty minutes early for an away game, and he said no, it would be 'disruptive.'"

Nicole Corriero, a Canadian who was Harvard's high scorer on a series of nationally contending women's hockey teams, wrote a sociology paper on the low regard in which she and other athletes were held at Harvard. Acting out the dumb jock image, she argued, was often a self-fulfilling prophecy. "This mentality is extremely prevalent in Harvard athletes," she wrote. Expected to behave in a certain manner consistent with others' expectations, jocks who might well have other talents and traits "downplay these attributes in favor of their primary mode of distinction, their athletic talents. Any academic discrepancy between athletes and nonathletes at Harvard University is not due to a discrepancy in intelligence or lack of academic ambition," Nicole wrote, "but rather to prevailing opinions and expectations that instructors and peers have of these athletes."

Ramona Shelburne, a recruited softball player at Stanford, echoed that view. "It's difficult to combat a stereotype," she wrote in a piece that ran in the university's alumni magazine. "For many student-athletes, it's a task too daunting to undertake. The stereotype then becomes a self-fulfilling prophecy. In my three years on the softball team, I've seen some of the smartest, most interesting people I've met at Stanford adopt a 'why try?' attitude toward academics simply because someone else made them feel stupid."

It echoes an argument sometimes made on behalf of African Americans and women by scholars who believe that lower test scores on standardized tests are the result of anxiety produced by racial and gender stereotypes. Indeed, student-athletes experience a bonding pattern and institutionalized isolation "not dissimilar to those of students of color," contended Paula Krebs, chair of the English department at Wheaton College in Massachussets and the college's faculty representative to the NCAA.

Like minority groups, athletes build their social lives around each other. With all the time they spend "across the river," as Harvard athletes refer to the undergraduate athletic complex on the other side of the Charles, the Crimson's women's ice hockey team has little time to develop friendships with anyone other than themselves and the male hockey players who share the same facilities. The widely observed forty-eight-hour rule that prohibits alcohol consumption for two days leading up to a game keeps them from joining in on a lot of the big parties in Cambridge. "For Harvard athletes, half the social scene is in the training and weight rooms across the river," said Mina Pell, class of 2004, who lettered in both ice and field hockey.

Soccer player Mike Wilson explained how his team's three-day nondrinking rule during the season prevented him and his teammates from joining in on prime party nights at Stanford. "Sunday and Monday nights were typically the only legal nights for us, while 90 percent of students partied on Thursday, Friday, and Saturday," said Wilson. "So we usually kept to ourselves."

At more remote campuses like Dartmouth and Hamilton, the correlation between athletic teams and fraternities seems much stronger than it had been in my day. At Hamilton in recent years, almost all the hockey players join Psi Upsilon; lacrosse players, Theta Delta Chi; and football players, Delta Upsilon. I saw the same pattern at Dartmouth. Sports teams at Williams have become virtual substitutes for long-banned fraternities—a mechanism for bonding and the organizing principle for campus parties.

Social bonding within the framework of a team is hardly new. But like so much else in college these days, it has become more intense, and, to a disconcerting degree, more exclusionary. Beginning on an athlete's first days on campus, membership on a team at Dartmouth is a conduit to a particular fraternity or sorority that involves not just an affinity for a sport but a whole package of social characteristics and expectations. Even the smell of teammates' hair evoked a connection for one team member because part of the ritual (hazing, if you will) for incoming freshmen was to buy shampoo for the team to use after practice. Team leaders make it known to their fraternity brothers or sorority sisters that a certain new first-year is welcome in the house for parties simply because he or she is a member of the team.

Changing attitudes toward sports in the larger society have had a profound influence on college sports. Throughout the last three decades, kids' sports programs have gone from being simple leagues of local teams to a series of parallel leagues with various tiers of proficiency in virtually every sport. The isolation of talented athletes begins in grade school, with select travel squads and summer camps employing the kind of rigorous training regimens I had always associated with Olympic-level figure skaters and gymnasts. Knowing that every advantage their child could offer an admissions committee could be a leg up in the ever more competitive race to get into the best schools, ambitious parents push their kids to the highest levels. Instead of working with whatever the admissions office gives them, even small college coaches recruit as if they were building a bowl contender, seeking out the best of these prodigies and asking for special dispensations in the admissions process.

Certainly I noticed that the football and hockey players I saw at Hamilton were much bigger and faster than what I had remembered. But I didn't realize how much bigger and faster until one Saturday afternoon in 1995 when I happened upon an ESPN broadcast of the football game between Amherst and Williams, two of Hamilton's NESCAC rivals. In the course of the broadcast, the ESPN commentator noted that the average weight that year of the starting offensive line for Amherst was seventeen pounds heavier than the average weight of the equivalent linemen on the 1975 University of Okalahoma national championship team. I recognized that college sports had become, as they say, a whole new ball game.

Some Division I schools with respectable academic reputations are taking bolder steps to rein in the jock culture. Vanderbilt's president, Gordon Gee, shook up a lot of coaches and athletic directors across the United States by putting his entire athletic program under the Division of Student Life. "For too long, college athletics has been segregated from the core mission of the university," Gee said in a statement at the beginning of the 2003–2004 academic year. "As a result, we have created a culture both on this campus and nationally that is disconnected from our students, faculty, and other constituents, where responsibility is diffuse, the potential for abuse considerable, and the costs—both financial and academic—unsustainable."

For the selective institutions, Bowen and his allies put forth a very specific program of reforms to reclaim the balance between sports and education. With a goal of making athletes more truly representative of their school's overall student body, they advocate an end to the special advantage athletes have been given in the admissions process, including preferential treatment in the awarding of scholarships. By curtailing recruitment of athletes, they envision intercollegiate athletes as being once again available to what are now known as walk-ons, which is to say nonrecruited athletes. Similarly, they advocate fewer coaches overall and more coaches who understand the culture of the institution that employs them. They want to shorten seasons and limit postseason play to regional competitions more closely coordinated with class and exam schedules rather than set up by outside athletic bodies (the NCAA) that in the past have shown little regard for the academic process.

Their goal is to bring athletics at selective schools back to what they were in the 1950s and 1960s. Their closest existing model of success is the University Athletic Association (UAA), a consortium of eight top-level private research universities formed in 1986 that recruit world-class scholars, some of whom play sports. Data used in the Mellon study from four UAA schools— Carnegie Mellon, University of Chicago, Emory, and Washington University of St. Louis—revealed almost none of the distorting effects of athletics found in the Ivy League and NESCAC. The authors surmise that the absence of intense traditional rivalries within the league and the fact that the league monitors the academic outcomes of its athletes may account for these differences.

Russ Reilly, the athletic director at Middlebury, had a copy of *Reclaiming the Game* on his desk when I met with him in the fall of 2003. "The thing that troubles me is that the authors are suggesting that schools like this have to be exclusively for the intellectually elite," Reilly said. "We all don't have to be Swarth-mores. It seems to be that the authors think this is a problem created by the colleges. I don't think so. I think it's a societal problem—what a family thinks it needs to do to get a son or daughter into a place like this." Reilly decried the emphasis on recruiting but noted that it is a two-way street, where high school coaches and parents send out videotapes and e-mails promoting athletes even at the Division III level. He regretted the over-specialization of athletes that winnows sports out of kids' skills repertoires beginning at the sixth- and seventh-grade levels. And yet, he noted, research shows that kids who play more than one sport are better all-round athletes. "I don't want specialists," he said, "because that's not life." Unfortunately, he's probably wrong about that, but I applaud him for the sentiment.

As important as the need for recruiting and admissions re-forms, however, are steps colleges can take to close the cultural divide between athletes and everyone else on campus. Though I used to favor the idea of rooming blocks in which groups of stu-dents can apply to live in adjacent rooms as an alternative to fra-ternity houses, I now believe these blocks promote isolation of whole segments of the population, from fraternity members to minority students to athletes. Any cluster of twelve or twenty stu-dents united by a special nonacademic interest seems like a recipe for trouble.

Even more critical are steps that bring faculty and student-athletes together so that they perceive each other as something beyond their respective stereotypes. Players and coaches at sev-eral institutions are trying to bridge the gap. Harvard's women's hockey team regularly invites professors to sit on the bench with them during games. Middlebury has created a similar faculty/team affiliates program with positive results. Russ Reilly recalled how one professor was reluctant to join Middlebury's hockey team on an away trip because he thought he'd have to endure a long bus ride surrounded by beer-guzzling goons. "Instead, he was shocked by the number of players reading and using their laptops on the bus," said Reilly. "They'd have a little pizza and then get their computers back out."

Virginia football coach Al Groh also asks professors to be the team's coach for a day. A lot turn him down. One who accepted was political science professor Larry Sabato, who spent two full days with the players. "I loved it!" he reported afterward. "You have no idea what those guys go through."

Sadly, neither do the vast majority of Sabato's faculty colleagues or most U-VA students. The jocks still live in a world unto themselves and pay a price for it.

11

What's the Right Drinking Age?

Recent campus crackdowns, bad publicity, and the passage of intrusive laws all reflect growing frustration with an almost universal inability to get a handle on underage drinking in the United States—what Harvard's former dean of the college Harry Lewis called "one of those unresolved issues in society that gets visited upon colleges." Those frustrations only grew following the publication in 2002 of *Dying to Drink: Confronting Binge Drinking on College Campuses*, a tirade of a book coauthored by Dr. Henry Wechsler of the Harvard School of Public Health. (I will discuss drinking in Canada and abroad later in this chapter.)

Dying to Drink paints a picture of contemporary campus life as one dominated by a significant clique of degenerate drunks whose dangerous and irresponsible behaviors spill into the lives of all those around them, including almost 20 percent of their fellow students who drink no alcohol at all. Wechsler did not personally invent the term *binge drinker*, but he employed it in a way that caught people's attention. According to his data gathered four different times over the course of a decade, a fairly consistent 44 percent of college students throughout the 1990s fit this description. Most of them, he noted, were members of Greek organizations and athletes.

Who qualifies as a binge drinker? For many of us, the term evokes the image of a chronic alcoholic who periodically goes on a binge, drinking steadily for days, even weeks at a time, before drying out for a spell and then repeating the cycle. For survey purposes, however, a binge drinker is a male who consumes five or more alcoholic beverages at one sitting or a female who consumes four or more—generally referred to by statistical experts as the 5/4 standard. A student who meets that standard twice in a two-week period qualifies as an occasional binge drinker. One who does so more than twice in two weeks is categorized as frequent.

Setting aside the issue of whether the 5/4 standard reflects what actually happens on college campuses, the pattern of drinking behavior reflected in Wechsler's data is indeed worrisome: after almost a decade, the problem appeared to have gotten worse. While the percentage of students defined as moderate binge drinkers stayed about the same, that of frequent binge drinkers more than doubled from 1993 to 2001.

Dr. Wechsler, whose book is a package of dizzying statistics interspersed with lurid accounts of alcohol-induced disasters, had no reservations about pointing a finger of blame in several directions. "Most college presidents," he wrote, "are afraid to take on the problem of alcohol abuse on their campuses," fearing they will "hurt enrollment and offend alumni." He faulted the alcoholic beverage industry not just for its predatory advertising but also for its "drink responsibly" public service advertising campaign, which he effectively called a pro-drinking message in disguise. Membership in Greek organizations, he said, was the single strongest predictor of bingeing behavior.

I was fascinated by Wechsler's findings but suspicious of his analysis. Certainly his assertion that there is serious drinking on campuses matched what I was seeing. But I was skeptical that a group of nineteen-year-olds with big appetites and speedy metabolisms drinking five beers in the course of a Saturday night could be the source of so much mayhem. Indeed, by that standard I could think of plenty of civilized dinner parties I've attended where a fair number of guests, myself included, consumed a couple of glasses of wine as aperitifs before dinner and several more with the meal. A total of three dinner parties like that in a fortnight qualifies a lot of otherwise responsible and successful people I know as frequent binge drinkers.

Many experts in the field, including Res Life people who had observed student drinking behavior firsthand, took issue with the binge standard as well. So-called 5/4 drinkers aren't the real problem, they said. In a field study done at San Diego State University in 2002, researchers conducting voluntary Breathalyzer tests on some three thousand students as they left area bars and parties on weekend nights found that those whose consumption fell within the 5/4 range rarely even approached the 0.08 percent level used in most states as the maximum allowable for driving. It took at least seven to ten drinks to get to 0.08, they found. What they discovered, however, was that many of the students had consumed between seven and twenty drinks. The kids causing most of the problems—the ones puking in dorms, wandering into snowbanks, and falling out of windows—were downing a lot more than five drinks at a sitting. Though relatively few in number, these were the college drinkers who were setting the parameters of socially acceptable behavior on campus. They were the source not only of the tragic deaths and hospitalizations but also of a great majority of the vandalism and riots that have plagued colleges in recent years.

The other dynamic buried beneath Wechsler's charges of carnage and catastrophe was a shifting pattern of college drinking behavior. Wechsler himself acknowledged early on in his book that "the majority—56%—(of college students) do not binge drink, including 20% who abstain from alcohol altogether." That category is being significantly bolstered by the increase in minority enrollments across North America, reflecting other data indicating that blacks, Hispanics, and members of other racial/ethnic groups coming to college are from cultures that tend to drink less alcohol, if any. Over the past ten to fifteen years, however, the middle segment of the distribution curve—call it the moderate middle—has been steadily shrinking.

Statisticians call it a barbell effect. Sociologists might interpret it as yet another example of American society's cultural flight to the extremes: more and more young people choosing abstinence, countered by a roughly equal number choosing to drink with abandon, leaving fewer moderate drinkers in the middle. One college-drinking expert who took note of this was David Anderson, a respected statistician at Virginia's George Mason University. "If that is the result of all the work that's been done," said Anderson, "then it's been a hollow victory."

Another phenomenon Wechsler's data fail to explain is that the worst drinking behavior often occurs at the best schools. Sure, there are massive alcohol-soaked parties at the big beer-and-circus universities. But some of the highest bingeing rates are coming out of the elite schools to which the best and brightest high school students aspire. John Chandler, who served as president of both Williams and Hamilton, recalled raising the drinking issue with the president of a less prestigious college not far from Williams. "What drinking problem?" replied the other president, whose students' average SAT scores were easily several hundred points below Williams's. "Our students are usually working at least part-time and can't afford to go out and get drunk."

Everywhere I went in the United States, I found colleges employing just about every technique to curb dangerous drinking and for the most part getting nowhere in their efforts. Even the schools that utilize the full arsenal of weapons—stricter enforcement, social norming, aggressive counseling and education—still face a daunting enemy. "We struggle over what degree of violations we can live with," Larry Moneta told me when I was at Duke, admitting that he still worries every day about another Raheem Bath, who died of pneumonia after inhaling his own vomit. "The problem is that we've exhausted our containment efforts."

Every dean will tell you that enforcement to the letter of the law against underage drinking doesn't work. Even at small schools, there are just too many students—otherwise functioning on their own accord and otherwise deemed to be adults—to enforce a ban on a substance that is perfectly legal for adults who happen to be twenty-one or older. There are some fundamentalist colleges that punish drinkers with immediate expulsion. But their applicants know what they're getting into. Mainstream institutions generally pursue a policy of containment, which is to say they place as many obstacles as they can between students and alcohol and then go after the obvious violations. Those that come down hard usually get a hard reaction.

In the spring of 2003, Gene Awakuni, newly installed as vice provost for student affairs at Stanford, approved a new rule effective in the fall that banned alcohol consumption in all public places—lounges, patios, and corridors—of the university's ten freshman residences. Never mind that virtually all of Stanford first-year students are underage. Put aside the fact that under the new rule these students would still be able to drink in their rooms. They were outraged. Twenty-two hundred people signed an on-line petition protesting the ban.

As an article in the nearby *San Jose Mercury News* noted, Stanford has historically been "loose on enforcement" of its alcohol regulations, perhaps with some justification. Compared to most of the American colleges I visited, Stanford's alcohol problems were minor: hospitalizations in recent years have averaged only a few dozen a year for a student body of sixty-seven hundred. But the atmosphere had been deteriorating. Over an eighteen-month period, six Greek organizations had been placed on probation for alcohol-related violations. Even Stanford's notoriously irreverent marching band was put on probation for alcohol violations. Worried about reports of unruly behavior during Thursday senior pub nights, the administration started carding students as they climbed on board the Marguerite for the ride downtown, not only checking their IDs but also barring anyone from bringing alcohol on the bus. According to one group of sophomores I talked to one afternoon, the administration also put a stop that fall to the tradition of returning sophomores welcoming their successors into the freshman halls with gifts of beer and booze. "It was a very successful way to break the ice," complained one. "Now, instead of mingling, the freshmen drink on their own."

The high dudgeon with which students received the news of the crackdown reverberated in the editorial pages of the Stanford *Daily* student newspaper. "If Stanford truly wants to decrease the role alcohol plays in the social life of Stanford undergraduates," the paper's editors wrote in October 2003, "it must provide students with alternative activities and ways to have fun. . . . A quick scan of this weekend's events reveals nothing that could even remotely be considered a substitute for a good party."

It was an unfortunate comparison to make in defense of a legally proscribed activity. But once I got over the sense of entitlement conveyed by the editorial, I began to understand the context in which it was written. Alcohol had become a symbol of adulthood at Stanford and at colleges all across the United States. To have it taken away was to be pushed back toward childhood.

The results at Stanford were much like the results of alcohol crackdowns everywhere: the drinking simply moved to a new venue. All fall, the freshmen started moving in on upper-class apartment parties and frontloading in their rooms. Everywhere they've been implemented, keg bans and complex minimum standards for party approval have led to more pregaming—only with hard liquor instead of beer. And restrictions on the use of college-owned space have driven a lot of the drinking off campus. "Undercover cops are now working the tailgate parties," reported senior Jessie Duncan in the fall of 2004. "It feels like they're out to get you."

Off-campus parties have plagued college towns for years. Recently, residents in many adjacent neighborhoods are saying it's gotten much worse as colleges crack down on campus drinking. In the Trinity Park and Trinity Heights neighborhoods off Duke's East Campus, local Durham residents report hundreds of students spilling out of rented homes onto the streets at least three nights out of every week, especially early in the fall semester, littering bottles and cans on the streets and lawns, throwing up, passing out, and driving away dangerously. After Harvard began tightening underage drinking enforcement, students began renting clubs and hotel spaces in downtown Boston for their revelries, far from the watchful eyes of the university police.

Recognizing the dilemma they faced, the deans must have decided sometime during the past decade that the best way to reduce risk is through a strategy of distraction. The theory seems to be that the more programming they put on that attracts student interest, the less likely it is that students will sit in their rooms or wander off campus and drink. From a Res Life point of view, effective programming should feel like it came from students but still have some relationship to the academic mission of the college.

Hoping to stave off the usual early autumn mayhem, Duke vice president for student affairs Larry Moneta threw $50,000 in front of Duke's Campus Council in the spring of 2003, instructing the body to work up twenty-one consecutive substance-free events covering the first three weeks of the fall term. It didn't work. Whether because there wasn't enough time to plan such an ambitious schedule or because the ideas were lame, the characterizations I heard from a lot of students about the so-called twenty-one-night stand ranged from ineffective to a joke. A particular target of derision was a trivia contest run by entry-level Res Life staffers. Parking a Blue Devil blue Chrysler PT Cruiser in the middle of the main quad, they invited passing students to take a seat in the car and answer curriculum-based trivia questions until they were eliminated. Some bemused Dukies deigned to take part, but most jeered from the sidelines. Joost Borland, a sophomore from the Netherlands, panned the event as "a Disney theme park version of intellectual life."

After witnessing several similar efforts elsewhere, I began to look at the lavish amenities colleges have been adding at a frantic pace in recent years in a new light. Yes, the whirlpools, climbing walls, and indoor water parks are great eye candy on the admissions tours. But maybe their real value is akin to that of midnight basketball programs designed specifically to keep inner city kids from getting in trouble. I happened upon a small example at the University of Wisconsin: an arts and crafts program, of all things. Around midnight on a Friday of a football weekend, there were nearly seventy students packed into a makeshift studio on the fourth floor of UW's lakeside Memorial Union, each making some form of pottery. At least half of them were guys, and there wasn't a beer can in sight. Wisconsin's student affairs staffers had picked up the late-night crafts idea from their counterparts at the University of Missouri, where a similar program designed to counter the campus boozing scene had first attracted only women—until the men found out that's where the women were hanging out at night and followed suit.

This is not a risk-free enterprise. Any college party can fail. But when an administration-endorsed, nonalcoholic event fails, the reverberations are wider. As an alternative to the beer bashes that had become increasingly obstreperous, in 2003 Pomona College's deans decided to counter the usual Halloween rush to drink with a substance-free party. Originally planned to be outdoors in the north campus's broad plaza, the gathering was designed around lots of games and activities including laser tag. But it was cold and rainy that night, and Harwood Halloween, as the festivity was called, got moved into the nearby Frary dining hall, a large, oak-paneled cavern of a room that reminds students of the refectory in Harry Potter's Hogwarts School of Witchcraft and Wizardry. The laser tag had to be canceled, and the remaining activities struck students who ventured in as childish. It was, admitted Pomona's vice president for student affairs Ann Quinley, "genuinely lame. . . . The message was, 'If you're not big enough to drink, we'll give you these games to do.'"

That was the message about college alcohol policies I kept getting from the students themselves, most of whom, it should be stressed, drank in ways that kept their behavior within what I would consider an acceptable range, and some of whom didn't drink at all. What they really didn't like was being told that they couldn't drink and then being treated like a child. "I'm not about to say there aren't problems with alcohol on this campus," said Dave Gordon, a twenty-one-year-old Hamilton senior who was written up for having an open container in the lounge of his dorm. "But a large part of the problem is the policy itself. People who get hospitalized aren't at large parties. They're sitting in their rooms."

The rite of passage is not drunkenness, students insisted, but rather simply having the right to drink. A scotch and soda, a beer, or a glass of Chardonnay have become the symbols of acceptance into the adult world beyond homeroom, curfew, and hall monitors.

The American college obsession with underage drinking seems perverse to me—first, the students' intense relationship with the symbolic status it has achieved, and second, the enormous resources spent fighting it. Whole new employment opportunities have grown up around drinking. Every college, it seems, has jobs dedicated to alcohol: AOD (alcohol and other drugs) coordinators, alcohol education specialists, wellness coordinators, and so on. And every Res Life job seems to have a significant element of alcohol prevention built into it.

The bureaucratic requirements of campus rules and state and federal laws carry further burdens: the expense of tracing the origins of beer kegs, the complications of hosting parties where minors have to be separated out, insurance, and the sheer amount of time spent enforcing these laws.

I was riding along with a University of Wisconsin police officer well past midnight when we came upon a white Toyota sedan stopped in the middle of a four-lane road. Its rear door was open and a young woman was leaning over the pavement, apparently throwing up. On went the flashing lights.

All told, there were four college women in the Toyota, and with reason to suspect the presence of alcohol, the officer asked each of them to get out of the car and submit to a Breathalyzer test. Sure enough, the two in the back seat, including the one who was sick, blew blood alcohol contents (BACs) of 0.15 percent and 0.12 percent respectively. Because they were under age, they were subject to the state's zero-tolerance law, which makes it illegal for anyone under twenty-one to have any trace of alcohol. Each would be subject to a fine of several hundred dollars.

I had no problem with the officer's commitment of time to a possible drunk-driving situation. But then I learned that the driver of the Toyota had blown a zero; she was cold sober. How sadly ironic that these young women who were faithfully obeying years of designated driver lectures were now standing out there in the cold Wisconsin night while a campus police officer spent forty-five minutes writing them up.

Drinking and driving—more accurately, drinking and then driving—was the issue behind the twenty-one-year-old national drinking age law in the first place. The argument that persuaded Congress to act in 1984 was that there was a direct causal relationship between lowering of the drinking age to eighteen in those states that had previously been twenty-one a decade earlier and the steadily increasing carnage on the nation's highways. Mothers Against Drunk Driving (MADD), a major player in the lobbying effort to restore the twenty-one age limit, marshaled statistics that seemed to indict the youngest cohort of drivers involved in fatal drunk-driving accidents. MADD claimed that alcohol played a role in 55 percent of the fatal accidents in which the driver was a minor.

Following full implementation of the change (it took three years for all fifty states to comply), there was a sharp dip in highway fatalities, for which MADD and other supporters of the twenty-one age limit took full credit. "Researchers found that teenage deaths in fatal car crashes dropped considerably—in some cases up to 28%—when the laws were moved back to 21," claimed the organization's Web site. "Like it or not, it is clear that more young people were killed on the highways when the drinking age was 18." In the summer of 2004, MADD celebrated the twentieth anniversary of the National Uniform 21 Minimum Drinking Age Act, claiming that the law had saved twenty thousand lives.

I have no doubt that making it illegal for eighteen-, nineteen-, and twenty-year-olds to purchase alcohol played some role in the drop in highway fatalities that took place between 1987 and 1995. But like many others, I suspect that safer cars and roads, airbags, wider use of seatbelts, and tougher enforcement of BAC laws for drivers of all ages played an even greater part. I also believe that a nationwide advertising campaign to promote designated drivers was more significant than raising the legal drinking age.

Drinking and driving—drinking *while* driving—was something my contemporaries were far guiltier of than recent generations of college students. We thought nothing of throwing a six-pack or two ("roadies") in the back seat of a car for a two- or three-hour trip to some women's college. In contrast, the students I've met have been drilled since they were preteens about the dangers of driving after drinking. They got it—not that it had any effect on whether they drank or not. But when they knew they were going to be drinking, they took taxis, had nondrinking friends lined up to chauffeur them, and even rented buses.

Another argument MADD offers in defense of the twenty-one drinking age is that alcohol affects young, developing brains more than it does mature brains, and that the longer you postpone the onset of drinking, the less likely it is that damage and dysfunction will follow later in life. But most of the evidence is based on an association between alcohol consumption at very early ages—nine, ten, and eleven—and alcoholism later in life. What that says about people who don't start drinking until they are seventeen or eighteen is very unclear. As for a relationship between drinking in college and problems with alcohol later in life, there is only sketchy evidence that one leads to the other except among those genetically disposed to alcoholism in the first place. But the alcohol-as-predictor-of-disease argument was an afterthought to the highway safety argument. And it is indisputable that anyone at any age who has more than two drinks should not get behind the wheel of a car. The question was how much age has to do with it.

Other countries came to the establishment of minimum drinking ages differently, and quite a number still have no minimum legal age at all. One of the most common arguments against the American twenty-one-year-old limit is that these other countries don't seem to have suffered as a result. Many American college students who have spent a semester abroad come home to report that the most egregious misuse they witnessed—in Spain or Germany or Japan—was by visiting Americans who went nuts at the prospect of unfettered access to alcohol.

Conversely, I asked foreign students at the colleges I visited what they thought of American drinking habits and laws. Javier, a Duke student from a European country, where the drinking age is sixteen, said the excessive drinking he saw among his fellow collegians reminded him of his high school classmates back home. "College in the United States," he said, "is much more like a continuation of high school." Christina Scolli, the Norwegian student at Indiana, concurred: "In Europe, it's not that way. Kids drink but not just to get drunk." She was particularly baffled by the enforcement policies she saw in Bloomington, where police would raid a student apartment and arrest underage drinkers where they lived. "In Norway, everything is geared so that if you drink, you drink at home where it's safe," she said. "Here they come and arrest you for drinking in your own home."

Those who challenge the American law by citing Europe's more liberal policies risk the wrath of the well-organized alcohol abuse prevention community, however. One who did so was journalist T. R. Reid, who spent tours as a *Washington Post* correspondent in London and Tokyo. Citing his experiences with his own children who as teenagers took advantage of their ability to drink legally in London pubs, Reid wrote:

Some countries have no minimum drinking age, a conservative approach that leaves the issue up to families rather than government bureaucrats. In most Western democracies, drinking becomes legal in the late teens. In Britain, a 16-year-old can have a beer in a pub if the drink accompanies a meal. Most publicans we knew were willing to call a single bag of potato chips—sorry, "crisps"—a full meal for purposes of that law. And yet teen drinking tends to be a far more dangerous problem in the prohibitionist United States than in those more tolerant countries. The reason lies in the law itself. Because of our nationwide ban on drinking before age 21, American teenagers tend to do their drinking secretly, in the worst possible places—in a dark corner of the park, at the one house in the neighborhood where the adults have left for the weekend or, most commonly, in the car.

Amid a national outcry over an epidemic of "binge drinking," politicians don't like to admit the problem is largely a product of the liquor laws. Kids know they have to do all their drinking before they get to the dance or the concert, where adults will be present.

Within days of Reid's column, Joseph A. Califano Jr., secretary of health, education, and welfare during the Carter administration and president of the National Center on Addiction and Substance Abuse at Columbia University, fired back with a statistics-chocked rebuttal, the essence of which was: Don't look to Europe for examples of good alcohol policies. British sixteen-year-olds, he said, were twice as likely as Americans to binge drink; fifteen-year-old Americans were less likely to get drunk than their counterparts in eighteen other nations. "Rather than paint rosy but unrealistic pictures of life in countries where teens can legally buy alcohol," wrote Califano, "we need to get serious about preventing underage drinking."

His argument was essentially the same one made by Henry Wechsler, who claimed that Europeans were rapidly developing their own youth drinking crisis. These nearly identical conclusions were based on the same 2001 U.S. Department of Justice report comparing drinking behaviors in Europe and the United States.

Because my own anecdotal information and personal experiences put me on Reid's side of the argument, I looked at the data and talked to the person recommended by the World Health Organization in Geneva as a leading authority on comparative drinking behaviors and policies around the world: Dr. Robin Room, the author of several books on drinking and leader of the Alcohol Research Group at the Medical Research Institute of San Francisco before joining the faculty at the University of Stockholm.

Acknowledging that the U.S. drinking rates among young people are just below halfway down a list of eighteen countries, Dr. Room observed that a cross-check of legal drinking ages in these countries reveals no pattern. Ukraine, the only other country with a twenty-one age limit, has a slightly worse overall record for risky teen drinking. Incongruously, Denmark, where it is legal to purchase alcohol at age fifteen, has a better record than Ukraine. If there is a discernible pattern, it runs longitudinally: kids in northern European countries generally drink more, while those in the south tend to drink less. "Teen drinking reflects what goes on in the larger society in each country," said Dr. Room.

Denmark is the only example of a country that has recently tightened its laws with some effect after a media-inspired debate over the use of "alco-pops" by children as young as ten and eleven led to the passage of the fifteen-year-old purchasing limit. After the law passed, said Dr. Room, there was indeed a decline in teen drinking not only among those younger than fifteen but also among sixteen- and seventeen-year-olds, who were still legal. It wasn't the law that most likely changed the behavior, Room surmised, so much as it was a highly visible airing of the issue and the resultant attention parents paid to their children's behavior.

"Europeans don't think much of the U.S. twenty-one policy," Room told me. They view the law as a misplaced effort to solve a traffic safety issue with a broad cultural policy that brings a number of collateral consequences. They have chosen to combat abuse by raising "sin taxes" on alcoholic beverages, by limiting purchasing hours, and most effectively through strict enforcement of severe penalties for drunk driving. Convicted Swedes and Norwegians do serious jail time.

Dr. Room is not alone in questioning the American strategy. "In a 'wet culture' where young people are early socialized to drinking, they simultaneously learn how to drink moderately, how and why to avoid drunkenness, not to expect magical transformations from drink, and to view excesses as inappropriate and illustrative of weakness (generally the opposite of what supposedly 'protected' youths in the United States learn)," argued Brown University anthropologist Dwight Heath, who has studied alcohol use and initiation patterns in different societies. "In short, the early-onset theory is accurate but only in those few parts of the world in which the legal and normative system makes it so. In the rest of the world, the opposite is the case!"

To the extent that early-onset drinking is associated with alcohol abuse later, Heath contended, it is by way of separating out those inclined to rebel and take risks and setting them on an unchecked path toward later abuse. "The antidrink constituency has succeeded in structuring the situation in such a way that the fateful outcome (early drinking results in drinking problems) is all but inevitable."

On the second tier of the debate is the question of what the age limit should be if it were to be lowered again. Richard Lucey, the U.S. Department of Education's point man on alcohol, argued to me that repealing the national twenty-one age limit would put the question back to individual states to decide, "and we'd be right back to the blood border thing."

Lucey and other supporters of the existing limit further argue that lowering the age would actively invite the next group down to participate, to which advocates of change respond by noting that they are already drinking in high school. Experts on both sides of the issue agree that whatever age is set, those just below it will seek and probably obtain alcohol illegally. The Libertarian view is that there ought not to be any drinking age at all precisely because of these tendencies; that it should be up to parents and teachers and all adults to make the decision as to when and whether a young person is ready to drink. The best answer I heard came from University of Wisconsin chancellor John Wiley, who told a student forum on campus drinking, "Anyone who tells you they have an easy solution has not spent enough time around the problem."

Of all the opponents of the twenty-one-year-old drinking law, the most surprising to me were the presidents and deans of the American colleges and universities, the people who have to deal with the law's consequences. I did not meet with the president of every college and university I visited, but I met with many, as I met with almost all of the top-ranking student affairs officers. Of those with whom I spoke, not one thought the twenty-one age limit was a good idea. "For colleges," said Pomona president David Oxtoby, "an eighteen-year-old drinking age would be much better."

In 2000, Middlebury president John McCardell proposed to the Vermont legislature that the state forgo its share of federal highway funds held under threat by the Uniform Drinking Age Act and allow the state's colleges and universities to make up the difference. When he realized that they were talking about $125 million or so, McCardell suggested that the state designate Middlebury and other residential colleges as "laboratories of progressivism" in which various social reforms might be tested, one of which was supervised underage drinking. "Hold us accountable for violating our own territorial boundaries, but allow us to make our own regulations and enforce them within those boundaries," he pleaded. Legislators said no, voicing concerns about underage local townspeople coming onto campuses to violate the law—not to mention the certain wrath of MADD and other powerful prevention groups. Shortly after retiring as Middlebury's president,

McCardell went public with his opposition to the drinking law, using the op-ed page of the *New York Times* to call it "bad social policy and terrible law" that had made college campuses "depending on the enthusiasm of local law enforcement, either arms of the law or havens from the law. . . . Neither state is desirable."

The case for lowering or even dropping the drinking age altogether is straightforward. Purchasing and consuming alcohol is the only activity withheld from majority citizens, who can otherwise drive, marry, vote, and serve in the military. The ban has artificially imbued drinking with a mystical quality—the last tile that completes the puzzle we call adulthood. "It creates this aura around alcohol," said Luolo Hong, Wisconsin's dean of students, another opponent of the law.

Yet because alcoholic beverages are legal for all other citizens, they are easily obtained. College officials find themselves cut off from engaging students on the issue of responsible drinking by the threat of liability, so they end up turning a blind eye toward behavior they can't control. "It's very difficult to say that we choose to disobey the law," said Sue Wasiolek, Duke's dean of students and a lawyer herself. "Frankly, we've danced around this ever since the passage of the twenty-one law." Since then, she told me, "I've seen no improvement and frankly much more harm."

First on the list of harms is pregaming. It encourages rapid consumption of highly concentrated alcoholic beverages, which virtually guarantees impairment and starts students down a path to the hospital emergency room. The second is the legal removal of adults from situations in which young people drink. A college professor or administrator who allows herself to be so much as in the presence of underage drinkers is subjecting the institution to legal risk. The result is that many students never see how alcohol is supposed to be handled; they never learn that it is not only possible but proper to have one or two drinks and then stop. And so they don't.

A third consequence has been the clandestinization of student social events like fraternity parties. The law has had the effect of turning these private societies into secret societies—speakeasies, really. When I was at Indiana, several students regaled me with stories of being at parties when the house "shutdown drill" went into effect. They laughed about being herded into rooms where the doors were shut and locked while outside the brothers moved with well-practiced efficiency to cover up all signs of alcohol consumption. I met one freshman pledge who was on his way to stand guard outside his new fraternity, either in a car or up in a tree from which he would alert his brothers by two-way radio or cell phone if the authorities were in sight.

Here's how it works at one IU fraternity: before the party gets under way, the house gets reconfigured into a maze, using furniture and strategically placed brothers to slowly guide guests to the party room. Uninvited guests, say a university dean or party patrol, are shown the same path, which gives members more time to react.

During the party, only one door to the house—the side door—is left open, allowing members to control who comes and goes. The first line of defense is a member who occupies a table at the end of the chapter's driveway. He must be someone who is cool under pressure and knows who he's looking for—even what cars people drive. He's armed with a muted, hidden walkie-talkie and a blue laser light. If he sees the dean's office employee on duty to patrol parties, he signals the door staff with the laser light and hits the panic button on his walkie-talkie. Between that outer table and the door, there are two other tables staffed by members and pledges that the university employee must pass, further slowing his progress. Once he reaches the front door, protocol requires him to ask for the fraternity president and have him paged. By the time the president's pager goes off, the shutdown is already well under way.

Once they hear the siren through their walkie-talkies, members in the party room spring to action. Their first job is to immediately close and lock an eight-by-ten-foot alcohol room built into a wall to look like a small closet. The outside door is designed to blend in with the brick wall around it and can only be closed from the inside, which means two members are locked inside the alcohol room for the duration of the shutdown. But they have company—trash barrels of punch made from about six bottles of grain alcohol, a case of fruit punch mix, buckets of ice, and garden hose water mixed together with a broomstick handle.

If asked about the liquor closet during an inspection, the president (who has the only key to the room) says he doesn't have a key and doesn't know who does. While he is taking his sweet time to make sure the alcohol room is locked and all other evidence of alcohol is hidden, other brothers are deploying the dummy punch, an alcohol-free fruit punch also served from trash barrels in red plastic cups. Armed with trash bags, pledges start collecting cups containing the real stuff. They're not concerned about missing some cups, though, since the university party patrol official doesn't have the time or energy to check every cup.

The dummy punch represents a gradual evolution of the shutdown drill. Earlier drills left a bunch of people standing around conspicuously doing nothing. Now it looks as if nothing has changed, and most of the hundreds of people at the party don't even know the party has gone through a shutdown drill.

Once the chapter president is satisfied that the shutdown is fully in place, he makes his way to the side door to meet the party patrol for a tour. Precisely because of this responsibility, the president never drinks during parties. He must be cool, calm, and stone sober to answer the university official's questions and lead him through the house. Of course, alumni attorneys also keep house leadership well versed in their rights and prepared for any question.

"Dry event? Yes, here's the fruit punch we're serving tonight. Too many people? No, here's the door counter showing 302 in attendance." (Of course, the counter is permanently set to 302 to hide the fact that anywhere from six hundred to twelve hundred people are packed into the house during a typical party.)

Over the course of a semester, the house practices shutdown drills twenty or thirty times. The results vary: members hosted one party without a single shutdown and another where there were seven or eight. It's just a cost of doing business. "You won't be able to draw enough people into your house at this university with dry events," said a former chapter president, "because every other house is having wet events."

The account reminded me of descriptions I'd read of drinking during Prohibition, the period between 1920 and 1933 when alcohol was illegal for all Americans, regardless of age. Indeed, according to Paula Fass, a professor of history at Berkeley, the similarities between college life in the 1920s and today are uncanny.

In the beginning of the Roaring Twenties, wrote Fass, "Drunkenness was considered obnoxious and ungentlemanly. By the end of the decade, it was a declaration of independence." For a college student to be seen drunk in public was a sign of membership in an elite peer group and an act of rebellion. Prohibition, according to Fass, "exacerbated the affectation of drunkenness, if for no other reason than that the young were forced to substitute whiskey for beer, and when liquor was available, the tendency was to drink more of it." Women, who rarely drank in the decade before, drank almost as much as the men in the twenties. "This new drinking spirit was peer-sanctioned, and drinking was, in general, most prevalent in the fraternities where peer pressure was most intense."

One of the more compelling arguments for repealing the Eighteenth Amendment was that Prohibition had only exacerbated drinking, particularly among the young. A 1926 poll of twenty-five hundred Yale students revealed that by a margin of four to one they believed that Prohibition had increased rather than decreased the amount of drinking at school.

Generally speaking, most of the scholarship devoted to alcohol and its effects on people concentrates on the medical and public health aspects, not on the sociological impact. There are only a handful of scholars who have pursued the question of whether age-specific prohibition might have the same effect that full Prohibition did in the 1920s. In addition to Dwight Heath at Brown are recently retired sociologist David Hanson of the State University of New York at Potsdam and Dr. Ruth Engs, a professor of sociology at Indiana University.

Engs has written extensively on the subject and maintains a Web site (www.indiana.edu/~engs/). Like her colleagues, she has refused financial support from nonacademic sources, particularly the alcoholic beverage industry. "My research," she told me, "is not sponsored by anyone except IU." She believes the United States is in the midst of its third "clean living movement" since the Revolution in which forces within society pursue campaigns to curb bad habits like drinking and smoking. The first was between 1830 and 1860; the second ran from about 1890 until 1920. The most recent began in the 1970s and like its predecessor movements was motivated by excesses and public displays of moral turpitude—the whole sixties/seventies sex, drugs, and rock 'n' roll scene perpetrated by none other than the parents of today's college students.

"The contemporary 'movement' is not an organized whole," wrote Engs. "It is a sum of various single-issue topics associated with community and national groups. Many, but not all, have as their agenda legislative limitation of individual choice in various health and lifestyle issues. Examples include Right to Life, which advocates legislation to eliminate choice concerning pregnancy termination, Citizens Against Tobacco, which lobbied for federal legislation to ban smoking on virtually all domestic airline flights, and Concerned Parents for Children's Education, which advocates abolishment of all sexuality, alcohol, and drug education in local schools." It also includes MADD, Henry Wechsler, Joe Califano, and a handful of private groups, in particular the Robert Wood Johnson Foundation, which has contributed hundreds of millions of dollars over the past two decades, largely toward organizations and research that promote healthy ideals.

No one I know seriously advocates bad health practices, including excessive drinking. And the modern clean living movement deserves enormous credit for making Americans more aware of the dangers of eating rich foods, smoking, and driving under the influence of drugs or alcohol. Whether the movement has led American society or simply reflected a general societal trend toward healthiness, the positive results are the same: among adults, per capital alcohol consumption has been declining and more people have switched from hard liquor to wine and beer. Generally, life expectancy in the United States has risen significantly over the past three decades.

But in their take-no-prisoners approach to the issue, the members of the clean living movement seem determined to ignore the possibility of the unintended collateral consequences of their efforts to limit individual choice.

If nothing else convinced me of the counterproductive effects of American drinking laws on college life, my experience at McGill University in Montreal did. On a warm night in late August 2003, I walked down the hill from McGill's first-year residence cluster with Flo Tracy, the university's veteran director of housing. We were on our way to a welcome-back dinner for the seventy-some resident fellows, undergraduate floor assistants called RAs in most American schools, who were about to commence their week's worth of intensive training on how to handle whatever would come up when some four thousand eighteen- and nineteen-year-olds descended upon the Montreal campus in a little over a week's time.

Flo was running down the list of issues that student life administrators like her deal with in college these days: the increasing indications of stress among students, the growing number of visits to the health clinic for psychological services, a slight increase in the use of soft drugs—marijuana, hashish, " 'shrooms"—by undergrads, roommate problems . . . the usual stuff. Sure, there were occasional problems with alcohol, but nothing compared to what she had heard was going on in the States.

Most of these fellows were still eighteen and nineteen themselves, having been recruited as freshmen to stay on in campus housing to oversee the next wave of newcomers. And there they were, seated at a dozen or so long tables at an outdoor bistro, waiting for Flo, whom they greeted warmly when we walked onto the patio. Every table had carafes of wine and pitchers of beer, and while Flo (who was picking up the tab) kept a watchful eye over the frequency of their orders, the students were free to refill as they saw fit.

By eight-thirty P.M., after Steve, an American from Marble-head, Massachusetts, successfully challenged Flo to down a glass of beer for the group, the dinner slowly began to break up. Some headed into Montreal to dance at clubs; others went back to campus. I found myself seated next to Liz, an American from Long Beach, Long Island, who told me she had ended up at McGill after being turned down by a couple of Ivy League schools. Uninterested in any of her safeties, she came north and had no regrets.

Liz asked me what I thought of the evening's event. I told her the first thing that came to my mind was what happened that evening in Montreal simply couldn't happen at an American school; the law wouldn't allow it. Liz smiled and told me how when she goes home to New York, she refuses to do the usual scam, which is to get a fake ID and drink as much as possible to flout the system.

I asked her what she thought would happen if the United States went to an eighteen- or nineteen-year age limit as the Canadians had. She thought for a while and said that she feared American kids would go crazy for a while and that it would take maybe six or seven years before they settled into a normal relationship with alcohol—"where Canadians are now."

Later in the week, I asked if McGill kept statistics on hospitalizations for alcohol overdoses—a measure I had found useful in my research. It did. Compared to Dartmouth's average of two hundred a year and Middlebury's one hundred, McGill, with an undergraduate population of about twenty thousand, had twelve transports the year before.

If a major Canadian university can marginalize high-risk drinking to that extent with an eighteen-year-old age limit, surely Americans can.

12

Who's in Charge?

A baker's dozen of Dartmouth undergraduates trickled into the first-floor lounge of Fayerweather Hall on a Monday evening in May for a meeting. As they came through the door, Kiera Kant, one of eight Dartmouth community directors (CDs) working under the Office of the Dean of Students, handed each of them a manila folder and invited them to choose a couple of coloring devices from a basket of crayons and markers.

The purpose of the meeting was to begin planning for the following fall, when these thirteen students would return under Kiera's watchful eye as undergraduate advisors, or UGAs, Dartmouth's term for residential advisors (RAs). These peer proctors are the front line of the multilayered support system colleges have established to manage the vicissitudes and challenges of modern campus life. At most institutions, the Res Life professionals to whom these student advisors report tend to view them more as agents than as colleagues. Student affairs professionals these days typically hold master's degrees in higher education specializing in one of three areas: counseling, administration, or student development, which espouses the holistic approach most administrations take to education beyond the classroom.

Several of the UGAs were still in their first year and would just be sophomores in the fall when they would take responsibility for about thirty fellow students, some of whom would be senior to them in age and class rank. More than a hundred UGAs in all would return to Dartmouth in mid-August for a week of intensive training before the new first-years arrived.

After everyone was seated, Kiera asked them to put their name at the top of the manila folder and then to draw a picture on the jacket—something about themselves that she would ask them to explain later. The students showed neither surprise nor enthusiasm for the art assignment. It was just another icebreaker, a standard student affairs technique at virtually every college and university. Icebreakers are used to break down shyness and to foster interpersonal connectedness. One person might draw a lakeside scene, for example, and under Kiera's subsequent coaxing would explain to the group that she was looking forward to being a camp counselor in the summer just ahead. Another might draw a mountain slope, indicating that he was a member of the varsity ski team. Kiera would follow up by asking everyone to describe a high and a low moment they had had in the last two weeks. The object was to get them to open up to their peers and to her. There is no room for reticence as a Dartmouth UGA.

Community directors, variously called area coordinators or residential directors at other colleges, are entry-level student affairs professionals. They usually live in student residence halls and act as the adult advisor to the undergraduate advisors. They are also local judges in small internal residential disputes as well as on-the-ground agents for the student affairs hierarchy of the college. If she were promoted from within, Kiera's next job might be as assistant director of residential life, overseeing CDs and reporting to the director of residential life. Or she might become a dean for one of the specialty groups on campus—Greeks or gays, for example. All eventually report to the dean of the college, Jim Larimore, who reports to the provost, the university's chief operating officer, a level below that of president. It is a chain of command entirely separate from the teaching faculty as well as from athletics, admissions, development, or any of the other collateral functions at Dartmouth.

Only a few years older than her charges, with eyes that crinkled from a lot of smiling, Kiera clearly loved to be around students. She had been an RA herself at Gettysburg College in Pennsylvania, from which she received her BA in 1995. She went on to get her master's degree in education at the University of Virginia, concentrating in counseling. Like most student affairs professionals, she so loved campus life that she didn't want to leave it.

Kiera may spend the rest of her career at Dartmouth. But young student affairs professionals tend to move around a lot. While that mobility gives them breadth as practitioners, it does not foster much loyalty to any single institution. Over the course of a career, their association with an institution is likely to be less important than their relations with other Res Life colleagues who are fellow members of NASPA, the National Association of Student Personnel Administrators. With NASPA's professional guidance, Kiera might end up as a dean of students or even a vice president of student affairs someplace. That is what she aspires to be.

Working out of a two-room apartment on the ground floor of Ripley Hall and a small office in Fayerweather Hall next door, Kiera spent much of her time running from one meeting to the next. On Mondays, she would meet with the entire UGA staff as a group and listen for patterns that might indicate a larger behavioral trend—signs of discord, rumors of drug use, whatever might threaten the peace and harmony of the cluster. Monday was also the day for the weekend round-up report from Safety & Security, Dartmouth's campus police force. If one of her charges were cited in a report for a drinking violation, vandalism, or any other transgression, Kiera would get a full report and ask to see the student personally. If alcohol was involved, she would ask the offending student, "What kind of an effect does this have on your community?"

Tuesday mornings, often over coffee in downtown Hanover, she met with her immediate supervisor, the assistant residential life director. She checked in daily with the central office in Parkhurst Hall, where she had frequent staff meetings with her superiors. Once every other week, she met individually for an hour with each of her thirteen UGAs. These sessions offered them each a chance to unload whatever issues they were having with their charges, to report on who seemed to be having or developing problems. Kiera wanted to know who might not be getting along with others or who was inclined to party too much—any behavioral patterns that warranted further scrutiny or intervention. "It could be routine," Kiera explained to me, "or it could be a crisis—like the woman in Fayerweather this week who thinks she was given a roofie." Crises were rare. More often, she dealt with the personal problems of her UGAs and helped them to plan activities.

Matt Nicholson, class of 2005, was one of Kiera's returning UGAs for the fall. As a sophomore, he had been responsible for thirty-some students, most of whom were at least a year older than he was. But Matt was physically big, a recruited lacrosse player from Maryland, with the self-assurance and poise to handle most situations. To fulfill his programming obligations, Matt would typically rent a thought-provoking film, like *American History X* or *Philadelphia*, get some pizza, and invite his hall mates to talk about the movie afterward. He had two quads of senior women on either side of his room. At Kiera's suggestion, he got them to talk to the sophomores and juniors on the hall about how to go about researching and writing a thesis. The routine was different, I was assured, for UGAs who oversee a hall full of first-years. Their programming typically focused on practical matters like how to use the library. Matt admitted that his required biweekly sessions with Kiera "can be a pain if you're pressed for time." But he had learned to enjoy them. "It's an opportunity to vent."

During her UGA planning session, Kiera asked her charges if they knew what her role was as a community director. The evening before, I had been with a group of first- and second-year students. After a community director had left the room, one of the students confided: "We have all these residential life people. I mean, who are they? I don't know them. They don't know me. What do they do?" Clementine James, who spent three years living in Dartmouth dorms before moving to an off-campus apartment with friends, told me that in all those years, "I have met only one of my community directors. That was when my family was visiting and the CD informed me that the family dog was not allowed in the dormitory. Other than that, I don't feel as though they had any presence whatsoever for me."

So I was interested in hearing whether these UGAs, the people who work directly for community directors, had an idea what CDs did. There was a brief, uncomfortable silence before someone ventured an answer to Kiera's question:

"Not really."

But then Kevin, a veteran advisor from the current year, came to the rescue: "CDs are here to support us," he stated. "They listen to the problems of UGAs, who listen to the problem of the residents." Cat, another resident advisor, added: "They provide a sense of continuity within the cluster. . . . It's nice to know that you're always backed up."

Kiera had a more modest view of her own role: "The students are driving their own experiences," she explained to me later. "I'm just the guard rail."

Modern Res Life people are good at what they do. They have been significant sources for many of the assessments and comparisons I have made about contemporary campus life. After all, part of their job is to measure the mood on campus, to understand the patterns of behavior, to recognize who is at risk of having a breakdown or drinking himself or herself to death. But as I traveled from campus to campus, I began to wonder whether they had gotten to be such good guard rails for students that they were unwittingly preventing their charges from learning how to drive.

To be sure, for fragile first-years, community directors by whatever name they're called can be lifelines. After that, their usefulness to most undergraduates declines rapidly. By the time they were juniors and seniors, most of the college students I met had grown pretty cynical about their presence. Alexa Hansen, no slouch as class president when it came to community building and name recall, told me that she had overheard a new community director ask one of his UGAs, "Have you memorized their birthdays yet?"

"There's just too much control," complained Alexa. "But people pretty much ignore it." With a mildly conspiratorial wink she added, "You receive a lot of nurturing at Dartmouth."

Student affairs professionals believe deeply that constant vigilance is not only helpful to the cause of higher education but also vital. They see their educational role as no less important than that of teaching faculty. Mike Lord, one of Kiera's community director colleagues, told me that when he tells people that he works at Dartmouth, they often ask whether he teaches. His response: "I say, 'Oh, in a different way.'"

Do today's undergraduates really need that much attention? One student affairs specialist at Duke conceded that they spend 90 percent of their time on 20 percent of the students. But some contend the Res Life culture is now so deeply entrenched that pulling the plug on the level of services provided and expected would be socially chaotic and perhaps both legally and competitively suicidal. "For all their struggles to gain freedom over the years," said Dartmouth's emeritus president James Freedman, "young people today still yearn enormously to be taken care of. Ignoring them gets them angry."

Res Life people play many roles. With titles like orientation director, student activities technology coordinator, and alcohol education director, they are the den mothers, advisors, impresarios, booking agents, counselors, prosecutors, and cheerleaders; they are the ubiquitous adult face of residential college life today. Coed housing aside, their ascendance as a dominating force in campus life constitutes the greatest single change I found from the time I was in college. During my stay at Hamilton, I met with the student affairs staff—twenty six people in all—whose jobs ranged from the dean of students to counseling services to campus safety. For a student body of less than seventeen hundred, Hamilton's wasn't a particularly big contingent by today's standards. But as I remarked to the assembled staffers, when I was a student all the tasks performed by the group before me that afternoon were done by just three people.

Quite understandably, coming from a member of the board of trustees, that observation was not happily received. It did, however, spark a lively discussion about the changing nature of Res Life: coed housing, the growing demand for psychological services and career advice, and the heightened risk of liability in an increasingly litigious society. The group argued in defense of its expanded numbers that Americans had come to expect a lot from their colleges and universities and it was the college's job to meet those expectations. There was another reason for this expanding influence over the years, pointed out a dean: "The absence of faculty in students' daily lives," she said, "is a real factor."

As broadly encompassing as I had found their roles on individual campuses, I did not truly begin to appreciate the scope of the student affairs professionals until I saw staff members together at conventions. Like most conventions, each of three such events I attended had its share of orchestrated gatherings with speeches and awards over lunch or dinner. But the real action was in scores of workshops devoted to the multivaried concerns of the profession. There were sessions on best practices and latest tactics to support the campus's LGBT community or racial/ethnic groups, on how to keep athletes in line, on sexual assault, on the Federal Educational Right to Privacy Act (FERPA) and its many interpretations, on career planning for junior student affairs personnel, on Greek issues, and so on. At NASPA's national meeting in Denver, I visited workshops on subjects ranging from "helicopter" parents (so called because they constantly hover over their child's college experience) to how to understand the language of instant messaging, and even one titled Love Gone Wrong: Management of Obsessive Relationships, a lively discussion of stalking.

At a regional convention in New York, I dropped in on a session entitled Your First Position in Student Affairs, presented by residential life staffers from St. John's University's Staten Island campus. Before I was seated, I was handed a piece of hard candy wrapped in cellophane. "Everyone has to take a candy," said Rosa Rizzo, an assistant dean at St. John's. "As student affairs people, we have to do icebreakers." This one was relatively simple: as a green candy holder, I had to tell the group what I hoped to get out of the meeting.

At another session, Will & Grace: The College Years, two young New York University Res Life staffers proffered a plan for mixed-gender housing that effectively allowed anyone of any sexual orientation to live with anyone else. Here too we used interactive listening techniques. I got to play a lesbian who was rooming with a gay man, played by Angelo, who was seated next to me. Asked to discuss first with each other and then with the whole group which rooming issues might divide us and which might bring us together, Angelo and I decided that because we were not a threat to one another and shared the common bond of belonging to a minority group, we could make our rooming situation work.

The national convention in Colorado, attended by thirty-five hundred men and women from all levels of the student affairs hierarchy, even more fully illustrated the scope of this huge industry within American higher education. On the lower level of the convention hotel, several acres were devoted to commercial displays by the businesses that sell to Residential Life: giant food services such as Aramark and Chartwells, whose representatives handed out free samples of their latest dining hall offerings; manufacturers of dormitory security systems and furniture; and one-person consulting firms hawking the latest theories on alcohol abuse prevention training or leadership development. One publishing house had a large booth featuring the latest titles on student affairs.

In another wing of the hotel were vast hiring halls where colleges from all over the United States had set up interview sites. In a sea of tables draped with the variously colored banners of small midwestern colleges and big state universities, I found Kiera Kant and Mike Lord looking to hire the next wave of Dartmouth community directors, as the two of them were about to be promoted to newly created associate supervisory positions.

Like any other culture, the Res Life profession tends to its own survival. At a roundtable discussion in Denver, I got a sense of their priorities: how to beat the deepening budget cuts, particularly at state schools; how to retain authority amid a growing movement toward merging student affairs with academic affairs, with the academic folks coming out on top; and how to fend off the scourge of well-financed right-wing provocateurs like David Horowitz and his Academic Bill of Rights campaign to remove liberal bias from the classroom. Many student affairs administrators view the political right as a threat to their way of life. If Horowitz and organizations like FIRE (Foundation for Individual Rights in Education) continued to make inroads, predicted one dean, "It could get ugly."

There was a lot of talk about parents at these conventions. Everywhere I went, Res Life administrators told stories about them: the mother of a Berkeley freshman who threatened to maintain a sit-in in the housing director's office until her daughter's roommate conflict was resolved, the Indiana mother who threatened to withdraw her daughter from college unless her upper bunk bed was lowered to the floor. Many parents don't bother complaining to administrators at the Res Life level—they go to the top. Presidents, chancellors, and deans of students are constantly called by parents whose children have gotten C's on tests when in their view they clearly deserved A's, parents whose son or daughter didn't make the varsity team or the chorus or who ran afoul of rules and regulations. Bruce Poch, admissions director at Pomona, remarked that *in loco parentis* is not a dead concept.

It has merely been retranslated and now means *The parents are still here.*

"One of the things that's very, very different from the college I knew," said Harry Lewis, Harvard class of 1968 and dean of the college until 2003, "is the level of expectation by students and their families that we would be structuring the social life of students." Richard Fass, dean of students at Pomona from 1973 until 1990, observed that in the 1970s, "Parents were absent from the picture. It was mutually agreed upon. But parents have come back with a vengeance." Once Americans reconceived college education as a consumer item, they began to demand high standards of performance and delivery.

When I arrived on Duke University's campus some five months after visiting Dartmouth, I found a Res Life system evolving in a direction remarkably similar to what I had seen in New Hampshire. The main difference was that Duke's Res Life staff under vice president for student affairs Larry Moneta had managed to avoid most of the publicity and subsequent suspicion and rancor that accompanied Dartmouth's student life initiative (SLI). No one at Duke ever threatened to close down an athletic team, and few spoke openly about the future of the Greek system.

Until 2002, fraternities occupied most of the original West Campus quads that opened onto the main lawn, Duke's central and signature piece of real estate. Then the administration broke up the Greek housing monopoly, redistributed the quads to non-affiliated students or to other non-Greek selective living groups (SLGs), and established separate governing bodies for each. The quad concept was exported to the two other Duke campuses: the East Campus, now home to all first-year students, and Central, which comprises apartment complexes occupied mostly by upperclassmen and some graduate students.

When the fraternities controlled prime West Campus real estate, their member-funded parties were the most visible form of social life at Duke. The creation of quad governments and the removal of fraternities from prime housing effectively shifted control of social life at Duke from the financially independent Greeks to the quad governments, whose finances came through student activities fees. The quad governments, each representing four hundred fifty to five hundred students, in turn were represented on a new Campus Council, which along with the existing Duke Student Government (DSG) became the distributor of activities funds for the entire campus and the ostensible arbiter of social life.

It was into this new configuration that junior Anthony Vitarelli stepped in the fall of 2003. An honors student from the New Jersey suburbs of Philadelphia, double majoring in public policy and economics and winner of a prestigious Truman scholarship, Anthony is a born leader. As we went through the food line at the Great Hall on the evening I first met him, he exchanged familiar greetings with dozens of other students, often with substantive comments about one issue or another that was percolating on the Duke campus. Over dinner, he explained to me the complexities of student government: the powerful but "remarkably bureaucratic" DSG and its links to the administration, the money—more than half a million dollars—which he as recently elected president of the Campus Council along with the DSG got to divvy up; and the subtle but effective control the university maintained over the events he and his fellow students allegedly controlled. When I remarked on the complexity and scope of student government, he put down his knife and fork and pronounced, "Student leaders are only as powerful as the administration allows us to be."

Watching Vitarelli preside over the biweekly session of the Campus Council later that evening, I came to see what he meant. After Deb LoBiondo, one of two Res Life staffers who regularly attended the council's meetings, reported on the previous weekend's alcohol violations, one of which shut down a council-funded quad party, Anthony and a dozen or so other undergrads got down to business, which essentially was spending other people's money. For almost two hours, members exchanged views on whether to sponsor more trivia nights to which faculty were invited, more movie screenings, an international food night, or dance instruction. There was talk of an academically based scavenger hunt in which clues would be derived from popular course subjects. There were a few nonentertainment topics, including Vitarelli's motion to rename the recently completed West Eden's Link quad after university president Nan Keohane, who would retire at the end of the year. But mostly they talked about programming.

In Res Life parlance, programming refers to an organized entertainment event that in its purest form has some discernible pedagogical link. In students' hands, that link can be tenuous. In 2004, the West Eden's Link council attracted several hundred to a ninety-minute program featuring a talk by two experts on female orgasm. The only expense was for the complimentary pizza and soft drinks. Residents of Few Quad threw a very clever Lack of Talent Show (mediocre slam poetry, guitar playing, karaoke, etc.), and a multicultural SLG event funded by the council featured dancers and vocalists performing African, Asian, and Latin acts. As with the orgasm experts, most of the talent at these events came from within the Duke community and therefore was at no charge, so virtually all the money allocated went toward consumables—pizza, ice cream, tacos, soft drinks, and more pizza.

Campus Council steers money to small functions like these but also produces campus-wide events. The last day of classes is always a great excuse for a party. For 2004, Vitarelli's Campus Council pumped in $58,000, of which $30,000 went toward booking the rising rap star Kanye West. There was plenty of food provided by Blue Devil Concessions, the official Duke snack vendor, and students of age could buy beer using their Duke dining debit cards. The council also asked for and got a video center and game room in the tower of West Eden's Link when it was still in the design stage. A year later, it engineered a cable TV package for dorm rooms at a cost of $100 per student per year beginning in the fall of 2005.

Student government has had some influence over university policy. At Vitarelli's initiative, the DSG persuaded Duke to agree to use nationally standardized green technologies and energy efficiencies in all its new construction. But most such initiatives deal with minor matters: adjusting the quiet rules for Central Campus residents, getting the Duke Parking and Transportation Office to e-mail students whose cars it tickets, or extending dorm cleaning services to include Sundays. When it comes to serious matters, Moneta and his professional staff accept or reject student government initiatives depending on whether the students' interests coincide with those of the administration.

A case in point occurred when Campus Council passed a resolution revamping the annual review process by which fraternities and sororities are evaluated. Instituted only a few years earlier, the annual review tied recognition of SLGs to a yearly demonstration of their good citizenship in seven categories, ranging from an acceptable disciplinary record to indications of support for such goals as campus diversity and community service. Its proponents contended that the review encouraged these organizations to live up to their own often idealistic charters. But many Greeks saw it as a joke—a tedious process of checking off a list of do-good activities, like eating dinner one night with members of a black sorority as a way of knocking off the diversity requirement, or inviting a professor over for the requisite display of faculty interaction.

Because so many of his fellow students saw the review process as flawed, Vitarelli, himself a fraternity member, and his colleagues devoted a good deal of time to reformulating it. In response to their resolution, the administration simply suspended annual review altogether unilaterally and indefinitely. Students who had once been dismissive of the review as an artificial burden on Greek organizations now grew suspicious that its suspension would remove the one mechanism fraternities had to show they were more than party machines. They reckoned the move was a calculated if subtle step in the direction of eliminating the Greek system at Duke.

Two months after they asked for a clarification and one day after the year's last issue of the student newspaper, the *Chronicle*, came out, Duke's director of housing sent the council a three-page single-spaced letter explaining the philosophy of the quad system. As for the annual review, the letter said, "The process for evaluating selectives (e.g., fraternities) . . . will be replaced as we continue to consider the importance of selectives to students and their relationship to the quad model."

The Res Life presence at Duke was as visible and purposeful as at any campus I visited. For several years, Duke has had safety squads known as A-teams, drawn from a pool of some twenty-five student affairs professionals, health services staffers, and trained student volunteers who fan out on party nights with walkie-talkies to keep a lid on the evening's excesses and tend to the wounded. While changes in housing had been under way before he arrived from Penn in 2001, Moneta accelerated reform and used it as an opportunity to build staff. He hired a crew of residential coordinators much like Dartmouth's community directors to oversee each of the new quads. As at Dartmouth, students reacted with a blend of suspicion and bemusement. When I asked Joost Borland, a sophomore from the Netherlands, how he would describe the role of the new residential coordinators, he smiled wryly. "How do I put this civilly?" he began. "They're there to create a more livable, more entertaining life."

As did his counterpart Jim Larimore at Dartmouth, Moneta brought in more affinity deans as well as a new director of housing and residential life. The expansion did not go unnoticed. Will Willimon, Duke's folksy, often outspoken chaplain, remarked that his university's student affairs organization chart "looks like General Motors in the 1950s."

In one morning meeting with residential staff members, I interrupted a lengthy recitation of their plans for more student activities to ask what they thought might happen if they abandoned programming altogether and just let students fend for themselves. There was a pause as these professionals pondered this bit of libertarian-inspired heresy, until one ventured a prediction: Student life, she guessed, would become "more haphazard."

The differences in approach and control between Dartmouth and Duke and the other American colleges I visited were mostly a matter of degree. Few of the colleges I visited or even heard about allowed their student governments much real power. Middlebury's multilayered Student Government Association, consisting of a seventeen-member senate with a presidential cabinet and six standing committees covering every major aspect of campus life, merely passed nonbinding resolutions on to a separate body called the Community Council made up of other students but also faculty and staff. Erin Sullivan, a senior from Lake Forest, Illinois, said the legislative actions on the student side "carry no weight. Tons of bills are passed that are never followed up on." The Community Council, however, "is where the real action takes place," said Sullivan. Policy changes that really affect students' lives—for example, a recently enacted modification of the judicial process that allows students to work off up to three alcohol citations by taking an online alcohol program—come out of the Community Council with the requisite imprimatur of the administration.

Even at the University of Wisconsin, a school where students have historically wielded quite a bit of power, I didn't see much evidence of student government authority. I sat in on a meeting of the ASM (Association of Students at Madison) in which members spent the bulk of their time listening to their peers speak in support of a referendum to raise the minimum wage in the City of Madison to $7.75 an hour—an issue over which ASM had no direct control and one that would have at best a tertiary effect on student life. The next most significant block of time was given over to a series of lengthy breaks called by the chair because the body kept falling short of the sixteen members out of thirty-two needed to constitute a quorum. I was told such interruptions, triggered by members wandering in and out of the meeting, happened regularly.

Ineffective as they sound, the machinations of these student governing bodies are very time-consuming; the young men and women in leadership positions I spoke with were putting in hours and hours of work. Carey Mignery, head of U-VA's Honor Committee and a university guide, told me that he spent forty hours a week in these roles—"at a minimum; if I had a trial on a Saturday, it could be fifty-plus." Virginia Student Council president Daisy Lundy estimated that she was logging sixty hours a week at her job—"and I still have school," she added. When did she sleep, I asked. "I don't sleep," she said. "I spend time with friends and I do my homework on weekends."

Why would a smart young person take on a job that generated so few meaningful results? In part, because leadership is a centerpiece of the student affairs curriculum. Regardless of what they might learn in the classroom, students at our most selective colleges are taught to lead. Their ability to demonstrate leadership—whether by chairing their high school student council or getting elected captain of the field hockey team—was probably a significant factor in their admission to these schools in the first place. For many of them, mastery of physics or philosophy had become subordinate to the attainment of leadership skills and credentials long before they set foot on campus. Res Life administrators promote that. Some feel as U-VA's vice president of student affairs Pat Lampkin does that the need is almost remedial: "We absolutely want to have our students involved" in leadership roles, she told me. "But it is difficult with this generation because they've been so coached."

Now and again, the elements of real student power bubble to the surface. It takes an issue that means something to a significant number of students, not an external issue. Earlier generations got fired up about the Vietnam War or apartheid or women's rights. Today's galvanizing issues are almost always internal, like the loss of a swimming team, the firing of a popular coach, or another tightening of alcohol policy.

"If enough students make noise, they can get things done," Middlebury's Erin Sullivan maintained. She recounted the story of what students refer to as the lockdown of the college after an assault on a student back in the fall of 2000. No doubt in large part because of liability concerns, the administration slapped locks on residence halls. That got the entire student body up in arms, demanding a return to the open atmosphere in which anyone could wander in and out of the dorms. Their protests led to the creation of a committee including students, which eventually recommended the current security system using electronic swipe cards. It was a compromise—not quite at the level of reversing a free speech ban, as Mario Savio and radical students at Berkeley succeeded in doing in 1964—but I got the feeling listening to Erin that it was nonetheless heady stuff, a lot like Dartmouth students felt after their protests saved the swim team.

Constant attention to student needs by Res Life professionals keeps such triumphs to a minimum. Campus leaders often find themselves serving as fronts for the administration. Some are content with that; others aren't. Frustrated that her role as president of Hamilton's Student Assembly had devolved into what she saw as a series of PR assignments to sell administration policy decisions to her fellow students, Elizabeth Dolan complained, "There is very little incentive to take a leadership position other than resume building."

Anthony Vitarelli felt far better about his role at Duke: "When I graduate, I will have been Campus Council president for exactly half of my college career. I wouldn't have done it if I didn't feel I was helping to make this a better place. The frustrating moments are really outweighed by the fun. Even with the annual review, I don't look back on it as time wasted. The whole thing made us more influential on campus. And what a great learning process for us!"

As different as their assessments of their roles in respective student governments are, Dolan and Vitarelli share an appreciation for the role of Res Life professionals and the relative contributions of these nonacademic adults versus those of teachers on campus. "Student life people are phenomenal," said Dolan. "They are constantly working to make life better here. They show up at our games and plays, which faculty don't do much—I guess because that's not going to get them tenure."

"Student affairs people are great relationship builders," said Vitarelli. "By training, they're empathetic, caring, and good mentors. Rather than holding doctorates in economics or European history, these professionals have dedicated their lives to learning how to be better listeners and to improve student life. We hold them to that standard."

Sadly, students have come to expect less from their professors. If a student is fortunate enough to develop a personal relationship with a professor outside the classroom, he or she is likely to cherish it. "Students crave the attention of the faculty outside the classroom," said Elizabeth Dolan, whose father is on the faculty of the University of Richmond. Many other students I talked to recalled with enthusiasm a meal at a professor's home and the sense of privilege they felt from conversations about matters other than their classes. "When you encounter a professor who genuinely cares about nurturing a student's academic development, it's perceived as truly remarkable," said Vitarelli. "Likewise, if a professor is an engaging lecturer who illuminates lessons with relevant anecdotes of life experience and offers meaningful feedback on a student's work, we feel like we've arrived at an academic mecca."

They don't say those things about student affairs people, even the ones they lean on constantly. And student life people know it. "We're managers. We're administrators. We're not scholars," said Sue Wasiolek, Duke's veteran dean of students. "That's something only faculty can do—and that's missing."

That message has been delivered to the community of professors more than once, but to date it has largely fallen on deaf ears.

13

Improving the Undergraduate Experience

I n 1997, in what insiders call the "secret speech" to his board of trustees, Middlebury College president John McCardell outlined his vision of developing a Commons system at the college that would subdivide the student population into five housing and dining units where they would reside for all four years. While expensive—a new Commons built from scratch with all the envisioned elements including dining facilities had a price tag of $80,000 to $100,000 a bed—the plan would pay for itself in part by expanding the student body from nineteen hundred students to twenty-three hundred.

When word of the proposal began to spread around the campus, the initial assumption was that student life professionals—the ones used to dealing with domestic issues and skilled in handling personal crises—would manage these new entities. But McCardell envisioned something different: smaller communities each headed up by a faculty member—like a Harvard master—assisted by a dean who would look after personnel matters including discipline. The real value he saw in these Commons was their capacity to reconnect students and their teachers.

Not surprisingly, the initial resistance came from the faculty, most of whom were content to live quiet, scholarly, family-oriented lives in bucolic central Vermont. Also not surprisingly, some of the first volunteers to serve as heads of Commons were older professors who were willing to step back into student lives now that their own children were grown up and gone. Their willingness was appreciated, but McCardell wanted young faculty so that Middlebury students would be exposed not only to professors but also to their families—their personal lives. He knew it would be a tough sell because of the necessary sacrifice of privacy and because the added duties threatened to make it that much harder for young professors to meet the scholarly standards deemed essential to advancement.

His chief recruiter in this effort was Tim Spears, professor of American literature, associate provost, and a former college football player who was a product of residential college life at Yale's Branford College. Spears was also concerned by the growing separation of faculty and the subordination of teaching to all the other aspects of student life. "It used to be that the faculty *was* the academy," he said to me as we walked across the Middlebury campus. "Now it's no longer seamless. I view the Commons system as an opportunity for the faculty to take back the college. It should be our responsibility."

Two of his recruits were Steve Abbott, a math professor, and his wife, Katy Smith Abbott, who taught art history at the college. Spears considered recruiting the Abbotts as a real breakthrough in the governance of Commons. Steve Abbott had grown up on the campus of Davidson, another first-rate liberal arts college, had done his undergraduate work at Colgate, and was a product in almost every way of a tradition that placed faculty in close proximity to their students.

But he'd never experienced anything quite this close. A good ten years younger than previous faculty appointments as Commons heads, he and Katy were in their mid-thirties, had small children, and enjoyed their privacy. Even though the Middlebury model did not physically place faculty heads and their families in the Commons, they were provided housing very close by and were expected not only to spend a portion of their days in the Commons but also to host social events at their home to which students would be invited.

"To me it boiled down to this: I was teaching math using an MIT text and a Web site with clips of the author giving lectures," Steve Abbott told me as we sat in his office of the newly built Ross Commons. "What am I doing, I asked myself, that the students need? The answer for me was that it's all about the connections that you make. So few hours of a student's life are spent in the classroom—you can figure that out quickly enough. The people who end school the most mature are the ones who lead the least segregated lives. I contrasted this with my own experience. I was not an adult when I left college. I'm interested in setting aside a certain portion of my academic career because I find it is a critical link in what the college experience is supposed to be."

The additional responsibilities allowed the Abbotts to set aside one course a semester and all their faculty committee work. In exchange, they came in contact with segments of the Middlebury community who Steve admits he might otherwise not have known—students, staff, dining hall people. He said he has gained insights from his casual conversations with students into what works and doesn't work in the classroom, which he can then share with his faculty colleagues.

The Abbotts' tour as faculty heads of Ross was scheduled for three years, after which they would take stock and decide whether to finish out the five-year term, as Tim Spears hoped they would. The take on their performance after the first two years was that they had created an open and light interaction with students. "We're much more in the mode of camp counselors," Steve said, "the meet-students-at-their-own-level types."

That was the point. By chatting with students in the dining hall or over family-style dinners in their home, the Abbotts and other faculty heads were getting a multidimensional view of them as people.

Middlebury's Commons system was not designed to render the student affairs profession obsolete. Each Commons has a dean, and a central Res Life staff continues to manage campus-wide issues. Faculty heads have come to appreciate what the deans bring to Commons life. "Before this job, the extent of my contact with Residential Life was that I knew who to call among the five deans when there was a specific problem," confessed Steve Abbott. His role as a faculty head was teaching him to appreciate the expertise these professionals bring. "The deans really know their students."

Cynthia Atherton, a professor of art history and a faculty head of neighboring Wonnacott Commons, agreed. "I never really knew who the deans were," she confessed. "Prior to decentralizing, they were just out there and useful only when students were in trouble." Like the Abbotts, Atherton, her husband, and two children lived rent-free in a house about a quarter of a mile from Wonnacott. They regularly invited students over for meals and events. Initially reluctant to involve herself in students' personal issues, she gradually gained confidence, at one point summoning up the courage to tell a student who was hanging out all night, missing classes, and spending his time in the gym that he was wasting his time in college. It was tough, but it was the kind of message students told me they are likely to take far more seriously when it comes from a faculty member rather than from a student affairs staff member. "I wouldn't want this job to be a figurehead," Atherton insisted. "On the other hand, I wouldn't want this job if I were just another dean."

In an effort to spread contact beyond the chosen faculty heads, other Middlebury professors are assigned as affiliates of one or another of the five Commons. But if the administration is to reach its goal of reintegrating faculty and students outside the classroom, its going to have to prove that there is career value in doing so. Currently, the compensation for a faculty Commons head consists of a free home, a reduction in teaching load, and a discretionary budget of around $10,000. More than a few professors are waiting to see if the added work pays off in Commons heads' future promotion and compensation.

The Commons experiment at Middlebury will not solve all the problems of contemporary student life. And it's not necessarily right for every college or university. Without the integrated residential and dining complexes and, more importantly, the overt commitment to faculty/student engagement, Middlebury's isn't much different from the residential models at Duke and Dartmouth, campuses that have been subdivided respectively into Quads or Clusters instead of Commons.

Some students complained about the system's potential to limit their contacts in a student body that was still pretty small. "Getting stuck in one Commons for all four years can feel isolating," one senior told me. It's one thing at Harvard, which is nearly three times Middlebury's size. It's another at a small college in the hills of central Vermont.

The residential college concept has been gathering supporters both in North America and overseas. According to one of its chief supporters, Middlebury biology professor Robert J. O'Hara, who maintains a Web site (www.collegiateway.org), there were about four hundred practitioners worldwide in 2004. With Yale's dean of the college, Richard Broadhead, on his way to Duke, where he was to succeed president Nan Keohane, O'Hara was speculating that residential colleges might be in Duke's future.

In many respects, Duke was already moving that way. Larry Moneta's quad system (students call it "College-lite") incorporated the collegiate system's concept of unit self-governance. With fraternities no longer dominating the West Campus, Moneta claimed that students were beginning to identify themselves by quads. Duke also had some faculty in residence, but almost entirely on the East Campus, which was given over to first-year students. Moneta told me that he would love to move faculty into the West Campus quads but speculated that he would end up settling for a fellows program like the Middlebury model. "What I hope to do is hire a cross-section of student affairs professionals and academics," he told me.

It will take a concerted effort to convince three separate constituencies—students, student affairs professionals, and faculty—that if colleges are to deliver on their promises, their lives and roles must be integrated.

Large public universities, where many upperclass students live off-campus and bear a greater burden of self-sufficiency, face a different set of issues. With inevitably large lecture classes and the pull of graduate school, it is much more difficult for faculty to focus on undergraduates. Creating more Chadbourne Colleges and other residential models for first- and second-year students that foster closer ties to teaching faculty is the best answer.

The key to success in all these places lies largely with the faculty. Students' high regard and respect for their achievements and knowledge offer the potential to bridge the divide that separates academic life from social life on most campuses, imbuing faculty members with an influence beyond their role as classroom teachers. Students and professors getting to know each other better isn't going to stop dangerous drinking, drug use, or date rape. Nor will it reverse the rise in depression and general anxiety that reflect larger cultural traits. But it can serve to curtail abuses by keeping the focus of campus life on the fundamental purpose of college, which is to learn and to grow while learning. And it just might influence how students behave in their own world. "If students knew that their professors were going to sit in judgment of their Saturday night drunk fests," said higher education expert John Gardner, "they just might act differently."

I believe students would act differently and make the transition to adulthood faster if the law didn't actively prevent adults from helping them learn the limits of responsible drinking. I recognize that the odds are stacked heavily against politicians demonstrating the courage needed to undo bad law. The best I can suggest is that college presidents keep the campus conversation going about the dangers of alcohol abuse, that administrators concentrate their enforcement efforts on the bad behaviors that result from abusive drinking rather than the act of drinking itself, and that the faculty do its part by holding students to reasonable academic standards. As I recall, there's nothing quite like a paper due to a professor known as a tough grader who seldom grants extensions to put a damper on an incipient party.

"It takes kids four years to figure out that they didn't have any power," observed Larry Sabato, the U-VA political scientist and a popular professor among Virginia undergrads. It isn't just power they lack. Despite all the activities and time they have at their disposal, they lack freedom.

Most of the students I met didn't recognize that they weren't free. As far as they could tell, they were. They could stay up all night, have sex pretty much when they wanted, study as much or almost as little as they wanted, eat whenever they wanted, and take part in a wide range of activities that provided great entertainment.

Few recognized that all these ostensible acts of free will are taking place within carefully prescribed boundaries. One who did was David Weigel, Northwestern class of 2004, who discovered midway through college that the heady power exerted by students in his parents' generation had since been effectively co-opted. "*In loco parentis* has been rejuvenated and returned," Weigel pronounced in an essay eventually published in the libertarian magazine *Reason*. "Administrators have tapped into the devaluation of personal responsibility illustrated by smoking bans and fast food lawsuits, coupling it with bullish political correctness. The resulting dearth of individual liberties on campuses would have seemed impossible to college students of 25 years ago."

Tracing the evolution of what he labeled "the contemporary nanny university," Weigel alleged that a new breed of college administrator—ironically often men and women who came of age in the turbulent sixties—employed three tools to regain control of the campuses its own generation had "liberated" only a few decades earlier. "The first involved intoxicants, including the escalating war on drugs and the mid-'80s change in the drinking age from 18 to 21. The second was an attempt to stave off liability for student mental health problems by intervening with students who were seen as being at risk of breakdowns. The third and most well-known was a rigid enforcement of political correctness that set standards for just how rowdy students could get." Though slightly put off by the broad ideological sweep of his analysis, I thought Weigel had a point.

Writing to his fellow Duke students at the beginning of his senior year in 2004, Christopher Scoville articulated another unintended by-product of the undergraduate experience that top colleges like his have embellished over the past three decades. "In case it wasn't abundantly clear in the college view books you pored over," he wrote, "the 'undergraduate experience' is college-speak for the four years of extracurricular activities, roommates, university-sponsored arts and cultural events, partying, student fairs, athletics and, of course, academics. Well, actually, what is so 'of course' about academics anymore?"

Scoville concluded that traditional book learning had somehow become the less important piece of the collegiate puzzle. "For students who pour their hearts and souls into student groups, community service or dance troupes, sitting in class or writing a term paper is a welcome break from this appointment or that meeting," Scoville asserted. "The point of academics today: 'I need something to do when I'm not saving the world during my undergraduate experience.' Has the undergraduate experience evolved into this self-obsessed menace that places academics at the end of the list in its definition?"

Scoville and Weigel had some allies among their elders in academia. In the winter of 2003, the *Chronicle of Higher Education* ran a pair of articles under the rubric of "Our Coddled Students." One was a lament about the changing character of Kenyon College by P. F. Kluge, an alumnus and writer in residence at the Ohio liberal arts college, who had previously written a diary of his first year back on the campus entitled *Alma Mater*. Kluge juxtaposed the intellectually challenging Kenyon he remembered as a student with the "Kamp Kenyon" he saw when he returned a few decades later: an "institution that lets students get away with a lot, that coddles and gets conned. Kamp Kenyon deals with campus life and student problems: drugs, date rape, harassment, gender bias, dyslexia, dysfunction, angst, anger, homesickness, seasickness."

The enablers at Kamp Kenyon, Kluge wrote, came from the growing cadre of counselors, mediators, and advisors whose job is to see to students' every need. "These people are thoughtful and hard-working, and much of what they do has developed in response to real problems. Yet I wonder whether their initially useful presence does not signal the piecemeal mutation of Kenyon College, and other institutions, into a therapeutic kibbutz—ultimately compromising the purpose of a college education."

The accompanying piece by Harvard's noted faculty conservative, government professor Harvey Mansfield, took his fellow professors to task for their failure to challenge Harvard's brilliant students, who he declared with some justification are the best of any college in the United States. "What happens at Harvard sometimes presages, sometimes reflects, what happens at other colleges and universities," wrote Mansfield. "And today, what I see occurring on the campus signals the damage that may result when higher-education institutions compromise their virtue to minister to the self-esteem of students." Grade inflation, course evaluations, a hollow core curriculum that allows professors to "teach what they have chosen as their own research," in Mansfield's words, advances a culture of self-esteem that ultimately diminishes the value of a Harvard education.

As provocative as the articles were the responses from readers, many of whom are college professors themselves. There was hardly a hint of protest against the coddling charge. Instead, the paired opinion pieces stirred up a rash of resentful anecdotes about entitled, ignorant, underprepared students supported in their whining by administrators who have adopted a nonconfrontational, consumerist approach to higher education. They are at fault; students are at fault; the K–12 school system is at fault.

These rants and laments came mostly out of second- and third-tier colleges and universities that operate in the wake of top schools like the ones I visited. The rare exceptions to this finger-pointing came from people who taught at community or commuter colleges or other institutions where most students come from less privileged backgrounds, many of whom have to work for a living and see college as a way to better themselves, often at great personal cost. These were schools where students had neither the time nor the inclination to indulge in binge drinking or crafting cocurricular entertainment packages. These were schools whose students tended to be older—students who were in college because they needed not just a credential but also a no-nonsense skill, whether it was accounting or code-writing or clinical training. Had I chosen twelve of these colleges, I doubt I would have found many of the behaviors so common to the classic residential campuses I have represented in this book.

The trouble is, our best and brightest students don't aspire to go to commuter schools. They strive to enroll in the most prestigious and selective institutions they can get into and afford. If we can change them, we will have changed the model, and North American society as a whole will be the better for it.

Many counselors and professors with whom I met on campuses spoke of a widespread, inchoate sense among today's students that the world under their feet is shaky. As Harvard senior tutor Rena Fonseca said about the *uber*-achieving undergraduates over whom she kept watch, "On the one hand they want independence, freedom of action. On the other, they want someone to hold their hand and keep them from falling. There's a level of hand-holding students need now that they didn't need ten years ago. . . . These children are much more worldly, much more savvy in terms of knowing how to produce a résumé or how to do career networking. But they seem to me to have less perspective. The resilience isn't there."

No doubt, Columbine, the disputed 2000 presidential election, and especially 9/11 have contributed to this angst. We who came of age in the sixties and seventies had our own milestones of insecurity: John F. Kennedy's assassination and those of his brother Bobby and Martin Luther King Jr., the race riots of 1967–1968, the 1973 Arab oil embargo, and the running threat of nuclear annihilation. My generation's response, however inept it might have been, was to try to change that world. Today's students seem to want simply to survive theirs.

Assertions of childhood insecurity will come as no surprise to anyone who has read from the library of self-help parenting books that were snapped up by anxious boomer parents in the 1990s, which is when today's college students were coming of age. The titles alone—*Parenting 911*; *Parents under Siege: Why You Are Not the Problem in Your Child's Life*; *The Second Family: Dealing with Peer Power, Pop Culture, the Wall of Silence—and Other Challenges of Raising Today's Teens*; *Another Planet: A Year in the Life of a Suburban High School*—limned a portrait of American family life as a running series of eating disorders, depression, sexual promiscuity, and drug use among kids while clueless moms and dads, too distracted by their own ambitions to devote time to everyday family rituals, delegated these responsibilities to surrogates—nannies, day care workers, school psychologists, and somebody else's dad as soccer coach. Because these kids were shunted off to the care of "professional kid wranglers who were paid to teach, encourage, amuse or monitor them," they had too little opportunity to develop a meaningful relationship with any adult. And so they turned to the one constant they had: their peers.

According to these books, comfort is this generation's end goal—one most efficiently reached by avoiding confrontation. Afraid of anything that will further alienate them from their children, parents silently conspire by withholding judgments and by refusing to exert their own values. Children pick up on it. In the suburban high school that is the setting for *Another Planet,* parents obsessed with their children's academic success feel no compunction about bullying teachers into raising their kids' mediocre grades. Questioning his profession's obsession with adolescent self-esteem, one teacher asked, "If you never let anybody fail, how can they not be afraid of failure?"

There is a link between this tableau of dysfunctional family life and the overprotective nature of the Res Life structure that awaits this handed-off generation in college. Still unnerved by the near-anarchy of earlier, more active generations and bruised by the barrage of lawsuits filed by the families of young people who tripped up in the process of growing up, administrators have been operating from a defensive posture for more than a decade. The court-enforced duty to protect students from harm has fostered an elaborate prophylactic bureaucracy made up of specialists who monitor, counsel, cajole, and distract young people who are in all respects but one already legally adults. But in doing so, they are not helping students to slip the bonds of adolescence; they are prolonging it. "It's okay to help them grow up," physics professor Larry Evans said he once told Duke's recently retired president, Nan Keohane, "but don't prevent them from growing up."

Most administrators don't want to take that risk. Instead, they are counting on a change in the character of the young men and women headed their way: the Millennials. Demographers Neil Howe and William Strauss, codifiers of generational cohorts (the G.I., dubbed the Greatest Generation; the Silent Generation that came of age in the fifties; the Baby Boomers; followed by Generation X), have recently profiled this latest cohort, formerly known as Gen Y. These are the kids born in the Reagan years who came of age during the Clinton administration and who began to populate our residential colleges around 2001.

Unlike the milquetoast conformists of the Silent Generation, the narcissistic, rebellious Boomers, or the angry, abandoned, latchkey Gen Xers, the Howe and Strauss Millennials promise greatness—maybe even greatness greater than that of the Greatest Generation. The researchers attribute seven core traits to them: "special, sheltered, confident, team-oriented, conventional, pressured and achieving." The products of hovering, nurturing, protective parents, this generation will be a conforming, risk-averse bunch, respectful of authority yet demanding that it deliver on its promises. Having lived highly structured lives, Millennials will readily obey instructions and toe the line, but cheerfully and productively so, engaging in community service, embracing difference, shunning drugs and alcohol. Beginning with the first batch, born around 1982 (the graduating college class of 2004), some 80 to 100 million of them will span a twenty-year period in which they will redress many of the ills that had befallen campuses during the raucous years of the Boomer reign and the desultory age of Gen X negativists.

Howe and Strauss concede that Millennials might be more emotionally fragile and demanding of attention to their stress-induced psychological needs, less interested in the act of learning than in the results, more brand conscious, and more likely to use crude language. But all in all, they averred, colleges could expect for the first two decades of the twenty-first century a more malleable and fun-to-be-with crop of kids than anything they'd seen in decades.

I certainly met students who came close to matching this promising profile. Their virtues and achievements were reflected in the observations of the deans and professors who dealt with them every day. Many of them displayed boundless energy, logging in hours in student government jobs or newspaper editing or hockey practice or community service yet still finding time to party and (somehow) get their class work done. But I also met ones who had mutilated themselves, been date raped, hospitalized for alcohol poisoning, or caught cheating. In the end, I could not share the deanly hope that society was in the process of delivering a new, low-maintenance cohort of students.

A more plausible portrait emerges from surveys done by the Cooperative Institutional Research Program (CIRP), run out of UCLA. Since 1966, CIRP has been asking a battery of questions of more than 275,000 students at over four hundred colleges and universities, including many of those I visited.

Over that long period, CIRP has captured several interesting trends and the subsequent reversal of some of those trends. It has tracked three decades of progressive disengagement from political activism as well as from substantive academics. Students don't get involved and they don't study as much as they did in the 1960s or in the 1970s or 1980s. And yet their record of doing well in high school has improved and their expectations of doing well in college are higher than ever.

Their values appear to have shifted dramatically over time as well. The first CIRP survey in 1966 showed that "developing a meaningful philosophy of life" was the number-one priority for more than 80 percent of freshmen, while "being well off financially" was way down the list, less than 45 percent seeing it as a very important or essential life goal. Since then, those priorities have flipped: by 2001, financial well-being had become the top priority, at nearly 74 percent. Over the next two surveys, the importance of raising a family overtook financial security, which finished a close second and still at another record-high percentage, while the old "philosophy of life" business slipped to an all-time low of under 40 percent.

The best I could ascertain is that this first batch of real Millennials, those who have recently graduated from college, went there expecting good grades but were not planning to work very hard to get them and apparently didn't much care what they learned as long as it got them a job that would comfortably finance their family aspirations. I suspect that if the statistics could be broken out on the high-end colleges I looked at, they would reflect a higher degree of anxiety, maybe more idealism, but essentially the same expectations.

One afternoon while I was waiting to meet someone in the Great Hall, a soaring, multistoried atrium in Middlebury College's Bicentennial Hall, I came upon a large leather-bound tome sitting on a shelf in the lounge area. It was called the Commonplace Book, and I later learned that it was left there intentionally as an invitation to students to write anything they wanted in it—a kind of communal diary. I thumbed through the entries, which ranged from deep philosophical musings no doubt penned in the wee hours of a Vermont winter night to mundane gripes about one aspect or another of college life. One, dated in the spring of 2003, struck me:

> I've got three, maybe four Fridays left as a Midd student. HOLY SHIT! I have to graduate in 23 or so days. When the hell did that come about? I'd like to know where my childhood went . . . and if anyone's seen my time at college, let me know where it is. . . . I missed the part where I was supposed to grow up. I still like cartoons, videogames, lazing about, making stupid jokes. I'm not ready to wear ties to work, to read the *Wall Street Journal*, and to have educated opinions on things like presenting, 401(k) plans and such.

I don't know who wrote that entry in the Commonplace Book; for all I know he may be wise beyond his years and pulling down a quarter of a million a year already at Morgan Stanley or on his way to becoming an oncologist. But one of his sentences—"I missed the part where I was supposed to grow up"—struck me as emblematic of his generation.

It's hard to judge how grown up I was when I left college or how grown up I was during college. Over the ensuing decade, a series of life events—enlisting in the Navy, going to graduate school, getting married, getting a real job, having a child—pushed me a good way up the ladder toward maturity. But a lot of growing got done in college. Those four years helped make me confident, resilient, wiser, and tougher. I had been treated like an adult, and whether or not I always acted like one, I believe I came to know the difference.

The vast majority of the students I met while researching this book seemed destined to make that transition too. Many are already now wearing business outfits, reading the *Wall Street Journal*, and living up to the commitments of the real world. Dean Sue Wasiolek spoke with wonderment about alums returning to Duke—"guys in frats who drank unbelievably then"—exuding newfound maturity as they kept a watchful eye on their children.

It is not easy to reconcile a view that North American colleges and universities are being dealt a hand of dysfunctional and over-anxious children with a simultaneous view that these institutions, perhaps especially the best ones, are babying their students. But this journey has led me to believe that the higher education establishment has lost focus on an essential mission of college: to provide young people with the tools to obtain knowledge about the world and about themselves.

Fixing it will not be easy. Moderate shifts—more rigorous academic standards to match the quality of the students accepted, a greater degree of faculty involvement with students' lives outside the classroom, and a reduction in the Res Life proctoring function—will spur important and positive changes in the culture of campus life.

There are some issues colleges alone cannot control. The traditional age of college attendance appears to coincide with a time in human development when people are psychologically vulnerable. For whatever combination of reasons, that vulnerability has gotten deeper and more widespread. Colleges can't be expected to fix that, but parents will continue to expect them to provide a safety net for their children. It's important, however, that psychological support not become a substitute for academic standards. There are times when some people ought not to be in college, especially at residential colleges.

It would also help a lot if the courts and the litigious society that feeds them would back off and let young people make mistakes and learn from them without suffering artificially dire consequences. The time and resources spent on policing "underage" drinking and the general overproctoring of student life could be so much better spent on teaching and learning. These shifts do not yet appear to be happening.

The American system of higher education remains the best and most diverse of any in the world, and four-year residential colleges are at the heart of that system. All of us need to be vigilant in keeping these treasured institutions on their essential mission: to help bright, ambitious adolescents make the transition into responsible, discerning, and enlightened adults. I am hopeful that if we stay vigilant, that mission can be achieved.

Notes

Chapter 1
Daily Res Life

33   *A college student in Pennsylvania admitted*   Reynol Junco, "Technology and Today's First-year Students," in *Challenging and Supporting the First-Year Student: A Handbook for Improving the First Year of College*, ed. M. L. Upcraft, J. N. Gardner, B. O. Barefoot, and Associates (San Francisco: Jossey-Bass, 2004).

34   *"i want 2 b a counselor because i love 2 work with kids"*   Steve Friess, "'Yo, can u plz help me write English?': Parents Fear Online Chatting Ruins Kids' Language Skills," *USA Today*, Apr. 1, 2003.

34   A prototypical emoticon is a smile or frown drawn with punctuation marks, as in :-) for a smile; :-(for a frown; or <3 for a horizontal rendition of a heart.

35   *Colleges and universities today are in the catering business*   Greg Winter, "Jacuzzi U.? A Battle of Perks to Lure Students," *New York Times*, Oct. 5, 2003.

36   *Northwestern and Dartmouth, among others*   Jeffrey Young, "Don't Touch That Virtual Dial," *Chronicle of Higher Education*, July 2, 2004.

Chapter 2
Hooking Up: Sex on Campus

41   *It is nine-thirty on a Wednesday night in a dorm room at Dartmouth* A composite of descriptions reported by various students in papers written for Prof. Hoyt Alverson's Anthropology 20 (Introduction to Ethnographic Field Research, fall term 2002

and 2003) at Dartmouth College. The events and quotes have been reproduced from separate accounts but did not necessarily involve the same group of students on the same evening.

43   *A study done by Norvall Glenn, a sociologist at the University of Texas, and Elizabeth Marquardt*   Norval Glenn and Elizabeth Marquardt, *Hooking Up, Hanging Out, and Hoping for Mr. Right: College Women on Dating and Mating Today* (Institute for American Values, 2001).

46   *A survey of housing policies at forty-nine representative institutions*   David A. Hoekema, *Campus Rules and Moral Community* (Lanham, MD: Roman & Littlefield, 1994), pp. 14–15, 52.

47   *"I was positively overwhelmed with letters and e-mail messages"*   Wendy Shalit, *A Return to Modesty* (New York: Simon & Schuster, 1999), p. 233.

50   *the ratio of women to men in college would continue to rise*   Center for Labor Market Studies at Northeastern University, 2003.

56   *"Here at Harvard," said Carol, a lesbian student*   Carol is an alias, as requested by the source.

Chapter 3
How Hard Are Students Studying?

57   *only 11 percent of college students spend 25 or more hours a week studying*   National Survey of Student Engagement Survey Web site, reported in the *Chronicle of Higher Education*, Nov. 25, 2004.

59   *2:00 A.M.   Drop by a final club*   Final clubs are Harvard's fraternity-like private societies with their own clubhouses.

60   *"the Lake Wobegon of higher education"*   Patrick Healy, "Harvard's Quiet Secret: Rampant Grade Inflation," *Boston Globe*, Oct. 7, 2001.

60   *a senior with a solid B average at Princeton*   Brian Henn, "Committee Reports Grade Inflation on the Increase," *Daily Princetonian*, July 14, 2003.

61   *Stuart Rojstaczer . . . did a study*   The sample of thirty-four included Dartmouth, Duke, Harvard, Pomona, and Stanford.

63   *By the 1990s, some college students were graduating*   Charles J.
        Sykes, "How Colleges Are Failing Our Students," from *Impri-
        mis*, the monthly journal of Hillsdale College, Vol. 19, No. 7,
        July 1990.

63   *Professors frequently build courses around popular cultural icons*
        James M. O'Neill, "Pop Culture Cracks College Curriculums:
        Your Tuition and Tax Dollars Go Down the Drain," *Philadel-
        phia Inquirer*, Dec. 28, 2003.

64   *"many students graduate from college with less knowledge about the
        world"*   "The Hollow Core: Failure of the General Education
        Curriculum, A Fifty College Study," published by the Ameri-
        can Council of Trustees and Alumni (ACTA), founded by
        Lynne Cheney and Richard Lamm, Apr. 2004.

64   *Defenders of the more fluid curricula counter*   Walter P. Metzger,
        emeritus professor of history at Columbia University, "Critics
        of College Teaching," *Almanac of Higher Education* (National
        Endowment for the Arts, 1996).

65   *"Today, what I see occurring on the campus"*   Harvey C. Mans-
        field, "Our Coddled Students: How Harvard Compromised Its
        Virtue," *Chronicle of Higher Education*, Feb. 21, 2003.

67   *an outright majority of college students*   Augustus E. Jordan,
        "College Student Cheating: The Role of Motivation, Perceived
        Norms, Attitudes, and Knowledge of Institutional Policy,"
        Journal of Ethics and Behavior, Vol. 11, No. 3, 2001, pp. 233–
        247.

67   *more than a third . . . is Internet-based cut-and-paste plagiarism*
        Donald L. McCabe, Linda Klebe Trevino, and Kenneth D.
        Butterfield, "Cheating in Academic Institutions: A Decade of
        Research," *Journal of Ethics and Behavior*, Vol. 11, No. 3, 2001,
        pp. 219–232.

73   *"One former student's degree had been revoked"*   Erich Wasser-
        man, "Keeping the Honor in U-VA's Honor Code," *Washington
        Post*, Dec. 28, 2000, p. A-23.

74   *"a time sink"*   Matt Kelly, "Bloomfield Challenges Students to
        Take More Responsibility for Honor," U-VA *News Daily*, Oct.
        14, 2003.

76   *Fraga is unusual for a big university faculty member*   The initial
        interview with Professor Luis Fraga, together with other Stan-
        ford resident fellows and students, was conducted for the
        author by Stanford *Daily* editor Michelle Keller, class of 2004.
78   *John Gardner, founder of the National Resource Center for the First-
        Year Experience*   Gardner is also distinguished professor emer-
        itus of library and information science at the University of
        South Carolina.

Chapter 4
Emotional Troubles

88   *"As soon as I suggested I wanted to leave, she was like, 'Go!'"*
        Katharine Kaplan, "Troubled Students Feel College Nudges
        Them Off Campus," Harvard *Crimson*, Feb. 23 and 24, 2004.
91   *"college lawyers discussed among themselves perhaps one or two pend-
        ing suicide cases"*   Ann H. Franke, "When Students Kill Them-
        selves, Colleges May Get the Blame," *Chronicle of Higher Edu-
        cation*, June 25, 2004.
93   *Nationally the number of students on such medications nearly tripled*
        Survey by the American College Health Association, *New York
        Times*, Oct. 26, 2004.
101   *"I sit here facing a blank screen with swollen eyes"*   Mary Adkins,
        "Discussing Eating Disorders," Duke *Chronicle*, Nov. 1, 2001.
101   *"Food has a grip on my mood, self-worth and schedule"*   Ibid.
105   For specific advice on mental health, several experts recom-
        mended contacting the HEATH Resource Center of George
        Washington University, 2121 K Street NW, Suite 220, Wash-
        ington, DC 20037. Web site: www.heath.gwu.edu.

Chapter 5
The College Alcohol Crisis

109   *alcohol accounts for the deaths of fourteen hundred college students a
        year*   "A Call to Action: Changing the Culture of Drinking at
        U.S. Colleges," National Institute on Alcohol Abuse and Alco-
        holism, July 9, 2003.
110   *That apparently is what happened over the 2004 Labor Day week-
        end*   The account of Samantha Spady's death is based on

numerous news reports in the *Denver Post*, the *Rocky Mountain News*, the University of Colorado's *Daily Camera* and the *Chronicle of Higher Education*.

110 *Not so for Daniel Reardon, who was allegedly forced to consume* From various 2002 media reports including the *Washington Post*, the *Washington Times*, the *Baltimore Sun*, and the University of Maryland's *Diamondback*.

110 *In the case of Alexander Klochkoff* Amy Argetsinger and Jamie Stockwell, "Teenager Hospitalized After U-Md. Rush Event," *Washington Post*, Feb. 9, 2002, p. B-1.

111 *Duke University junior Raheem Bath died of pneumonia* Duke *Chronicle*, Feb. 13, 2000.

111 *Owen Smith, a senior at Vermont's Champlain College, froze to death* Associated Press, Burlington, Vermont, Dec. 9, 2003.

111 *Freshman Jeffrey Shank, age eighteen, plunged from a fourth-floor balcony* Associated Press, Carlisle, Pennsylvania, Mar. 28, 2003.

111 *Brett Jensen, age nineteen, fell off the deck of the Pi Kappa Phi house* "Parents Settle Suit over Son's Death at UW Fraternity Party," *Seattle Post-Intelligencer*, Nov. 2, 2004.

111 *Indiana University sophomore Seth Korona died after performing* Indiana *Daily Student*, Feb. 3, 2003, as well as other accounts.

112 *Henry Adams recalls that his mid–nineteenth-century Harvard classmates drank* Henry Adams, *The Education of Henry Adams* (Houghton Mifflin, 1918), p. 58

112 F. Scott Fitzgerald, *This Side of Paradise*, Book One, Chapter Two (New York: Charles Scribner, 1920).

113 *The first two weekends of George Washington University's first semester* GW *Hatchet*, Sept. 11, 2003.

113 *"closer and closer to a major catastrophe"* North Adams (Mass.) *Advocate*, Nov. 5, 2003.

113 *At Harvard, the number of undergraduates carried into University Health Services' ER* Harvard *Crimson*, Dec. 12, 2003.

114 *Until then, Harvard health officials might have expected twenty-five* Associated Press, Oct. 5, 2003.

115 *"There were about ten of us sitting on the floor"* Excerpted from a paper submitted to Prof. Hoyt Alverson's Anthropology class in the 2002–2003 academic year.

115   *"Safety & Security"*   Dartmouth's campus police.

115   *"Students can feel anxious saying hello, sharing things about themselves"*   "Early Intervention: Confronting the Idea and Practice of Drinking to Drunkenness on College Campuses: A Next Step," *Journal of College Student Psychotherapy*, Vol. 7(1), 1992.

118   *"Should we wait until a student dies before we do something?"*   Tufts *Daily*, Feb. 21, 2003.

118   *"Seven students required treatment at Princeton Medical Center"* Princeton *Packet*, Mar. 9, 1999.

118   an *"annual festival of spit-swapping and nudity"*   Stanford *Daily*, Oct. 9, 2003.

119   *After MIT freshman Scott Krueger died*   The Kruegers filed a wrongful death suit against MIT and their son's fraternity and eventually settled for a total of $7.75 million.

120   *social norming takes a kind of cognitive dissonance approach* Cognitive dissonance theory, expounded by psychologist Leon Festinger, posits that individuals naturally seek consistency among their beliefs and opinions. When there is an inconsistency between attitudes or behaviors (dissonance), something must change to resolve the conflict. In the case of a discrepancy between attitudes and behavior, it is most likely that the attitude will change to accommodate the behavior.

121   *after* Time *magazine named Indiana one of its four Colleges of the Year*   *Time*, May 3, 2003.

122   *At the University of Colorado, insult was added to injury*   NBC's *Dateline* segment on college binge drinking aired Sept. 26, 2003.

122   *At the end of the six years, Colorado's binge drinking rate*   Associated Press, June 17, 2003.

122   *In January 2002, the Indiana legislature passed a law*   Indianapolis *Journal and Courier*, Jan. 30, 2002.

123   *"We will be bearing down and bearing down hard"*   *Dartmouth*, May 16, 2003.

123   *A week before the 2003 Thanksgiving break, undercover agents*   Rutland Herald & Times Argus, Nov. 14, 2003.

Chapter 6
The Date Rape Dilemma

128   *It was a warm August evening*   The story of Melissa at the University of Wisconsin employs alias names for all the students involved.

130   *"Women are not just drinking more"*   "Women on a Binge," *Time*, Apr. 1, 2002, p. 58.

132   *only 40 percent of U.S. colleges and universities have been meeting the requirements of the Clery Act*   Jeanne Clery was a nineteen-year old freshman at Lehigh who was raped and then strangled in her dorm room while she slept on April 5, 1986. Her assailant was a Lehigh sophomore. Incensed to learn afterward that in the previous three years Lehigh had been the scene of thirty-eight violent crimes, none of which had been reported to the student body or to applicants, the Clerys campaigned for legislation that would require all colleges and universities receiving state or federal funding to report incidences of violent crime to students, prospective students, and parents. The law was originally passed in 1990 as the Crime Awareness and Campus Security Act. The law was amended in 1992 to give sexual assault victims certain basic rights and it was amended again in 1998 to expand on those rights and make more requirements of colleges and universities reporting crimes. It was formally named the Jeanne Clery Act in 1998. The law was expanded again in 2000, stating that as of 2003 all universities must publish the names of registered sex offenders on campus.

133   *Between 1998 and 2000, emergency room admissions in the United States for GHB quadrupled*   Substance Abuse and Mental Health Administration Report, 2001.

134   *"sufficient independent corroboration"*   *Boston Globe*, Apr. 22, 2003, p. B6.

135   *"False accusations of rape do happen"*   Harvard *Crimson*, Apr. 17, 2003.

139   *"nothing more or less than a conscious process of intimidation"*   Susan Brownmiller, *Against Our Will: Men, Women and Rape* (New York: Simon & Schuster, 1975), chap. 1.

Chapter 7
Is Diversity Working?

143   *an offensive editorial cartoon the paper had run a week earlier*   The
      cartoon was drawn by Dan Carino, staff cartoonist for the San
      Diego State University *Aztec* and syndicated by Knight-Ridder
      Campus News Wire.

147   *an art director superimposed a 1994 picture of UW senior Diallo*
      Shabazz   "University Inserts Black Student among Whites in
      Photo," *Milwaukee Journal-Sentinel*, Sept. 21, 2000.

149   *UCLA agreed to create the Caesar Chavez Center*   "The Politics
      of Separation," *Time* special issue, *The New Face of America*, Fall
      1993, p. 74.

160   *"Apparently, the advice provided by class deans is inadequate"*
      "Dartmouth's Racial Separatism," Dartmouth *Review*, Feb. 12,
      2001.

164   *"I've been going to diversity retreats since high school"*   Christina
      Ng, "Students Find 'Common Ground,'" Duke *Chronicle*, Oct.
      17, 2003.

165   *As a result, Adams House acquired a reputation as artistic*   Based
      on various interviews but confirmed in the Harvard *Crimson*,
      Mar. 21, 2002.

166   *"We are increasing our happiness by segmenting off so rigorously"*
      "The Agenda: People Like Us," *Atlantic Monthly*, Sept. 2003.

Chapter 8
Fraternities and Sororities under Siege

170   *"ready-made administrative units"*   Paul S. Fass, *The Damned*
      and the Beautiful: American Youth in the 1920s (New York:
      Oxford University Press, 1977), pp. 144–145.

170   *Originally admirers of Greek societies*   The first Greek letter
      society was Phi Beta Kappa, founded at William & Mary in
      1776. Its motto: "Philosophy is the guide of life." The first
      social fraternity, the model of the modern-day fraternity, was
      Kappa Alpha, founded at Union College in Schenectady, New
      York, in 1825.

172 *a relatively small cadre of male society members*   Report of the Committee on Residential Life, Mar. 1995, p. 4.

175 *But four of the most prominent fraternities on campus*   The four plaintiff fraternities were Alpha Delta Phi, Psi Upsilon, Delta Kappa Epsilon, and Sigma Phi.

177 *a recommendation by yet another committee examining college alcohol policies*   The author was a member of the Campus Coalition on Alcohol and Other Drugs formed in spring 2003 and made recommendations to the president a year later.

177 *"disturbing increase in the reports of inappropriate behavior occurring at various final clubs"*   "The Final Club Scene," John Harvard's Journal, *Harvard* magazine, May/June 1997.

179 *"a full discussion about how we might introduce some fundamental changes"*   President Wright's address to the Alumni Council, May 21, 1999, as reprinted on the Dartmouth College Web site.

180 *"experienced extraordinary expressions of violent misogyny"*   Lucy Buford, class of 2000, "Feminism and Women's Activism at Dartmouth College: A History of the Emergence and Evolution of Women's Beliefs."

180 *"two basically distinct Dartmouths"*   The title and lyrics of the college alma mater were not changed from "Men of Dartmouth" to "Dear Old Dartmouth" until 1988, sixteen years after the first women enrolled.

183 *The copy of the "Zetemouth" dug out of the garbage behind the house*   "Zete's Graphic 'Sex Papers' Exposed," *Dartmouth*, Apr. 18, 2001.

189 *"I came to recognize later"*   Carla is an alias used at the request of the source, who did not wish to betray the confidences of her former sorority sisters.

Chapter 9
The Morphing Drug Scene

198 *"My freshman year, there were three guys dealing it on the same floor,"*   Ben Sweet, "Living the High Life," Vanderbilt *Hustler*, Apr. 23, 2004.

199   *In the fall of 2003, two freshmen at Hamilton* Jennifer Gonnerman, "Three Young Men, Two Coke Deliveries, One Prison Sentence: A Question of Justice," *Village Voice*, June 29, 2004, as well as from the author's interviews.

199   *Following a fifteen-month investigation into the sale of marijuana, cocaine* University of Virginia *Cavalier Daily*, Oct. 6 and 7, 2003, as well as campus interviews.

201   *including a* Time *magazine cover story* John Cloud, "Happiness Is . . . a Pill?" *Time*, June 5, 2000.

201   *In 2001, roughly 15 percent of college students reported using Ecstasy* Aaron M. White, PhD, assistant research professor, Department of Psychiatry, Duke University Medical Center, "Ecstasy: Weighing the Risk," June 9, 2003, published on NASPA's NetResults Web site.

201   *"They had been selling the tabs on campus for $15 to $20 apiece* Adam Aasen, "Members of Ecstasy Ring at Indiana U. Get Prison Sentences," Indiana *Daily Student*, Mar. 31, 2003.

201   *When the rave scene died, the same Michigan student, whom I'll call Steve* Steve's story first appeared in an article in the University of Michigan *Daily* ("High Life: A Former Addict's Path to Ruin and Back," October 29, 2004) by staff writer Victoria Edwards, who subsequently put the author in touch with the subject. The name is an alias.

203   *They are seeking to avoid the fate of people like Josh Duroff* Julie L. Nicklin, "The Latest Trend: Mixing Prescription Drugs with Other Substances," *Chronicle of Higher Education*, June 9, 2000.

205   *"It's helped me a lot"* David B. Rochelson, "Students Turn to Drugs to Study," Harvard *Crimson*, Jan. 26, 2004.

Chapter 10
College Sports and Res Life

210   *"a powerful synergy between big-time college sports and contemporary student life"* Murray Sperber, *Beer and Circus: How Big-Time*

College Sports Is Crippling Undergraduate Education (Henry Holt, 2000), p. xxii.

211   *It is a conclusion supported through research directed by William G. Bowen*   William G. Bowen coauthored *The Game of Life* with James L. Shulman (Princeton, N.J.: Princeton University Press, 2001) and *Reclaiming the Game* with Sarah A. Levin (Princeton, N.J.: Princeton University Press, 2003).

215   *"This mentality is extremely prevalent in Harvard athletes,"*   Nicole Corriero, "'Dumb Harvard Athlete': Oxymoron or Omnipresent? The 'Dumb Jock' Effect on Harvard Student-Athletes," written for Professor Seth Hannah's Sociology 40 course at Harvard University, 2003.

216   *It echoes an argument sometimes made on behalf of African Americans*   See "Improving Adolescents' Standardized Test Performance: An Intervention to Reduce the Effects of Stereotype Threat," by Catherine Good, a postdoctoral fellow at Columbia University, as published in the December 2003 issue of *Journal of Applied Developmental Psychology.*

216   *"not dissimilar to those of students of color"*   Paula M. Krebs, "Coaching the Student in the Student Athlete," *Chronicle of Higher Education*, Oct. 22, 2004.

218   *"For too long, college athletics has been segregated from the core mission of the university"*   Vanderbilt University press release issued Sept. 9, 2003.

219   *Their closest existing model of success is the University Athletic Association*   The University Athletic Association consists of Brandeis, Carnegie Mellon, Case Western Reserve, Emory, New York University, University of Chicago, University of Rochester, and Washington University of St. Louis. Johns Hopkins, an original member, left the league in 2001.

220   *"We all don't have to be Swarthmores"*   Swarthmore College in Pennsylvania is a Division III school that consistently ranks among the top three liberal arts colleges in the country, enrolling about fifteen hundred students. In December 2000, it dropped its football program, along with wrestling and badminton.

Chapter 11
What's the Right Drinking Age?

223   *Those frustrations only grew following the publication*   Henry
        Wechsler, PhD, and Bernice Wuethrich, *Dying to Drink: Con-*
        fronting Binge Drinking on College Campuses (Emmaus, Penn.:
        Rodale Press, 2002).

223   *According to his data gathered four different times over the course of*
        a decade   Wechsler's data come from a sample of two hundred
        students each at 140 four-year colleges.

224   *"Most college presidents," he wrote*   Ibid., p. 231.

225   *In a field study done at San Diego State University in 2002*   The
        San Diego study was reported at the November 2002 Depart-
        ment of Education AOD Prevention Conference, Seattle,
        Washington.

225   *"the majority—56%—(of college students) do not binge drink"*
        Dying to Drink, p. 21.

226   *"If that is the result of all the work that's been done"*   From a
        workshop at the November 2002 Department of Education
        AOD Prevention Conference, Seattle, Washington.

226   *beer-and-circus universities*   The phrase is borrowed from Mur-
        ray Sperber's book, *Beer and Circus: How Big-Time College Sports*
        Is Crippling Undergraduate Education (New York: Henry Holt,
        2000).

227   *As an article in the nearby* San Jose Mercury News   *San Jose*
        Mercury News, Apr. 29, 2003.

228   *"If Stanford truly wants to decrease the role alcohol plays"*   Stan-
        ford *Daily*, Oct. 3, 2003.

228   *In the Trinity Park and Trinity Heights neighborhoods off Duke's*
        East Campus   Duke *Chronicle*, Aug. 28, 2003.

235   *"Some countries have no minimum drinking age"*   Commentary
        by T. R. Reid, "Let Teens Drink Legally and Learn Responsi-
        bility," *Colorado Rocky Mountain News*, May 8, 2003.

235   *"Rather than paint rosy but unrealistic pictures of life in countries"*
        Joseph A. Califano Jr., "Don't Make Teen Drinking Easier,"
        Washington Post, May 11, 2003.

236   *Denmark is the only example of a country that has recently tightened its laws*   In 2000, New Zealand lowered its minimum drinking age from twenty to eighteen with three objectives: (1) to be able to target the abuse of alcohol, not the age of the drinker, by actively seeking to encourage sensible drinking patterns; (2) to clarify the law for ease of enforcement; and (3) to gain high levels of public acceptability for the new law by establishing fairness with regard to other restrictions on rights. It was too early, however, to assess the effect of this change.

239   *"bad social policy and terrible law"*   John M. McCardell Jr., "What Your College President Didn't Tell You," *New York Times*, Sept. 13, 2004.

240   *Here's how it works at one IU fraternity*   The shutdown drill account was provided by Corey Schouten, Indiana University, class of 2004, a reporter and editor for the Indiana *Daily Student.*

242   *"Drunkenness was considered obnoxious and ungentlemanly"*   Paula S. Fass, *The Damned and the Beautiful: American Youth in the 1920s* (New York: Oxford University Press, 1977), p. 318.

Chapter 12
Who's in Charge?

258   *virtually all the money allocated went toward consumables*   Alcohol can be purchased with student activities funds at Duke, but there is a 15 percent cap on the amount of money that can be allocated to alcohol.

261   *Even at the University of Wisconsin*   Not everything student governments spend time on is trivial. During 2002–2003, Pomona's administration relied heavily on the Association of Students of Pomona College (ASPC) to formulate a new alcohol policy. The ASPC conducted in-depth surveys of student attitudes toward drinking, ascertained differences in habits and outlook between new students and upperclassmen, and came up with a policy that both banned hard alcohol on campus and

loosened up rules on parties—a combination of sticks and car-
rots. "Students were instrumental in shaping the outcome,"
said Matt Taylor, the dean of Residential Life. "They were the
ones who said we should look at the culture." Pomona's new
president, David Oxtoby, was impressed. "Student leadership
here is much, much stronger than at [the University of] Chicago, where student government was something of a joke," he
told me. "Here, it has some impact."

Chapter 13
Improving the Undergraduate Experience

273   "In loco parentis *has been rejuvenated and returned*"   David
       Weigel, "Welcome to the Fun-Free University: The Return of
       In Loco Parentis Is Killing Student Freedom," *Reason* maga-
       zine, Oct. 2004.

274   *"In case it wasn't abundantly clear"*   Christopher Scoville,
       "Knowledge, Schmowledge: Topher's Parade," Duke *Chronicle*,
       Aug. 20, 2004.

274   *One was a lament about the changing character of Kenyon College*
       P. F. Kluge, *Alma Mater: A College Homecoming* (Addison-Wesley,
       1993).

275   *an "institution that lets students get away with a lot"*   P. F. Kluge,
       "Kamp Kenyon's Legacy: Death by Tinkering," *Chronicle of
       Higher Education*, Feb. 21, 2003.

275   *"What happens at Harvard sometimes presages"*   Harvey Mans-
       field, "Our Coddled Students: How Harvard Compromised Its
       Virtue," *Chronicle of Higher Education*, Feb. 21, 2003.

277   *"professional kid wranglers who were paid to teach, encourage, amuse
       or monitor them"*   Dr. Ron Taffel, with Melinda Blau, *The Sec-
       ond Family* (St. Martin's Press, 2001), pp. 45–46.

278   *"If you never let anybody fail, how can they not be afraid of failure?"*
       Elinor Burkett, *Another Planet: A Year in the Life of a Suburban
       High School* (Perennial Books, 2001), p. 96.

279   *The researchers attribute seven core traits to them*   Neil Howe and
       William Strauss, *The Millennials Go to College* (Life Course Asso-

ciates, 2003), p. ii.

280   *A more plausible portrait emerges from surveys*   Cooperative Institutional Research Program, sponsored by the American Council on Education and UCLA, "The American Freshman: Thirty-five Year Trends."

Index

Abbott, Katy Smith, 268
Abbott, Steve, 268–270
academics, 6–14, 57–59, 82–84, 276
  alcohol use correlated with, 226
  cheating, 66–72
  class schedules, 36, 65–66, 116–117
  faculty-student contact and, 76–82
  grade inflation, 59–63, 82
  graduation rate, diversity and, 162
  honor codes, 72–76
  prescription drugs as study aids,
    204–205
  priority of, 274
  sports and, 207–209, 213
Acampora, Thomas, 53, 157
activism, 37–39, 209, 263
Adams, Henry, 112
Adderall, 204–205
Adkins, Mary, 100–102
admissions, 102–104, 175–176,
    213–214, 218, 219
affinity deans, 152–153, 160–164
African American students, 143–145,
    154. *See also* diversity
Against Our Will (Brownmiller), 139
alcohol, 8, 21, 107–108, 112–114
  age limits for, 232–239, 272–273
  alcoholism, 233–234
  binge drinking, 176, 223–226
  date rape and, 130–131
  deaths from secondary effects,
    111–112
  drinking and driving, 231–233
  drinking games, 42, 115–116, 183

drugs and, 196, 203–204, 205
education campaigns about,
  120–122
fraternities and, 119, 171, 176, 182,
  184–185, 223, 240–242
international laws, 14, 234–237,
  244–246
law enforcement and, 114–115, 119,
  122–124, 226–231, 240–242
off-campus use, 176, 228–229
poisoning, 108–111, 119, 187, 226,
  246
pregaming, 41, 114, 239–240
rituals involving, 118–119
social norming, 120–121
sororities and, 187–189
sports and, 210, 216–217
weekend lifestyle and, 116–117
Ander, Steve, 34–35, 36
Anderson, David, 226
Andrew W. Mellon Foundation, 211,
  219
antidepressants, 87, 92–95, 203–204
AOD (alcohol and other drugs), 195.
  See also alcohol; drugs, illegal
Asian students, 152–153. *See also*
  diversity
Asperger's syndrome, 96–97
Association of Black Harvard Women,
  159
Atherton, Cynthia, 270
Auburn University, 199
authority. *See* Res Life professionals
Awakuni, Gene, 13, 227